My American Bride

OTHER BOOKS BY ELIE A. SALEM:

The Political Theory and Institutions of the Khawarij
Modernization Without Revolution – Lebanon 1943–1970
The Rules and Regulations of the Abbasid Court
Violence and Diplomacy in Lebanon 1982–1988

My American Bride

ELIE A. SALEM

QUARTET

First published in 2008 by
Quartet Books Limited
A member of the Namara Group
27 Goodge Street, London W1T 2LD

Copyright © Elie A. Salem 2008

A catalogue record for this book
is available from the British Library

ISBN   978 0 7043 7137 8

Typeset by Antony Gray
Printed and bound in Great Britain by
T J International Ltd, Padstow, Cornwall

Preface

I sit in the same small village where I was born, some ten miles from the biblical Cedars of Lebanon. I reflect on my life from the vantage point of more than seventy years. I find that when I stop and dwell for a moment or so on a particular memory it often leads on to another until I am recalling things I have not thought of for many years. I survey the happy times of my life and the sad ones, the exciting and the miserable. I wonder if there is value in writing my story. Why write it? Why tell it?

I look at pictures that take me through the stations of my life – some recent, some now quite distant in time but vibrant in memory. Photographs can be iconic. I look and often see what lay behind them, going inwards, upwards, sideways. I am a Lebanese man of the twentieth century. I was a national leader in times of un- imaginable unrest and strife. My story is inextricably bound up with the story of an American girl from the Midwest who became my wife and the partner of my life's work. I write not merely to tell my own story, and hers, but to offer our experience as a human one with universal qualities.

Like the loner in Robert Frost's poem 'The Mountain', I look out with wonder. The object of my contemplation is the highest in the mountain chain in Lebanon, and indeed the highest in an Arab World stretching from Morocco to Kuwait, 'from the roaring ocean to the rebellious Gulf ', as the nationalists put it. And like that loner, I note that my children have grown up and departed each in his or her own way. My wife, the woman I loved and who is the reason I think of writing this account, died three years ago. I find myself in dialogue with myself. The more lonely I am, the more intense the dialogue.

I am very much alone here and hence I am very busy. Indeed my mind seems crowded with stories, ideas and anecdotes. And I think often of when I crossed the Atlantic for the first time so long ago to study in the United States. America transformed me and I loved it. There I met the girl who became my wife, and she too was transformed. She loved Lebanon. My brother Kamal says that she came to us as an American, but she died a Lebanese. To tell our story now in the context of this unlikely and transformational love between an American girl and an Arab boy may be of particular interest.

This is not a good time for Arabs and Americans. Indeed a wave of hatred and abject misunderstanding permeates the sphere between them. I write in the hope that it is useful to tell our story, essentially a love story, at such a time. Of all of the writings of St Paul, which I read often, none is more eloquent than the passage where he speaks of love in his First Epistle to the Corinthians: 'Love is patient and kind. Love is not jealous or boastful; it is not arrogant or rude. Love does not insist on its own way; it is not irritable or resentful; it does not rejoice at wrong, but rejoices in the right. Love bears all things, believes all things, hopes all things, endures all things.'

As I loved that American girl, I must relate my story through her. I met her exactly one year after my arrival in the New World.

1

She was with a group of four or five other girls on Florida Avenue, an unimposing street in Washington DC. She stood out, not because she was more beautiful than the others, nor because she was taller. Neither. But to me she looked more distinguished, more reflective, more pensive, as though she did not belong with them at all. In an unexpected flash, I realized she belonged with me. Although I risked only a quick glance, it revealed that her eyes were kind, somehow sad and remarkably piercing. How could it be that I saw so suddenly and so clearly that I would spend my life with this girl? Yet I truly did. God, I love her! We will be together – build a home, join our families, raise children. These convictions came to me as certainties even though they faded like the multitude of thoughts and images that crowd themselves into our mysterious, unfathomable and unconscious world every day.

'Are you from Baghdad?' she asked me.

I thought it a strange question, but an intelligent one. Was it obvious I was an Arab? I could have passed as Southern Mediterranean or as Iranian. But clearly she wanted to talk to me, to pursue the question.

'No,' I answered, 'I am Lebanese.' I wondered silently if she had ever heard of my tiny little mountainous country proudly standing guard on the Eastern Mediterranean at the very gate of Asia. Aloud I asked, 'How do you know about Baghdad?'

'Oh,' she said, 'my father works for an Armenian who came from Baghdad to Pottstown.' Pottstown turned out to be her home in Pennsylvania, not far from Philadelphia.

'And what is your name?' I found the courage to ask.

'Phyllis,' she volunteered a bit shyly. 'Phyllis Sell.'

Though my knowledge of German scholarship was somewhat slight, it prompted me to ask her if she was related to the famous Islamic scholar Sell who translated the Qur'an into English.

'No, I don't think so,' she replied.

Our conversation took place on the street in front of 1906 Florida

Avenue, the original home of the School of Advanced International Studies (SAIS). Now a division of the Johns Hopkins University, the school was founded during World War II by Paul H. Nitze and Christian Herter. It was devoted to developing new methods and systematic theories of international relations. The curriculum was both scholarly and practical, with the underlying vision of preparing men and women for international responsibilities so that a war of such cataclysmic proportions could never come again. When SAIS joined Johns Hopkins University in 1950, they remained for several years at 1906 Florida Avenue. The modest red-brick building served as school, library and administrative office. It was also the dormitory for twenty of the ninety-eight students enrolled at the time we were there.

Next door, 1908 Florida was the women's dormitory – a typical Washington building of the 1920s with a small welcoming living-room, five bedrooms on the second floor, and three bedrooms on the third. The friends were girls of average families from all over America in their early twenties. They came to Washington, the nation's capital, seeking employment in the Foreign Service. At the centre of the world's most powerful seat of government they sought adventure and a role in the making of the lasting peace promised by the United Nations at the end of a catastrophic war. The United States was a major architect of the post-colonial world and plans were emerging for an international order, free of war and dependent on the rule of law among nations. Graduate students or aspiring members of the Foreign Service, we shared the purpose of shaping a just world for peaceful ends. In this one girl, that purpose and the ambition to be part of it were consuming passions that seemed to light her from within.

For a day or two I did not hear from Phyllis. Though I had been in the United States for a year, I was still too much the withdrawn Lebanese villager to take the initiative with American girls. Culturally, I was far removed from them and my most innocently intended words and actions too often ended in embarrassment.

My cultural ties were strengthened by the letters from home that arrived weekly without fail. My father clearly saw it as his duty to remind me why I was in the United States – to study, to gain a higher degree and to return to Lebanon to work so that I could earn a good income and help the family. My father was Christian

Orthodox and the equal of the most archetypal WASP as far as purpose, commitment and hard work were concerned. And these values he implanted in me through countless kindly sermons and spell-binding narratives, cleverly woven with lessons of the good and the evil in human behaviour. His teaching had prepared me well for many encounters, but not for this one.

The fleeting sense of destiny I experienced when I first saw Phyllis was indeed a glimpse of what lay ahead. No words could describe the joy I felt when I answered the phone in the corridor of the third floor of 1906 Florida Avenue and heard her voice.

'It's Phyllis,' she said. 'I am calling to find out what you're doing. Would you like to have coffee with me and my friends at 1908?'

'Yes, of course,' I blurted out in disbelief. 'Tomorrow afternoon at five would be fine. Yes, just after work.'

I arrived to find that Phyllis was clearly the organizer of the coffee *klatch*. She was vibrant, anxious and attentive. Her friends were deferential towards her, and naturally accepted her leadership. For me, stirrings of love began to complicate the issue. Telephone calls became more frequent. I acquired, under Phyllis's tutelage, a new insight into American mores, and we spoke of visiting her home in Philadelphia and of travelling together to her birthplace in Potts-town, where her grandparents, uncles and aunts lived.

After my year of social trial and error at the University of Cincinnati in Ohio, Phyllis was remarkably easy for me to talk to. She was curious, always keen to break new ground. I was curious too. I felt a great deal of empathy with her and was yet unsure whether empathy and love were the same, or only pretty close. As a Lebanese I saw each person in the context of his or her family, and the only concept of family I had to go on was the extended model. As a graduate student I was trained to enquire, to probe, to get quickly to the detail. So I asked all about her.

'What does your father do? What does your mother do? Who are your grandparents on your father's side, on your mother's side?' I asked with genuine interest. She answered readily; glad it seemed for someone to care in that way. Family conversation led naturally to other things and Phyllis and I talked and talked. We had an ideal setting for our meetings, living as we did in the vicinity of Dupont Circle. Although my budget was intended exclusively for my academic needs, I managed a few quiet dinners with Phyllis in some of the finest restaurants in the city.

Showing off was a part of my culture that I exercised with great personal pleasure, although sometimes with embarrassing consequences. Our fine dining excursions often ended with a restaurant bill that exceeded my expectations – and the cash in my pocket. Several times I had to choose between humbly asking Phyllis for a loan or excusing myself for a quiet talk with the manager to work out an arrangement for deferred payment. In time, with patience, love and a good deal of humour, Phyllis taught me to live within my means and to appreciate the frugality, the simplicity and the informality of the post-war American way of life.

I was truly in love with this five-foot-two American girl who amused me by singing a favourite song of her parents from the 1920s. It went something like this: 'Five foot two, eyes of blue, oh what those five feet can do!' As she sang it she did the Charleston, the crazy dance that went with it.

Yes, I decided, I was in love. The thought of marriage did not occur to me, however. It simply was not part of my father's plan for me when he sent me to the United States. It seems amazing now, but I saw the romance of being in love with this blue-eyed adorable being as an end in itself. The logic of next steps just did not enter my thoughts.

Perhaps it is not so amazing after all, considering who I was at that time – just twenty-one years old when I met Phyllis in October 1951. I had arrived by ship in New York Harbor in September 1950, only one year earlier, so the country too was still quite new to me. America and the Allies had just won the war against Germany, Italy and Japan, only to be drawn into a Cold War with the Soviet Union, a former ally. The Soviets were challenging the United States in Europe and in Asia. In Korea the challenge ended in war and heightened tension not only with the Soviets but with the Chinese as well. America was in a nervous mood when I arrived as a young, naïve, unjustifiably arrogant young student.

In the initial stages of my voyage to America, from Beirut to Naples, the sea was relatively calm. I was slightly seasick, but very much alive. From Naples to New York things got much worse. I was violently seasick, bedridden and thought I would die. The few apples I managed to swallow did not remain long inside me. Since I was always in bed, all I could do was read. I read constantly. I

arrived exhausted and disorientated, to face the New World somewhat shakily.

When we docked, New York police boarded the ship. One officer
in particular regarded me with suspicion. I was carrying *The Gathering
Storm*, the first of a number of volumes on the Second World War
written by Britain's wartime prime minister, Winston Churchill.

The burly Irish policeman looked at the weak and exhausted
traveller and asked, 'What are you reading, son?'

'*The Gathering Storm* by Churchill,' I replied.

'Why would you want to read about a storm?'

'*The Gathering Storm* by Prime Minister Winston Churchill, chron-
icling the causes of the Second World War, sir.' I assumed that the
reference to Churchill would ring a bell with the aggressive officer –
but I was wrong. He seemed to have missed the news that the
country was no longer at war.

'What are you coming here for?' he growled.

'I am coming, sir, to study political science.'

'Politics, heh!'

'No, sir, political science.' I was gradually losing my patience,
though I made a real effort not to lose my temper.

'You want to study politics? You wanna go back and lead the
Communists in your country?'

I was a young, proud and curiously immature scholar and lost
my battle for self-control as I retorted: 'Oh yes, sir, this is exactly
what I want to do.'

'And this is exactly why you cannot enter the US,' roared back
the Irish giant.

'Fine,' I responded. 'I no longer want to enter the United States,
and I am going right back to my cabin and back to my country.'

Angered and fiercely confused, I returned to my cabin – seething
as I considered my limited options. All the travellers on board
seemed to be moving in one direction, I in the other. It was
strangely worrying, though I was not yet fully aware of the gravity
of my action. I dived back into my cabin, closed the door and was
immediately submerged in an ocean of tumultuous thoughts. What
shall I do now? How can I return? How can I make new travel
arrangements, find another ship, and what if I cannot leave this
ship to get on another one?

Then came the most dreadful thought– what would my rational, calculating, Aristotelian father think? I remembered my boyhood friend Jamil. He dreamt of emigration to Venezuela, of making a fortune and returning home to build the biggest house in the village. He spoke often of how he would be the envy of all. Jamil boarded a ship, arrived in Venezuela, took a one-day walk on shore – and booked a return passage the very next day. We all laughed when he arrived, having spent the few liras he had accumulated. His parents reprimanded him severely for his immediate return. It was highly unusual behaviour and in the village context the unusual is most often regarded as stupid. Jamil was a happy-go-lucky guy. He enjoyed the laughter and skirted the reprimand. But I was no Jamil. To be a source of laughter was such punishment that I could hardly bear the thought of it. I could not imagine ever willingly disappointing my parents, especially when they had great expectations of me. I was the eldest, the first boy followed by five other boys, a privilege in ranking, a burden in responsibility.

I was thus in a state of utter disbelief as I sat on the ship. Perhaps as an Easterner I was waiting for a miracle. I certainly felt that I needed one. All nine hundred passengers had left the ship. Most of them were Italians who had embarked at Naples – villagers who carried with them all of their possessions, mostly food and clothes. The Italians were already ashore, hugging and kissing their waiting relatives. While a virtual Italian opera played out on land, I sat alone on a deserted ship. The loudspeaker finally broke the silence, summoning me – the young rebel – to the captain's cabin. With defiant steps I obeyed, hugging my *Gathering Storm*, my sin and my crime.

A young diplomat from the Lebanese embassy, sent by Dr Charles Malik, was there to meet me. Dr Malik was a close relative of my mother's and was Lebanon's ambassador to the United States and the United Nations. The young Lebanese diplomat had spoken to my tormentor and together the two of them concluded that I was in the wrong. My countryman asked me to apologize. 'The police officer will accept your apology and let you disembark.'

Apologize! The thought offended me. For what? I was now a pompous rebel and replied, 'The policeman should apologize to me!'

Lengthy diplomatic negotiations ensued. My patient representative explained to the captain who I was – a good student from a good family. To my chagrin the diplomat went to great lengths to assure him that my family was anti-Communist, and to stress how pro-American my whole neighbourhood was. If the sea had made me sick, I was now becoming even sicker.

But it was just what was required to satisfy the authorities that they did not have a bomb-throwing radical trying to enter the country and in due course we reached an understanding. There were suddenly smiles all around. The smile was still beaming from my face as I walked out to shake hands with the police officer. He heartily reciprocated, glad to see the last of this mess. Finally, peace restored, I walked from the ship a free man. The kind young diplomat even took me to a hotel to rest for a few days before I went on to my ultimate destination in Ohio.

He took me to the McAlpin Hotel, which was to me a veritable skyscraper. It was immense, huge, forbidding and more im-personal than any hotel I had ever set foot in. From my room on the twenty-fifth floor I looked down aghast from a very great height. I wondered how many floors could be stacked this way, one above the other. The people scurrying back and forth on the streets below made me think of Lilliputians. 'So, this is New York,' I repeated to myself, 'here below me is New York, the great city, the financial capital of the world. Look as far as you can and you see nothing but buildings – skyscrapers, bridges and monuments. Man has made everything you see. Truly astonishing. Here nature has been conquered by the will of that teeming multitude who fled Europe to build a new world across the sea.'

In utter, exhausted amazement, I explored the room in which I found myself. I turned the radio on. The song I heard was a happy one, upbeat. 'Lucky, lucky, lucky me, I am a lucky son of a gun: I work eight hours, I sleep eight hours and leave eight hours for fun.' It was sung in a jubilant mood by one who plainly believed every word of it. In my dazed and battered state, it was quite beyond my understanding. It was completely different from the music I knew. I was accustomed to songs of tortured love, of suffering, of lovers' separation.

I sat down and wrote the longest letter I had ever written to my parents. I explained the difference between the American song I was hearing and the songs I had grown up with. I explored that difference. From this one experience, I went on and on, regardless

13

of the fact that I based my whole philosophy on something I knew nothing about. Not that I ever confessed that. These people, I wrote, are happy, they are disciplined. They work, they rest, they have *fun*! Fun was not allowed to be part of our vocabulary as children.

When I had recovered my energy I went down to learn about the city, to walk its streets. After short rations on board ship I was looking forward to a good meal. As I walked I noted that I was strolling while everybody else was rushing, practically running. Many knocked into me in their hurry. One woman actually screamed at me – 'Move, move!'

'But where to?' I frantically asked myself.

I took refuge in a restaurant and I was somewhat soothed as a beautiful young maiden approached me – until she yelled: 'Whudyawant?'

'I want to eat,' I said.

'What number?' she demanded, already irritated.

'What do you mean what number? I want to eat food.'

'Order food by the numbers listed here,' and she slapped down a list and walked away.

In a minute she returned, threw a knife and a fork at me, and walked away again. I did not look at the list. I was determined to ask her what they had and to select what I wanted in the manner I chose. Wrong. She refused to speak with me about my meal. There was absolutely no chance of negotiation here. Order by number; get your meal – no conversation. The more I asked, the madder she got. I left two dollars on the table and walked out, hungry and frustrated.

Several visits by the young diplomat helped a bit, but not much. I was lost in this new culture. After all, I had no proper orientation. Everything was different. The young diplomat tried to help me understand. He spoke fervently about America. 'It is the greatest country in the world,' my new friend said. 'It is largely industrial and the people are imbued with the ethic of hard work and belief in individual effort. The Americans work hard, play hard and vacation hard.' The more he spoke, the more eloquent he became and he gave many examples to support his opinion.

'But what about food?' I enquired. 'Why do the waitresses not converse? Why does the system rely on numbers?'

'Yes, it's strange I know,' he said. 'But there is a good reason for it. Americans are very busy. They take only a short break for lunch. The menu has a list of some fifteen dishes. Each dish carries a number. You just tell the waitress the number or numbers you want, and she will serve you immediately. If you want to converse at a meal, you must go to a fancy restaurant, where you get a fancy meal and you pay a fancy price. That is how you will get your conversation. Everything has a fee.'

I was so shocked and alienated by my first experiences in New York that I hurried on to my destination – the University of Cincinnati – which I found to be a beautiful place with charming people.

It was now, having come from Cincinnati to SAIS just over a year later, that I found myself in Washington DC, in love with a young Pottstownian.

What was I to make of her desire for me to meet her family? Was she so keen to show me off? I feared instead that she mistrusted her attraction to me and perhaps needed family reassurance that I was in fact worth pursuing. Whatever her motivation, after only a few weeks of talking and walking the avenues of Washington together, Phyllis decided to bring me to Philadelphia and Pottstown and to do the rounds of the family.

She anxiously tried to prepare me for an encounter with small-town America. Of her large, extended family, only her father and mother had ever left Pottstown to settle in the greater city near by. She needn't have worried, for I required no introduction to the ways of provincial people. Throughout the world, they are much alike. Generally I have found that those who live in small communities tend to be suspicious and fearful of anyone who represents Otherness. The greater the Otherness, the greater the fear, the deeper the suspicion. And to the Pottstownians I was an Other far beyond any of their previous experience. Nevertheless, what was to them a cause for concern was to me a matter of intense pride.

The train was at that time the most common way to travel among the cities in the eastern United States. Trains were fast, luxurious and reliable. Thus, on a golden day in late October, the lovers took the train to Philadelphia, the City of Brotherly Love, for a meeting with the family. It was a glorious day and I was with a girl I adored, and yet I was apprehensive.

From the East we came to the West with little knowledge but with infinite pride. Play to the dignity of the Arab and you can rob him of everything – even his clothes. Assault that dignity only if you are prepared for battle. Much as I feared a fight with the family, I would not allow my dignity to be affronted. Phyllis knew me well enough to understand that I would not be humiliated without a fight. And yet she did not seem worried at all. She seemed oblivious to the dangers of my visit.

I was ambitious, volatile and wildly inspired with the idea of remaking the world. I was headed for an encounter with her average American family. Although they supported her ambitions, the members of Phyllis's family were not really interested in higher education, and certainly my PhD studies would not impress them. But Phyllis was completely sure of herself and of her parents. She was amused by my apprehensions, she was supremely confident and she was light-hearted to the point of giddiness. The day itself provided the perfect setting for her mood – it was simply beautiful.

The train carried us smoothly through the richly wooded country of eastern Pennsylvania. I sat facing my beloved, admiring her beauty, captivated by the shine of her spectacular eyes. Despite my seriousness, she giggled and laughed and we filled the time as we nearly always did – with endless conversation. Oh, how we loved to talk! Language was our tool of exploration, the one we used to excavate the hidden worlds reserved only for young lovers. I yearned to know everything about her, her family, her town, her people, how she had come to be the extraordinary young woman I loved. It was a rare ambition she had – to leave her small town behind, to fulfil herself and her duty to her country and the world in the Foreign Service. I longed to understand what made her choose this. I was more curious than I had ever been about anything to know what had lit the fire of resolution in this small-town girl. How had she become so determined to storm Washington and earn the right to serve her country in foreign lands? Her curiosity about me was just as strong. She was full of questions about the part of the world I came from, what culture had shaped me, what language framed my perceptions, what history animated my hopes and dreams, and most importantly what family I would return to. And I was pleased and proud to tell her all these things.

Although I laughed when she asked if I belonged to a tribe and lived in a tent, I understood why she asked. I used the question to spin her the story of Muhammad, my Saudi friend, who lived in Washington. She listened intently as I told his tale.

'Muhammad,' I began, 'is a student at Georgetown University. Like me he has fallen in love with a sweet American girl . . .'

It would probably have been more accurate to say that his girl, a stunning blonde named Betty, had fallen madly in love with Muhammad. My friend was much older, in his mid-thirties, mature, cautious and realistic. Betty was a romantic. Her dreamy imagination transformed Muhammad into a romantic figure, a Lawrence of Arabia. Never mind that unlike Lawrence, Muhammad was a dark and rugged tribesman, a man who lived in a tent in the desert some hundred miles from Mecca. I told Phyllis about the day Muhammad came to me in tears.

'Elie,' my friend pleaded, 'you have got to save Betty from disaster. There is no way I can marry her. I tell her all about my life – the tent, the desert, the sheep and the camels. She finds it all very exciting. I tell her that there is no electricity, no running water, no bathrooms. There are not even houses in the sense that she understands them. She gets more excited. I try to tell her about Islam and she just nods to tell me she has read an article on Islam and kind of liked it. I tell her about the Wahhabis – how reactionary they are, about the House of Saud and how authoritarian it is. I tell her about traditions that bind women to the home and free men to roam, and you know what her reaction is? She says, "Great – you and I will lead a reform movement!" She will not understand that her ideas would probably lead to us having our heads chopped off.'

As the train moved through the autumn sunshine, Phyllis hung on every detail of this story. 'And did you meet Betty?' she demanded to know. 'Did you dissuade her?'

'Well, I tried,' I told my avid listener. 'I really did. But the more I told her things I thought she would find intolerable about life in Saudi Arabia, the more determined she was to marry Muhammad.'

And so it was. Not even my description of how justice is meted out in Saudi Arabia, how the authorities cut off the hands of thieves and other minor offenders, could move Betty from her determination to marry my friend. She was certain that they could change the society he came from. Muhammad saw that his fate was sealed. He sank slowly into an abyss of despair, a black hole from which all light was extinguished.

The tale of Betty and Muhammad put Phyllis in a pensive mood. I could read her thoughts in her brilliant eyes as she considered the obvious moral of my story. 'Is he scaring me off?' she wondered. 'Is Lebanon like Saudi Arabia? Are we as incompatible as Muhammad and Betty?' She did not voice these fears. She was too loving, too concerned to demonstrate her trust in this untested youth to express the doubts that must have crowded into her mind. Reason was put aside until the future. Its turn would come as our romance matured and progressed towards marriage, parenthood, home and future careers. For now she wore an enigmatic smile on her angelic face and gazed out at the spectacular countryside between Washington and Philadelphia.

Pennsylvania is a beautiful state, with rolling hills, seemingly endless forests and a network of rivers nourishing the land. Even the roads seemed part of this organic system. Cars and trucks crowded the highways, carrying people to work and goods to their destination. A variety of craft thronged the rivers. I thought of the civilizations that rose and fell centuries ago on the Tigris, the Euphrates and the Nile. In this happy, contemplative state we arrived in Philadelphia. We disembarked at the North Philadelphia station. Phyllis held my hand and led me up to the happy, very happy mother waiting alone on the small platform. My first impression of Dorothy was of a gorgeous smile. Hugs and kisses for Phyllis, a warm handshake for me. Not a bad start, I thought, with some relief.

'This is Elie whom I've told you so much about,' Phyllis was saying, ' . . . and Elie, this is Dorothy, my mother.'

A blonde in her forties, Dorothy looked more like Phyllis's sister than her mother. I later discovered that Dorothy was married at the age of sixteen. Mother and daughter climbed into the front seat of the car and I got into the back. Soon the two of them were chattering about everything with only an occasional and brief allusion to their captive in the back seat. I immediately loved Dorothy. She was all motherhood, all kindness, all readiness to please the prized princess by her side, the child who had become, in her motherly eyes, a big shot in the capital.

In the small towns of Pennsylvania people bragged about their children working in Washington, just as villagers in Lebanon boasted about their sons and daughters who worked in Beirut. Parents everywhere stretched the truth, and who cared, as no one really knew what the sons and daughters were doing in the capital or whether they were big wheels or small ones? The message was in the effect. Parents tend to exaggerate, the better to impress their neighbours. We do that a lot in the village. I found that it was also common in the United States.

My professor at Johns Hopkins was from a small hamlet in Ohio, and he would often return home at weekends. When his mother received a call for him, she would always use the chance to show off a bit.

'Norman,' his mother cried out for all to hear, 'hurry up, Washington is calling.'

In an Ohio hamlet, Washington may be interpreted as a high government official, even the President, the Secretary of State, no one was too exalted in a mother's estimation. The same went for Pottstown, and its 'emigrants' to Philadelphia.

Beneath their chatter, the mother regarded her child in awe. The unspoken thoughts in her wondering gaze went something like, 'So you love Washington, and you will serve your country in the Foreign Service. So you will be leaving soon for a distant capital in Europe, in the Soviet Union, in Africa, in South-East Asia, in India . . . ' However Dorothy stretched her imagination to encompass her child's future, the Arab World did not really figure in the mother's mind. Israel, Palestine and the Arab–Israeli wars were just beginning to emerge as issues in Washington and New York. My entire world had not yet even dawned on the consciousness of most American minds: not in Philadelphia, and definitely not in Pottstown.

The Sell home was on Stratford Avenue in Melrose Park, a suburb of Philadelphia. It was pleasant and comfortable, well furnished for a family of limited means. A piano (for Phyllis, of course) was proudly exhibited by the winding stairs that led to two upper floors. As we arrived, the rest of the family assembled to meet me. Phyllis's father was Ernest – called Ernie – and her two brothers were William, called Bill, and Peter, called Pete. There was another daughter as well, Bonnie – called Bon. The Sells built their family in stages: Phyllis and Bill first, a respite of a dozen years, and then Bonnie and Peter.

If ever there was a typical American working man, it was Ernie. He had finished his high-school education and then joined the workforce. Ernie was a salesman who needed no training in salesmanship. He was a natural in it. He had worked hard to keep the family together during the Depression. Both father and mother had spent all their meagre earnings to provide milk and food for Phyllis and Bill. Jobs were rare, and Ernie had travelled from city to city, from town to town looking for temporary jobs at a time when the entire economy was on hold. He was versatile and handy, fixing machines, furniture – almost anything – with ease. He tried his hand at every possible opportunity that came his way. He worked as a milkman, as a construction supervisor overseeing the building of cheap houses, and now as a salesman for a series of different products.

I had learned that the early 1930s were extremely hard for most Americans. When the market collapsed, great investors jumped from skyscrapers in despair, preferring death to the frightening uncertainties of the Depression. Working people were hungry, homeless and desperate to provide for their families. One man stood out and gave the people hope. It was Franklin D. Roosevelt, the new president, the man of the New Deal. President Roosevelt told the American people, 'The only thing we have to fear is fear itself,' and inspired them to exhibit courage and endurance. Ernie, like so many Americans, loved Roosevelt and trusted his slogan. He was inspired to sacrifice and to work for the common good, secure in the hope of a better future. Thus traits of courage, endurance and personal sacrifice for the greater good were woven from her first breath into the character of Phyllis Sell.

Ernie, like all fathers, had a special weakness for his fragile baby daughter. She was, and would always be, his favourite. His highest hopes were for her future, and he looked with suspicion upon this stranger who accompanied her home. But he was clever; he did not lack perception, and he was not about to reach a hasty decision that he might come to regret. In the Sell home, Ernie spoke and Dorothy listened, or rather busied herself in running in and out of the kitchen making coffee, preparing dinner and washing dishes. Ernie's world was oceans away from mine, physically and figuratively – a Pottstownian facing a Lebanese; an experienced, hardened working man facing a graduate student; a cautious father facing an alien youth. And the alien triggered the instinctive fear of the unknown. Initially we shifted like combatants, seeking middle ground and finding none. Phyllis, too, was uncharacteristically reticent and still too inexperienced to help much. We struggled on.

I asked about his business and he spoke enthusiastically about the machine company founded by an Armenian from Iraq. Although Ernie was a sort of partner and a successful salesman, he complained that it was a family business. That fact made it difficult for him as an American to fit in, and to feel like a genuine partner to the clever Armenian.

'The Armenian family,' Ernie told me, 'are a mysterious bunch. They stick together, they whisper, they make deals, all behind my back.'

Since Ernie spoke English and they spoke Armenian, or Armenian mixed with their own home-made English, I could see that it was difficult for him but that he made the best of it.

He did not ask me about Johns Hopkins, about my field of study, about my country or my culture. Clearly Ernie did not know how to venture into my world. Years later I understood that one cannot ask about things that one does not know. If you have had no familiarity with higher education, you cannot easily ask a stranger about his college experience. Never having travelled outside the States, Ernie could not frame questions that made sense, even to himself. Such inner caution handicapped our first conversations. He would not venture only to fall. He lacked the words, the frame of reference and the necessary threads to connect questions and possible answers. He had no interest in these things aside from my relationship with his beloved daughter and that topic was still too tender to broach.

Out of the silence, he suddenly ventured, 'Son, what can you do with your hands?'

Though it startled me at the time, it was of course quite an appropriate question in America at that period. Here was a virgin continent of vast forests, plains and deserts. The European colonists came with axe and hammer and they tamed it. The Americans were first and foremost workers, clearers of forests, builders of roads, tillers of the land. The act came first. Thought as abstraction formalised by higher education came later, but had not yet replaced the tangible fact of the land and the art of dealing with it. What can you do with your hands? was a legitimate question from an axe-wielder.

Americans were self-sufficient. They chose a piece of land, they built their own homes, and they ploughed their own fields. In the early fifties, the American household was still quite self-supporting. It owned and operated virtually all the tools it needed. Father, mother and children painted the house, mowed the lawn, repaired broken chairs, planted their trees and shrubs, and kept their automobiles running. Only rarely did they call on others to come to the rescue. While vaguely aware of this aspect of American history, I still only partially grasped what Ernie was asking me.

I answered meekly, 'Well . . . nothing.'

Ernie was a great lover of antiques and he collected old chairs and tables, especially Pennsylvania Dutch furniture. He thought I had merely misunderstood and tried to simplify to the essentials of his question.

'Can you fix a broken chair?'

'No.'

'Can you polish wood?'

'No.'

'Can you frame pictures?'

'No.'

It could not have been easy for Ernie to grasp this unprecedented level of incompetence and he did not give up easily. He moved into another realm of the physical world.

'Can you mow the lawn?'

Now the perplexed student was utterly silenced, not by content but by nomenclature. Mow! Lawn! Two words I had never heard and said so. By that time Ernie had concluded that the candidate had miserably failed the interview. As was to happen again and again, Phyllis came to my rescue. In slow, simplified language, neither patronizing nor pedantic, she presented me to the Sells as a doctor might present a difficult case to his students. Her family listened politely, nodded occasionally and understood nothing.

The Sells really were average Americans, good people and good Christians. They were Lutheran and took their religion seriously. The Bible lay on the piano, and there was no dust on it. The Sells read their Bible regularly and conscientiously, applying it to their lives and believing its messages. The ritual of church every Sunday was welcomed and unquestioned. The family dressed up for church and joined with the choir in singing the great Protestant hymns: 'Onward, Christian Soldiers', 'Nearer, My God, to Thee', 'We Shall Gather at the River'.

As their pastor sermonized on all issues under the sun, the family listened respectfully and attentively. The Sells tried to see the world as through the eyes of Jesus. At the end of the service, they filed out one by one, shook the pastor's hand, exchanged warm greetings and congratulated him on his erudition. Then, they went home for a good meal. Grace before breaking bread was routine, and was never missed. Ernie's prayers were home-made and heartfelt. His prayer perfectly epitomized the man. Although he tried to lead his children to God through his example, he never succeeded in instilling quite the same authenticity of worship in them. Ernie's children never were able to pray as seriously or as humbly as he did.

But Ernie's kids followed his example more successfully in other ways. They finished high school and went to work. His children all left home at the age of eighteen. They were independent; they immediately got jobs and earned their own living – and they all married young. It was easily possible at that time for an American family to live well on a working man's income. A typical worker could own a house, a car, and command the amenities of comfortable living. He spent what he earned, and he enjoyed his life. He could even send a son or daughter to college – and many did.

No one seemed to worry about the future. The Sells were no exception. Phyllis's paternal grandfather worked on the railroad. He was a God-fearing man, a bit silent and something of a loner who had a steady job that allowed him to work throughout the Depression and retire with a small pension. Her Uncle Tom was a union electrician who also kept a steady job. Phyllis especially enjoyed the fact that her maternal grandmother worked in the box office at a movie theatre. Young Phyllis and Bill gained free access to the shows. Long before television hooked American children, the Sell family used the movies as a convenient babysitter during the 1930s and 1940s. Phyllis and her brother saw dozens, maybe hundreds of movies that opened up infinite horizons for them.

The Sells were Pennsylvania Dutch – so called through an Americanization of Deutsch, meaning German. This group of Lutheran migrants to Pennsylvania came from Germany at about the same time as the War of Independence in 1776. They were farmers who left the fields of Germany for life in the New World. They were still a close-knit community when I encountered them, living in Philadelphia and the surrounding countryside. The Pennsylvania Dutch are practical people and much more worldly than their neighbours, the exotic Mennonites.

Though deeply Christian, these Lutherans detested the Pope. Their love for Christ was balanced by a disdain for the Antichrist living in Rome. Nothing was more surprising than to see the sweet, round, cherub-like face of Phyllis's paternal grandmother twist into a sneer when the word 'Catholic' was mentioned. Her son Ernie seriously considered converting to Catholicism at one time. He might have gone through with it, just to shock the community, had he not been made to understand the scope of vengeance he would incur from his seemingly benign mother.

The most engaging characters in Phyllis's immediate family were her maternal grandmother Mary and her step-grandfather Dada. Mary was a tall buxom handsome woman, intelligent and a bon viveuse. She loved men and experimented generously in her day. She used men as sex objects and looked upon them with pity and a bit of scorn. She thought they were stupid, arrogant and, on the whole, overrated. Like her provincial peers in Pottstown, she was truly a bigot. She detested Catholics, Blacks, Mexicans, Poles, Jews, and all those unfortunate immigrants who had arrived of late in Pottstown and infected its pure air. Mary's prejudice was constantly reinforced as she daily played cards with a bunch of women of like mind. Naturally, they talked about their common enemy. They jeered at the foreign devil; they assigned him a place in hell, and they felt pretty good about themselves.

Phyllis faced a real challenge when it came to bringing her parents around to support her interest in me. But that challenge was less than nothing compared with the task of getting Mary to understand and it was a task Phyllis worked hard at tackling.

'He is such a nice boy, from a good family. He is a serious scholar – a PhD candidate, a man with a bright future,' Phyllis said earnestly to Mary. 'It really makes no difference that he's Lebanese! He is Christian Lebanese, Christian like us, but a bit different – like the Greeks you've heard of, Greek Orthodox and religious too. He does not go regularly to church like us, but his faith is deep. He knows a lot about the Bible and the New Testament.' Phyllis gained confidence. 'So what if he is an Arab!'

But the word Arab triggered Mary's fury and brought forth the full force of her anti-alien prejudice. 'An Arab?' she exclaimed vehemently. 'An Arab? Then he must be a Muslim, or whatever they call the followers of that imposter from the desert. If he is Arab, he must be black. How can I face my bridge partners if you marry a Black?'

Wounded, but not defeated, Phyllis fought back. 'He's not a Muslim – and anyhow there is nothing wrong with Muslims. He is not black.'

'What is he then?' Mary demanded. 'Is he white?'

'Yes, I think so,' Phyllis replied shakily. 'Oh, I don't know. He seems white to me, a bit baked more than us by the Mediterranean sun.'

But that was later. On this, our first visit, Phyllis understood intuitively that it was better not to meet Mary. Phyllis was content to let Dorothy, the daughter whom Mary adored, and Ernie, the son-in-law she tolerated, prepare the grandmother in advance. This was determined based on the dubious assumption that Dorothy and Ernie would form a good opinion of me as a boyfriend. No one was talking of marriage at this stage, though now I understand that the thought was in all their minds. I knew a lot about Mary from Phyllis's family stories, and was truly eager to cross swords with her. I would have my day in court.

As for Dada, he was exactly what Mary wanted him to be, a delightful nobody, eager to please, to go along with her and to help in the kitchen. His favourite occupation seemed to be washing dishes. In the Sell family the wife was the cook and the husband washed dishes. When Dada was around, all deferred to him at dishwashing time. In any case, Dada would not allow anyone to share in his cherished ritual. The lunch dishes he washed thorough-ly, carefully, and so slowly that he usually finished just before dinner. No one ever knew when he finished the dinner dishes, since by then we were all sound asleep. In time, the family came to know what caused the extended dishwashing sessions, though they kept it to themselves. Dada was too kind a man to be confronted with unpleasant truths, and thus his symbiotic ties to the dishes were accepted as a harmless mystery.

Peaceful, gentle Dada was a closet alcoholic. The compulsion to wash-up was not driven by the dish, the soap or the hot water, but by the bottle of bourbon whiskey in the closet above the sink. As an alcoholic Dada was like a sleepwalker, and that suited Mary just fine. He had not always been so. He had been changed by destiny. In a not too distant past he had been a handsome Catholic widower. He was a free man until Mary decided that she needed a consort. And without knowing what hit him Dada found himself married, Lutheran and oppressed. Mary made all family decisions, and Dada nodded gently. Mary took the master bedroom, and Dada was relegated to a tiny room, one that reminded me of a maid's room in an average Lebanese apartment. I never heard Dada curse, except once when he was watching a boxing match between a white boxer and one who was black. For the duration of the fight Dada was on the edge of his seat, eyes fixed on the tiny television screen, mouth wide open, and the veins of his neck on the verge of bursting. He screamed continuously, he was angry, he was up, he was down, he was gesturing. This was not the sweet figure we knew. This was Alexander at the gates of Sidon, Napoleon at Austerlitz, Hitler at Warsaw. Gentleman Dada had to hate someone, had to express his suppressed anger, and his victim of choice was this black fighter.

'Pound his black face, break his neck, kill the sonofabitch,' the raging spectator ordered the white boxer. But to Dada's dismay, his erstwhile champion was himself undergoing a pounding resulting from another rage, another anger, another oppression.

And yet, the more I knew Dada, the more I loved him. In years to come, Dada would be promoted from dishwashing to babysitting my children – in the distant capital of the great USA. This would prove to be a welcome vocation for him, with easy access to bourbon.

Phyllis had one uncle and two aunts. The uncle was a nice gentle soul, unemployed. He was never seen without a bottle of beer in his hand. He lived alone, and died a lonely man at an early age. Her Aunt Mimi was a jovial round woman, a great singer, an unequalled cook, always talking, always laughing. She was best known for her driving style. As she drove, she looked sideways and backwards at her passengers, gesturing, pointing this way and that and often bumping into trees, walls, cars and other objects that crossed her path. No matter how often this occurred, Mimi maintained her good spirits about the accidents. Mimi's husband Walt was a mailman, easygoing, earthy and primitive in a positive way. His favourite subject of conversation was food. 'Mimi what are we having for dinner?' was a frequent conversation starter. Aunt Suzie was a beauty, tall and imposing. She had just one problem, her husband Tom. Tom worked hard as an electrician and retired early. He was driving her crazy. She wanted children. He said no. She obeyed and stoically catered to all his needs. No complaints from long-suffering Suzie. Mimi and Suzie loved Phyllis and Phyllis adored them.

Phyllis's brother Bill, two years her junior, was finishing high school when I met him. Bill was angling for a job in sales, like his father's. As the first two children of Ernie and Dorothy, Phyllis and Bill had a wonderful childhood. The extended family was still close. The grandparents, the uncles, the aunts were all around, and were full of love and care for the two youngsters. Phyllis and Bill were buddies, and very, very close. Bill was relatively small, and when some tough peer of his bullied him, Phyllis automatically administered a stunning punch. She was always there ready to come to Bill's rescue, and she was always right. Bill grew up adoring his older sister, and the sister grew up holding him in a very special and deep affection.

At first encounter, Bill was suspicious of me. I was truly alien, ergo unpredictable, and could be a source of heartbreak, even tragedy, for his idol. He bravely challenged me, asking why I wanted to be Phyllis's boyfriend anyway. I believe I may have murmured that she wanted me to be. During that first visit to the Sell household, the adults all exercised extreme caution. Although everyone did his or her best to contain the tension, it silently reverberated from wall to wall.

There were two other children in the family: Bonnie aged seven and Peter aged four. And fortunately children do not reason, do not enquire and usually do not worry. They just cuddle; they want to love and be loved in return. I easily loved Bon and Petey, and they loved me back. This pleased Phyllis no end, this contact at the deepest human level. Children tend to have a basic understanding of others long before judgement carves a place for itself in their hearts. Christ had a deep regard for children. He paid special attention to them and welcomed them unto His divine presence.

Perhaps by nature or by imitation of the Crucified One, I too loved children. I felt at ease with them. I could easily and joyously descend from the height of my inflated ego to the elemental and self-sufficient world of the child, and there I could be at best childlike, at worst childish – two adjectives I have always loved.

Some friends have said that I am an accomplished actor. Perhaps it is so, but only if the acting is a natural unpremeditated type of behaviour. Perhaps acting is an integral part of being, a function acquired over our long journey from prehistory, useful for adjustment, for survival. I act, because I am, and being is not conscious acting.

This was a momentous weekend, both for the Sells and for me. It was unique. Poor Sells, I thought. Poor Elie, they must have thought back. The trip on the train back to Washington was a delight: two dazed young people analysing the thoughts, beliefs and times of the previous generation. Phyllis was happy with the visit. She thought the shock was bearable. I, too, thought the visit had been a relative success. No disaster had occurred. After all, Phyllis and I were friends with no long-term plans, at least none declared. The family visit somehow strengthened the bond between Phyllis and me; it added a serious dimension, and we talked about it. Lovers of such divergent backgrounds must talk, and I was, and still am, a big talker. Phyllis was curious, full of questions, and Socratic in her approach. Although her family lacked the means to send her to college, she took secretarial classes and was determined to make a larger life for herself than was possible in Pottstown. She was a voracious reader of novels of all types, and this of itself opens up horizons and arouses intellectual curiosity. She was exceptionally alert and culturally and intellectually mature.

Some couples court in restaurants, some in nightclubs. I courted Phyllis on Connecticut Avenue – a broad, long avenue in the nation's capital. In New York City, Fifth Avenue is the up-market street. In Washington it is Connecticut Avenue. Here are the luxury shops, the good bookstores, the fine restaurants and the highbrow hotels. Dupont Circle, which attracted artists, poets, loners and dreamy intellectuals, provided a respite for walkers and sitters alike. The Circle with its fountain, statue, trees and inviting benches was a good place for us to rest and pursue our seemingly endless intellectual explorations. Phyllis loved Dupont Circle, and after an intensive search, she and three of her girlfriends rented an apartment overlooking the prized site.

Many an evening I took my books and worked late into the evening at her apartment. Walking the few blocks from Dupont to Florida Avenue at midnight proved to be a hazardous undertaking. Somehow, parts of DC that were quite normal in the daytime turned exclusively gay at night. One evening we decided to have dinner in a favourite lunch-spot. When we arrived for dinner, it was very busy, nearly full. We found one lone vacant table, and took it. Just after we ordered our food, Phyllis looked at me and said, 'Let's get out of here.'

'But, why?' I enquired.

'Look,' she said, 'I am the only girl here.'

I looked. It was true. 'So what?' I asked innocently.

'Because this is a gay restaurant, this is a gay crowd,' she said. 'Some of your Hopkins colleagues may be here.'

'So what?' I was still mystified.

'What!' she exclaimed, now exasperated. 'They'll think you're a homosexual and I'm a lesbian.'

'Not bad,' I replied. 'The greater the rumour, the deeper the intrigue.'

Not one to allow love to affect her reason, my practical Phyllis was not amused. I rushed to the counter, paid for the food we did not eat, and we walked out.

Beautiful, artistic Dupont Circle turned out to be a gay hangout. I was disconcerted as I walked through the area at midnight from my girlfriend's home to be approached again and again. Phyllis was terrified. She thought it could be dangerous for me to arrive at her place after dark or to leave late. And, indeed, there came a time when I was approached by a transvestite who was desperate, persistent and, in the end, violent. I had to punch him/her pretty hard to get away.

It was a source of great speculation for Phyllis and the roommates – Why are they so interested in Elie? 'Obvious,' proclaimed tall, loud Suzie, the Californian. 'Let's face it. Elie is the exotic Arab. He is different, and these guys thrive on experiments. Elie is the experiment *par excellence*.' Someone piped up: 'Are you saying Elie might have those kind of tendencies?' but this suggestion was greeted with hysterical laughter from Phyllis as the joke of the century.

The room-mates loved to hear about my acclimatization to the United States and often urged me to talk about my previous year in Cincinnati.

'I have learned a lot about American customs,' I told them. 'I learned all about them in the first weeks and months of the academic year in 1950.' I explained to them that it was normal in Lebanon in my teenage days for friends to hold hands – boys would commonly hold hands with boys and girls with girls. We all did that in our villages, in our schools and in our universities in Beirut. It was utterly unacceptable for a boy and a girl to be seen holding hands in public and beyond imagining for them to be embracing or kissing. This was utterly taboo, dangerous for the boy, calamitous for the girl. I assumed Lebanese customs to be universal, and for that ignorance I paid dearly.

A few days after my arrival in Cincinnati (Cincy to the natives and soon to me as well), I asked my room-mate Elmer to go with me to a movie downtown. Jovially we took the bus and occupied two seats midway between the front and back. The bus was full. Unconsciously, and in perfect obedience to ingrained Lebanese norms, my left arm sailed over my friend and perched on his shoulder. Gently Elmer removed my arm. Gently my armed sailed again. Elmer was shocked and quite angry. He shouted for all to hear, 'Elie! I didn't know you were a homosexual.'

Equally shocked and angry, I screamed back, 'Who me? Homosexual!?'

'Yes, you!' he stormed, heedless of the now stunned audience on the Clifton Avenue bus. With a knee-jerk reaction, totally out of control, I punched Elmer smack on the nose. To my horror, blood gushed from his mouth and nose as I screamed wildly, cursing and threatening him for insulting me as he did. The driver stopped the bus and ordered us out, whereupon, as if from nowhere, two burly policemen appeared. They arrested Elmer and me and dragged us to the police station.

When I had been confronted with the Harbor Police on the ship in New York, I had been proud, I had stood tall, defending my identity and asserting my dignity in the face of a superpower. In the police station in Cincinnati, however, I felt shame. I was humiliated. I was sure I had done something wrong to drive Elmer to accuse me of homosexuality, but I did not know what. It began to dawn on me slowly that I had violated American propriety and consequently hurt a good friend. We were told to wait for a senior officer to interrogate us. When the detective arrived, he was sober and suspicious as he looked me straight in the eye and asked: 'So, what's going on?' And he listened as I told him.

He turned to Elmer, and Elmer confirmed my story about our battle on the bus.

'So you two are homos?'

'No, sir,' we answered in unison.

'Then why did you put your arm on his shoulder?' he asked, looking at me.

' I thought it was a friendly act. It is in Lebanon,' I answered.

'What Lebanon, where?' The detective was suddenly confused.

'Not Lebanon, Pennsylvania,' I answered.'Lebanon – in the Middle East.'

'Hmmm,' the officer was thoughtful. 'I hear most of you out there have queer habits.'

'No more, no less, sir, than you have here.' I was indignant, but still humbled.

'Why did you embrace him?' he struggled to make sense of it.

'I did not embrace him, I put my hand on his shoulder,' I replied. 'I'm sorry.'

'Why did you create such a commotion and disturb the peace?'

'It was beyond my control, sir, when he accused me of being queer.'

At that, the detective took a new approach. 'What are you doing in town?' he asked me.

'I am a graduate student at the University of Cincinnati.'

'Well, then. You should go back to school. No more trouble now, just go away.' He dismmissed us, shaking his head wearily.

'Great advice,' I murmured to myself and immediately followed his excellent counsel. Elmer and I walked out friends and I invited him for a cup of coffee. We both apologized for the misunderstanding.

But I had been sent to the United States to study, to get a doctorate and to return without delay and definitely without a scandal. So, not being one for taking chances, I went straight to my cherubic landlady, Mrs Dalzelle, and asked for the one private bedroom in her house, though I knew it would cost me. Although I could not afford it, even less could I afford any more misunderstandings. The fewer problems, the better.

My tale of Elmer delighted the gossip-loving girls in the apartment by Dupont Circle. They realized there was a wide cultural chasm between my country and theirs, and they wanted to hear more about my experiences in 'Cincy'. Phyllis was curious but anxious. She was obviously serious about me, and wanted to learn more about these encounters. 'Clearly he is not a homosexual,' she thought, 'but he could be nuts.'

They were all amused by the tale of Elmer and laughed at the dilemma I had found myself in. Phyllis egged me on. Truly I did not know how to begin and how much to say. The culture shock I experienced from the moment I set foot in New York was far greater than I had expected. It was a mistake to arrive in a country knowing as little as I did about its customs. I had got so much wrong – and suffered for it.

For the most part, I loved the Cincinnatians. They were friendly, ready to help, and generally ready to learn. But even with such friendly people, culture intervened. A sweet classmate named Ann invited me to have dinner with her family on a Friday night. 'I'm sorry,' I said, 'I can't.' She accepted my refusal and repeated the invitation the next week. Again I regretted, and she graciously accepted my regrets. This went on for several weeks. By then, I was furious and for days would not speak to her. When she asked why, I told her quite frankly. 'Clearly, you're not serious about your invitation, and I wish you would stop teasing me.' I scolded her. 'You don't insist on my presence, you don't pursue it. You just say OK and leave it at that. This is not fair to me and, in fact, this is insulting.'

Poor Ann, she was completely taken aback. She sat me down and gave me a long orientation lecture. Her father and her mother both wanted to meet me, Ann assured me. Dad was a high-school principal at Indian Hill, a luxurious suburb of this cosy American town, and she had told them about her foreign friend. 'They would like for you to dine with them. They really want you to come for dinner. They are eager to come and pick you up and drive you back. They are learned people. They are interested in other cultures, we all *want* you to say yes.'

I accepted, and Ann breathed a sigh of relief.

The Davisons received me well and we seemed to be doing all right until we were called for dinner. Mrs Davison must have worked hard to make things nice for the evening. The table looked very pretty, perfect in fact. There were four pieces of meat, four baked potatoes and four grilled tomatoes. I quickly saw that if each one of us took one of each, nothing would be left on the table. I knew this would be a catastrophe and I panicked.

In Lebanon, the dining-table is customarily loaded with a wide variety and abundance of food. It is expected that guests will hardly make a dent in all the food offered. To have nothing left would be a great embarrassment to the hosts, and I certainly did not want to embarrass them on my very first visit. I pretended that I had already eaten, that I had not been aware that the invitation was for dinner.

'Oh, what a shame,' said Mr Davison as they cheerfully shared my portion of the meal. My empty stomach brought home the fact that I had learned yet another lesson in American customs.

America, as de Tocqueville noted more than a century ago, is a country of clubs, societies and associations of all sorts. When Americans – both men and women – find that they have something in common, they associate and promote their shared interest. There must have been a dozen women's groups in Cincy that studied the Holy Land. Mrs Drake was a leader of one of these study groups.

She called me one day on Mrs Dalzelle's telephone. 'Oh, Mr Salem,' she cooed. 'We would like you to address our group on Sunday morning at eleven. We will pay you five dollars and provide you with a free meal.'

Upon hearing that I took a deep breath, slammed the telephone receiver on the wall as hard as I could and walked away from the phone. Mrs Dalzelle rushed to my rescue. I adored this kindly American woman and she loved me in return and looked out for me. She put the receiver in its place gently.

'What happened, Elie?' she enquired.

'You would not understand,' I said. 'But you must know that I am not a beggar to be paid for speaking, and I am not destitute to be offered a free meal.'

From that very moment the words 'free meal' still send a shudder up my spine. But Mrs Dalzelle was most reassuring. 'They don't mean to offend you, Elie; this is our custom. Next time they invite you, accept the invitation.'

'Do you know what it means,' I said defiantly, 'to be told that they will pay me back by feeding me? Don't you know this is very bad manners? This is condescending. I will never accept.'

'Poor Elie,' she smiled ruefully, 'you are going to have a difficult time.' And I surely did, for quite some time.

My Dupont Circle audience was greatly amused. As I finished each tale, they clamoured for more. So I launched into yet another of my stories.

On Thanksgiving Day, many of the families in the extensive Ohio farmland greatly enjoyed the chance to share their magnificent feast with foreign students. The University of Cincinnati strongly encouraged this tradition, for it introduced foreign students to one of America's most revered national holidays. I understood that this day honoured the Pilgrim Fathers, who had a tough time surviving and after their first good harvest wished to celebrate their good fortune by giving thanks to the Lord. I had read how neighbouring Indians, the erstwhile enemies of the pilgrims, were invited to partake in the meal after the Indians had shared their knowledge of local plants and hunting techniques. I believe the Thanksgiving feast to be the finest and richest of all meals ever concocted by man.

The Thomsons were the family that invited me to share Thanksgiving with them. They wanted to do a good deed by including a foreign student in their holiday. The Dean of Students told me that the Thomsons had a huge farm, and were quite well-to-do. They were Presbyterians, God-fearing and very kind. They were justifiably proud of their home, their way of life and their boundless and borderless farm and they wanted others to see it. To have a foreign student as a guest for an afternoon was a break from their normal routine, and they thought it a good way to introduce the family, and especially the children, to other cultures. Local farmers also took pride in working with the university. And, of course, there was the religious dimension, which in the 1950s permeated all aspects of American society. Some of my classmates kept the Bible with them at all times as their basic reference to healthy living. The local Ohio farmers were churchgoing and naturally charitable. So what could have been better than extending the family circle on

34

the occasion of giving thanks to the Almighty – the all-powerful Deity who spoke to them through the Good Book.

But the dear Thomsons had the misfortune of having Elie A. Salem assigned to them by the University Student Office as their guest for that joyous day. The Thomsons lived on a farm about fifty miles from the university with their two daughters and a son. The plan was for them to pick me up from the office at noon, and to return me at the end of the Thanksgiving festivities that evening. The entire family arrived in a brand-new Chevrolet, full of smiles and a warm and welcoming manner. The girls kissed and hugged me as if they had known me for years. The father and son shook hands, warmly. My Elmer encounter caused me to tone down the more passionate Lebanese salutation that I would customarily have given. I was placed in the honourary seat by the driver – the father, and the rest of the family crowded into the back seat and we set off.

The drive through the Ohio countryside was extraordinarily pleasant on that November day. The impression I had was one of space, of rich cultivated land. No fences, no road blocks, no mountains – just open space. My favourite American song of the time was 'Don't Fence Me In'. It began with the refrain, 'Oh, give me land, lots of land, under starry skies above . . . ' and extolled the virtues of open air and space. Throughout the ride, I looked out and conveyed my positive impressions of the land and people to my gracious hosts. They were most appreciative of my sentiments and we rolled merrily along.

'I love the vast horizons of Ohio,' I told them grandly. I was enraptured by the plains we crossed, the pastures, the cows and horses grazing freely as if they owned the entire place. Occasionally a farmhouse could be seen behind a ridge in the luscious farmland. Each house seemed to have a spirit of its own, an individualism representative of those who built it. By each house proudly stood a large barn, shelter for cows, bulls and horses and also the storage place for wheat, barley and corn. If in ancient times Syria and Mesopotamia could have been said to be the bread basket of the Eastern empires, by 1950 I perceived the American Midwest had become the bread basket of the world.

Father Thomson, placidly piloting his ship-of-the plains, then committed the grievous error of turning the radio on. Glaring joyous American music filled the air and my window was wide open. In subconscious obedience to Lebanese norms in car travel, I put my hand all the way out of that window, and began conducting the invisible orchestra with wide angular and circular sweeps of my arm, to the confusion of all the other passengers. I was enjoying the music immensely and expressing my joy both inside and outside the car. I was totally oblivious to driving rules, to possible danger to other cars and above all to the strictures of state laws. I had not yet learned that in America laws covered everything you could possibly think of, including putting your hand out of a car window. To do so, I was told later, is dangerous to you, and whether you wish it or not, the state wants to protect you. You put your hand out and you can be fined handsomely.

Mr Thomson, eyeing what was to him my very odd behaviour, said in a straightforward tone, not at all offensive, 'Put your hand inside the car, son. It's the law.'

'Please stop the car,' I said immediately.

'Stop?' He was baffled. 'Why?'

'Please stop the car,' I was emphatic.

The crowd in the back seat wondered what the problem could possibly be. 'Are you car sick?' someone asked solicitously.

'No, but please stop the car,' I insisted. 'I want to go back.'

'You cannot go back,' remonstrated Mrs Thomson.

'No you can't,' echoed the children.

'What's wrong?' enquired the father.

'Please just stop the car.'

Mr Thomson dubiously asked, 'But what are you going to do?'

'I am going to go back,' I answered mildly yet with absolute certainty.

Mr Thomson stopped the car. 'Son,' he explained, 'you can't go back, we are nearly thirty miles from the university. There is no bus, no train, no telephone.'

'I know,' I assured him as I turned and started walking the way we had come.

After a few minutes I looked back, and the poor Thomsons were gathered outside the car gazing in amazement after this idiot. They seemed to be exchanging glances and were probably wondering what would happen to the student who was now their runaway guest. What went wrong? Is it our fault?

A few minutes of walking and the car was no longer in view. If you ever think you might walk thirty miles on an American high-way, think twice. It is sheer hell. Cars pass you by at a speed of sixty miles an hour and more. If you do not hitchhike, and I certainly did not, no one will bother you, no one will stop to ask if you would like a lift. Cars pass like bullets. You dodge them, you make way, you are bombarded by noise and whipped by the windstorms they generate. I made it to Clifton Avenue in the early hours of the next morning, totally exhausted but jubilantly triumphant.

'But why,' asked Phyllis as I finished my perplexing story. 'Why did you leave the car, Elie? I don't understand what upset you.'

'It's difficult to explain,' I said. 'Perhaps it was the command in his voice, perhaps it was because he did not say please, perhaps he was too direct.' I pondered a moment. 'Well, Phyllis, there are some things that one simply does without knowing why, without reflection.'

Jane, the most opinionated and vocal of the girls, looked at Phyllis and counselled only half in jest, 'Sister, bail out now!' They all laughed uproariously. The laughter, I thought, was uneasy. Though it seemed merry enough, their mirth covered their doubts and fears about this young man from overseas and his effect on their innocent young friend from Pottstown.

With the perspective of time, I understand their bemusement now. There is really no good explanation when it comes to moods that arise from innate cultural habits. Perhaps it was the directness of the instruction. Had he said it as a joke first, explaining how stupid laws are and how, irritatingly, we all have to obey them, I would perhaps have reacted differently. There is so much indirection in the Arab mode of address, and the more there is of it, the less impact the statement has, especially when the statement is a negative one. 'Do not' is such a loaded term of command. It rouses the Arab temper. Awareness of this fact does not, unfortunately, help. Cultural reactions are visceral, not rational, and often have dire consequences. Cultural misunderstanding continues to have tragic results far beyond my Thanksgiving Day walk.

Phyllis was too serious to form a final opinion on the basis of culture-clash stories. She was curious because she was serious. She wanted to probe further. She and her friends had never met a foreign student before. Here was their chance to quiz and to experiment. We are told that we come to know ourselves better by

37

knowing others. The other is really the minor player. You may see yourself mirrored in a way that makes the reflection even more fascinating.

'What in the name of heaven brought you to Cincinnati, of all places in the United States?' they wondered. The girls were entranced with New York, Boston, Washington, Philadelphia, Los Angeles, San Francisco. But Cincinnati? They thought of that town as the pit, the bottomless pit. Why would anyone choose to go there of all the marvellous alternatives on offer?

I explained to my American friends that with us in the East personal contact is most important. I went to Cincy because a friend of mine, Hani al-Hindi, told me he had a friend who was studying there. Of all the schools where I was accepted, this was the only one where I had a personal contact, a cultural *point d'appui*. When I arrived, I discovered that the friend of the friend had actually left, and no one knew where he had gone. But there I was, and there I stayed. Indeed, one year later, I came to Johns Hopkins School of Advanced International Studies (SAIS) because a woman classmate at Cincinnati was coming. She recommended it and I followed her recommendation. As I write now and survey the turning points that led to new stations in my life, I realize that in each of them a person was central. The person made the difference.

My graduate work went well. I studied international affairs with many teachers and students who had come through the Second World War or from the still raging war in Korea. These students were older, most of them were married and many had children. Some were in their thirties and forties and were preparing for new careers after years of military service.

I was the only Arab in these classes, and I could see that my ethnicity added a new and intriguing dimension for many of my classmates. The rebellious Arabization element in my youth was fostered when I was a student at the American University of Beirut. The end of the 1940s was dominated by the Palestinian problem. Palestinian students attended the AUB in large numbers. As they had so recently become refugees, displaced in 1948, they were radicalized and they set the political mood on campus. I was very close to them. In small groups we organized cells and political movements. We dreamt of transforming the Arab World. The rise of Israel, as we saw it, was due to the failure of Arab regimes. I recall my friend George Habash buying a six-chamber pistol and bullets to kill the leader of each of the Arab states that failed in their duty to salvage Palestine from the Zionist Movement. George sat on my bed, counting the bullets as he verbally assassinated each of the villains. One for Bisharah al-Khuri, the president of Lebanon; one for Shukri Quwatly, the president of Syria; one for King Abdallah of Jordan; one for King Farouk of Egypt.

'I will have two left,' George concluded. 'I can select the targets, there are so many of them, traitors all.'

The British Council attempted to influence a few of the thousands of students then studying at AUB by inviting ten of them each year to live in the British Hostel. This was a form of scholarship and a welcome privilege as it provided nice rooms, good food, an excellent library and several cultural activities. The students living there at this period, including me, happened to be among the most politically active on campus. To the officers of the hostel council, we were a distinct challenge. We were not only rebels, but we were socially and culturally uncouth.

Tom Scott and his wife were in charge and Mr Scott was prone to enquire about my activities after a weekend in the village. 'Well, Elie, what did you do this weekend?'

'I went hunting, sir,' I replied.

'But of course, Elie, you did not shoot small birds?'

'Oh, yes, sir, I shoot only small birds.'

'You give them a chance to fly, don't you?' Mr Scott prompted me, 'otherwise it would not be sportsmanlike.'

'No, sir,' I was truly confused. 'If I let them fly I would not be able to kill them.' It made no sense when the point was to shoot the birds. But my practical perspective seemed to infuriate Mr Scott and offend his sense of fair play.

Mrs Scott arranged weekly dinners at her home and expected us to attend in groups of three or four. The idea was to introduce us to British table-manners. When it was my turn I arranged, in rebellious resistance, to enact scenes of stupidity with my dinner-mates. For example, she would want us to hold the fork in our left hand, the knife in our right. And so we did the opposite. As she instructed us to remain always calm, we feigned nervousness and continually dropped the fork, the knife, the spoon. 'It's not easy to change one's eating habits,' Mrs Scott kindly tried to calm us. 'Of course, if you're nervous, you're likely to drop the fork, the knife, the spoon.'

When it came to conversation, we were inclined to choose political issues and shout at each other at the table, like street people. The Scotts were determined Brits, however and I must admit they wore us down a bit. We graduated almost civilized and at least somewhat British-influenced. Some of the most radically honest leaders of the Arab East in subsequent years had been dinner guests at the Scotts in the late 1940s.

At Cincy, some of my teachers felt I was violent, iconoclastic and somehow immature. Professor Vinacke, a professor of international politics, in particular, wondered about me.

'Salem,' he would confide in the privacy of his office, 'I do not know what to make of you; you are either a genius or an idiot.'

'Genius, sir,' I would answer, half-believing my new negotiating posture.

Not interested in joking, Vinacke persisted in his train of thought.

'On the Graduate Record Exam you scored among the lowest ten per cent in the country.'

'This is good, sir,' I tried. 'It means I am different.'

'Perhaps it is good,' the professor mused, as if he had not heard me, 'and yet your grades in all your classes here are the best, definitely in the highest five per cent in the country.'

'This is certainly good, sir.'

'No,' he yelled, 'it is not good at all! How can I recommend you? No one will believe me.'

At this I put on the appearance of being deeply aggrieved. Vinacke reached for ice cream from a refrigerator he kept in his office and offered me some. A peace offering, I assumed, and still hoped for a good recommendation. My classmates referred to my relations with Vinacke as ice-cream diplomacy.

Professor Vinacke was a specialist on the Far East, but knew very little about the Middle East. I was so filled with Arab nationalism and with anti-Zionist fervour that I would find a way to introduce the conflict between the Arabs and the Israelis into every class discussion. In the early 1950s, this issue was a mere curiosity to most, and in Cincy, Palestine was as distant as the moon. On my first visit to a Cincinnati Post Office, in fact, the man at the counter put a two-cent stamp on a letter to Lebanon. I pointed out his error, telling him the letter was to go overseas, to Lebanon.

'No,' the man insisted. 'Lebanon is in Pennsylvania. I have been around, son, don't try to fool me.'

'But, sir, please,' I pleaded with him. 'My Lebanon is a small country in the Middle East – you know the Middle East, Egypt, Saudi-Arabia . . . oil?'

'Oh,' he said, comprehension dawning, 'near the Nile, you mean?'

'Yes, yes,' I encouraged him.

'Well, then. You'll need a ten-cent stamp.'

Ohio girls were pretty and so friendly. They'd say 'Howdy' for 'How do you do?' and 'Hey, guy, whacha doin'?' for 'Hello, sir, how are you?' Although I was pompous, a bit self-important and rather a moody character, I was also very shy with the opposite sex, having had no real experience with girls. Customs differ and I knew that errors in that department could be fatal.

Brave Ann from Indian Hill took the chance of developing a friendship with the newcomer. After the fiasco of the Davison dinner, Ann still took it upon herself to train me in American customs. On our first date, I thought it would be correct to compliment her.

'How nice you smell,' I offered.

'Perfume, you fool!' came the answer.

Ann took me to the movies and invited me to her dorm. The women's dormitory at the university had a nice cosy living-room for girls to meet their boyfriends, and I made frequent use of it. Ann taught me how to kiss passionately, and how to embrace.

'Was your relationship with Ann limited to kissing only?' my Washington audience had to know the answer.

'Oh yes,' I replied, and it was the honest truth.

In the 1950s, Cincy was a very conservative town, and Ann's mother called her frequently. Though they had been polite and curious about me, Ann's mother did not want her daughter to become serious with the alien. When we hugged in Ann's living-room at home, she discovered later that her mother had been peeping at us through the keyhole.

Cincy was close to several Kentucky towns with a lively nightlife, including bars and shady nightclubs. I often visited them at week-ends with friends. The girls in the clubs were young and beautiful. My friends were mostly Turks studying engineering at the expense of their government. True 'Young Turks', my friends idolized

Mustapha Kamal Atatürk, the founder of modern Turkey. Atatürk renounced Ottomanism and laid Islam aside in favour of a secular, material, more Westernized social organization. He aspired for the next generation of Turks to become engineers and scientists, not intellectuals or theologians. And so my friends the Turks laughed at me for specializing in political science.

'This is no science at all,' they scoffed. 'Knowledge is engineering.'

They looked down on Arabs not only because we sided with the British in World War I, but also because we retained the traits of Ottomanism – reaction, religion and tradition – which they now shunned without a backward glance. Though they hated 'the Arabs', they liked me, as Lebanese. They regarded me as a Christian with a sufficient tinge of Westernism.

One evening, in a foray to the illegal Kentucky cabarets, one of my Turkish friends recognized his venerable professor coming down the steps. The Turk melted in shame and tried without success to hide his face, but he was stunned by his good fortune when his professor offered him drunken encouragement. 'Nizam, it's OK, I am too god-damned drunk to care that you are here, too. Now, go ahead . . . and ask for Jenny, she is good!' But poor Nizam was too shocked to continue, and we had all to retreat. I deemed it a Turkish retreat, reminiscent of the Great War.

Often the nightclubs were raided by the police, and we made a few trips to the police station, which were invariably quite brief. We were students. We were aliens. We were clearly a source of confusion and pity among the cops and we were always soon released.

There were other foreign students besides the Turks. One that I will never forget was an Indian – Jamshad. A Gandhi-like character in appearance, he was skinny, angelic and a do-gooder, or so it seemed to me at first. 'Call me Jim,' he told us and nearly every evening he would come to my room to sit on my bed and regale me with Indian stories, at which he always laughed profusely.

Jamshad was always broke, and always borrowed money from me. I lent him money for food, to pay the rent, to pay his school fees. Before I knew it, he owed me two thousand five hundred dollars – in those days, a fortune! My father was skimping at home to send me money and I had lent it to my neighbour. Jamshad was always promising to pay it back next week or next month. After a year, I left Cincy for Washington to study and live at SAIS, and still there was no sign of payment. To the contrary, Jamshad was beginning to hint that he had never borrowed money from me. In despair, I wrote to him threatening to bring the matter to the attention of the Indian ambassador. In response, he wrote a most insolent letter. After a whole year of close friendship, I realized that he was a crook of the first order.

'I have handled guys like you before,' he wrote, 'and if you're going to see the Indian ambassador, why don't you also pay a visit to President Truman?'

I could not believe what I was reading. I expected a meek, apologetic letter promising payment in some distant future. Instead I got this pompous, mocking letter, virtually threatening me. I hit the ceiling. I wanted to kill the two-faced sonofabitch. The hell with my studies, I decided. I must avenge myself and crush the offender!

I took the first train to Cincy to look for the impostor. Mrs Dalzelle in Clifton Avenue revealed that he had not paid rent since I left and so she had evicted him. The Turks told me that Jamshad knew that I was crazy enough to come after him and so had run away to the large Indian community in Kentucky. My friends led me to his abandoned room. I looked over his remaining possessions to see if there was anything of value that might pay his huge debt to me. There was only a leather bag, a belt and a book – all worth less than fifty dollars. I took them anyway, and returned to Washington as angry as the moment I had gone to chase the Indian miscreant. I decided to consult with the dean of my school, Philip Thayer, a prominent lawyer of the time. I presented Dean Thayer with the full details of the case.

'You destroyed your case,' Thayer informed me, 'by entering his room and stealing his belongings.'

'I did not "steal" them, sir,' I replied indignantly. 'I took three items hardly worth fifty dollars.'

'Yes, Elie, this is your story,' Dean Thayer patiently explained, 'but your opponent's lawyer will say that you broke in, you searched his room, and you took all his belongings, especially as you say his room was virtually empty. They may claim the room was full of priceless Indian pearls and precious stones, and rare cashmere sweaters that his client brought for the cold winter weather of the American Midwest. Salem, you committed a crime. Just leave it at that. Now you are even.'

The verdict was devastating. The semitic maxim of an eye for an eye, which I had righteously pursued, could not be applied. My anger against Jamshad turned into anger against the Indian people, government and culture. This anger persisted until a chance encounter with the Indian ambassador at the home of my venerable dean.

'Sir,' I said to the ambassador, 'I want to tell you why I hate you and all Indians.' To my great surprise, he sat and listened intently, and then apologized profusely for the behaviour of an errant citizen. He then proceeded most lovingly to tell me about India and its people, eager for me to change my opinion.

'Do you have a girlfriend?' the ambassador enquired.

'Yes,' I said. 'Here she is, Phyllis Sell, a newcomer to the Foreign Service.'

'Will you two honour me by having lunch with me and my family tomorrow at the Indian embassy?'

'We would be delighted to accept,' volunteered Phyllis, faster than sound, fearing some further impropriety on my part.

'Yes,' I said humbly.

And the next day, we enjoyed an exquisite Indian meal and the most charming crowd of Indian men and women, nearly the entire staff of the embassy. The ambassador, a brilliant and jovial soul, joked merrily. 'Who knows, one day you may become a Lebanese diplomat,' he laughed. 'I want you to think well of India as we Indians are not all like that rogue in Cincinnati.'

What a fine gesture, I thought, and how potent is the personal dimension in the conduct of human affairs. I learned from the gentle ambassador not to make hasty judgements on an entire nation or culture because of one event or one person. Later on in my career, I often recalled the Jamshad abberation and the ambassadorial redemption. As I told the story to my friends in Washington a year later, I believed it to be as instructive to my audience as it was to me.

The more Phyllis learned about my cultural conflicts in America, the more concerned she was. Women at the age of twenty-one are often more serious than men at that age. I was learning that, in addition to this gravitas, Phyllis also possessed a practical streak of Pennsylvania Dutch. While she looked forward to the excitement of a Foreign Service career, as a woman she also hoped for a stable life with marriage and children. She fully expected to build her nest in an agreeable location with a responsible spouse. While we were in complete agreement that we were in love, we had yet to grapple with the fact that love comes in several dimensions.

To me, we were having a beautiful romance, while Phyllis experienced our courtship as the necessary prelude to a lasting commitment. She was completely serious. Over many a private dinner at the Sheraton Park Hotel across the Potomac Bridge, she probed deeply into my life, trying hard to understand my mind, my style and my relations with people. We were, as the poet put it, 'near to each other on mountains farthest apart'. Phyllis was a determined woman, however, and she was determined to bring the mountains together. After all, did not the Incarnate One teach us that love can move mountains?

Phyllis was not only a great listener, but also a great teacher and an unequalled choreographer. I have often thought that she would have been a masterful chess player had she ever taken up the game. She was skilful and patient in the game of life, making many strategic manoeuvres with one ultimate move in mind. Often it worked out splendidly. But when it did not, she became furious.

My beloved Phyllis was supremely rational and she held a balanced perspective in social matters. She decided to use her social network to better familiarize me with the attitudes and customs of America. So she held parties; she convened various groupings and invited me to learn at least enough to prevent my misunderstanding people and situations so often. The first such party in my honour was designed to introduce me discreetly, perhaps surreptitiously, to her friends. Phyllis arranged a cocktail party at her Dupont apartment. I was excited about the prospect, and was determined to blend in, although I was hardly the blending type.

Always in my head I heard the impassioned voice of my father, coming to me from my village far away: 'Remember, Elie, you are sent to America to study, not to socialize, not to blend in, and definitely not to fall in love.' The weekly letters from my father always ended with three words – actually one – study, study, study. Such linguistic repetition was common in Lebanon, for emphasis, and I had never seen it used this way in the Anglo-Saxon world.

I disregarded the nagging voice and looked forward to attending the gathering arranged by my American sweetheart. The party was jovial, about ten girls and ten boys, all in a happy-go-lucky mood. A party in America was special to me – good spirits, mixed company, lots of drink and nothing serious. Phyllis, the perfect hostess, spoke to everyone, while getting drinks for all and offering all the little titbits of food expected at a cocktail party. We felt merry and sophisticated, even though our drinks were limited to beer, wine and the soft variety.

'Elie,' Phyllis said brightly, 'let me introduce you to Bob, a former boyfriend, and still a good friend.' It was obviously her intent to make it perfectly clear that this was a past-tense boyfriend. I was meant to deduce that I was now her one and only love.

No matter how it was intended, the message was not unequivocal enough for a young lover, still unsure of himself. I acknowledged the introduction, and was especially friendly towards him as I anxiously searched for an escape route that would not be noticed by anyone. My escape had to be perfect. No scenes, please. I was quite aware that the escape itself, if unobtrusive would not create a scene. Soon I found a way. I acted as though I was looking for something in the hall and then quickly slipped away down the stairs. I jumped into a taxi, got to my room at 1906 Florida and gathered all the cash at my disposal. Things happened so quickly, I had no idea what I was doing or where I was heading. A deep preternatural force, a primitive one from the darkest recesses of prehistory, was driving me and guiding my steps. To the railway station, the force urged me – and it was an easy objective.

In half an hour I was in the Union Station, facing a booth where train schedules to virtually every nook and cranny in the USA were posted. Florida, the force within me insisted – that should be far enough. Fine, I was suddenly going to Florida – but what town, what village and what about accommodation? Understand that the force driving me was not precise, it ordered cash, no suitcase, no books, and no instructions to university authorities. And how long was this petulant, unexplained outing supposed to last? School was in high gear. Papers were due. Seminars were imminent in which I was expected to make presentations. But my mood crowded all these worthy obligations out, and distraction prevailed. Somehow, for some reason I was angry, jealous, suspicious, hurt. And deep down I was firmly convinced, if anyone can believe what I am about

46

to confess, that there was no cause for concern at all. It was just this mood. What a mysterious force, how compelling, how blind, and finally how irresistible.

'Jacksonville, Florida,' I blurted out to the ticket clerk.

And a schedule was quickly and easily prepared for me. 'Stop here, and change trains,' I was told. 'Stop there and change trains again, and you take a night train to . . . ' some God-forsaken city.

Why I had chosen Jacksonville I had no idea, unless it was that the name had emerged from my subconscious, as people from my village have emigrated to Jacksonville since the mid-nineteenth century. Every village seemed to have a specific location for their migrations. My Bterramis went to three cities – two in the US, Wilkes Barry (Pa) and Jacksonville (Fla), and one in Australia, Sydney. Most of them had no idea where Wilkes Barry and Jacksonville were. Some thought they were in Africa. They went to the towns and to their countrymen, not to the nations that claimed them. Somehow migrants heard of Jacksonville and got there. After reading the train schedules, there were many city names in my head. Jacksonville would do as well as any other for my purpose. Planning was not a strong point with me at that time.

The ride was particularly arduous, not because it was long, but because it was purposeless and senseless, an act of madness. My mind was confused. It was a battlefield of right against wrong, of the true against the false. It pained me to feel that I was in the wrong, on the other side of the truth, but I could reach no other conclusion. In my conflict between mood and reason, mood had triumphed. I am afraid that this is too often so. Emotional roots in our prehistoric past are deeper and stronger. Poor reason is a late-comer to our consciousness and not yet an equal opponent.

And so, here I was at the railway station in Jacksonville, Florida. I had made it. I had won. But now what? Naturally the thought of a hotel loomed large on my mental screen. It must be cheap, an inexpensive motel, as so much of my funds had been lost in my investment in the confidence trickster from Bombay. Not fond of sightseeing, not a particularly resourceful person, and not having been oriented to fun in my upbringing, I headed straight to a bookstore and bought a solid book that was bound to take my mind off the exasperating dilemma consuming my imagination. *The Decline of the West* by Oswald Spengler fitted the bill. It was deep, long and appropriately depressing. The motel in a quiet suburb was accommodating to my needs. It provided a spacious room, with a large desk, and secluded paths in the vicinity for an avid walker.

After three long days I decided that this was punishment enough for the victim, even if I was unsure who that might be. The ride back to Washington was more pleasant as I expected to see Phyllis, to go back to school and to return to the normal life of a student in a prestigious graduate school. Upon my arrival and with a high degree of fear and trembling, I immediately called Phyllis. Instead of screaming at me and blaming me for my bad behaviour, she was all affection and genuine concern, wanting only to know that I was all right.

'Is there anything wrong? Where have you been?' she asked anxiously. 'Elie, we need to talk now that you're back, but first I must stop the manhunt I initiated the moment you disappeared. You might have been kidnapped, for all I knew.'

She had no idea in this world why I had sneaked out of the party and disappeared, and I was too embarrassed to enlighten her. I concocted some story, which I am sure she did not believe. But she was wise enough to know that the matter was obviously beyond open discussion and was best left to return to in the distant future. I discovered that she had called the Lebanese Ambassador, who to my dismay was not particularly concerned.

Phyllis had spoken of my disappearance to some of my class-mates and they had advised her to call the police to report a missing person. Her instinct counselled against adding legal complications, however, to an already incomprehensible situation. She deduced that my behaviour must have been psychological, that perhaps the episodes of Elmer, Jamshad and the Thomsons had had a sequel of the same kind. Phyllis was too thoughtful to be distracted by silly events, or even by bad behaviour.

The idea of marriage was now at the forefront of Phyllis's mind and she needed to know where she stood. She was in training for a job in the Foreign Service and due to leave for Tripoli in Libya. She had delayed her departure for months, hoping that the idiot she loved would propose to her. She had no idea how long she could continue to postpone her departure without being fired. This job literally meant the world to her, it was her passport to a new life away from Pottstown. Phyllis had become part of the big city and she would not go back.

Mr Norman Burns was a lecturer at SAIS, a friend of mine, and a friend of the Arab World. Fortunately, he was also the director of the Foreign Service Institute, where Phyllis was doing her training. She told Norman that she loved me and wanted to marry me, but that I had not proposed. I was deeply in love, but I was not seriously thinking of marriage. Mr Burns was most understanding, and he played for time considering the various training programmes on offer – among them Tripoli, Libya or Tripoli, Lebanon, two dreadful prospects for those who knew the Middle East. Finally, Burns had to urge Phyllis to come to a decision or to move to a non-Foreign Service job. She was going to have to force the issue.

I was oblivious, quite happy with things as they were. I had no reason to look beyond the current situation. In fact, I was so content with our relationship that I saw no reason to change a thing. Especially since I felt that my future, given my background, was not fully in my hands.

One evening Phyllis chose a cosy restaurant downtown for our evening together. It was a rather romantic place with French cuisine and good wine. Phyllis told me in nervous giggles that she had just returned from a visit to her family in Melrose Park, and that she had had a most interesting conversation with her father, Ernie. She told him about her love for me, her love for her job, her desire to seek something new and exciting.

'I understand,' said the wise father, 'but decide what it is that you want most. Pick one goal at a time, and give it all of your attention.'

'I want to get married,' Phyllis told her father.

'Fine,' said Ernie. 'Work on it.'

'So,' Phyllis looked at me now, and hesitated just a bit, 'so I decided to work on it. I decided I want to get married.'

'That's great,' I answered. 'To whom?'

At that she rolled her eyes, and in one more desperate attempt at communicating with the enigma from the East, she said, 'To you, of course.'

To me! The idea, though flattering, was one that I had closed my mind to. No one in my position could rationally entertain marriage in his second year of graduate work, a year or two away from his academic objective, and perhaps years away from a job. This was a fact against which was set the fact of Phyllis, a lovely girl, an ideal partner, a person I loved and could not say no to. But marriage? In America, marriage was easy and so was divorce, no big deal. In Lebanon, in my village, marriage was a very big deal. While a marriage certainly involved a bride and a groom, it was really a union between two families, and once concluded it was for life. Divorce was a scandal to the man, a disaster for the woman.

Phyllis, however, had nothing to draw on but her own experience. She was virtually unconcerned about my background and my life in Lebanon. She clearly thought marriage possible. Two can live as cheaply as one, and all those other practical considerations. Instead of working for a Foreign Service, she figured, she would marry one. Foreign aid could be public or it could be private. The challenge was nearly the same. In the latter, the reward is visible and immediate. Furthermore, she could help me in my research and in typing my manuscript (for of course there were no computers then). Come to think of it, her generous offer was eminently reasonable. The huge Atlantic Ocean must have softened my brain, and for a moment rendered my village of Bterram dim and distant. I was lulled into thinking like an American. After all, I had been in the 'land of the free' for some two years, and was bound to be influenced by its norms.

In that transitional mood, swinging between the romantic and the real, I wrote a letter to my father. In matters of great consequence in patriarchal families, one must write to the father. Mine was the archetypal patriarch. To address the letter to father and mother would only infuriate the father and embarrass the mother. My mother was kind and could never say no to her first son. Were she to speak her true feelings, she would say 'by Elie's life', rather than 'by God's life' or 'by Christ's life'. This was a traditional way of affirming the truth. You swore by the life of your eldest son. Why the son and not the daughter? In our traditional society it was the son who would be expected to earn the living and provide for the family. My mother was also quite aware that our father relied on me as the family's 'racehorse'. Father knew that in matters of grave importance he was obliged to act rationally, coolly, and in the highest interests of the family. So I wrote to him what I thought was a rational, cool letter.

'Here I am far away from home and I have fallen in love with a great woman,' I told my father. 'She is intelligent, well balanced, hardworking, loving.' I emphasized the qualities father valued. While beauty, romance and love were the extras that I valued, they were not of interest to this practical, traditional man. 'Marriage in America,' I added, 'also has an economic factor. Two can live as cheaply as one, if not cheaper. Cooking at home is less expensive than eating in restaurants. Phyllis, an educated woman, will help me in my studies.' I decided to lay great stress on the economics, which were a top priority in my rather poor village. 'My wife will type my papers and my PhD thesis,' I concluded. The emphasis on the PhD thesis was intended to reassure him. I wanted him to know that soon I expected to finish my sojourn in this distant land and return to the fold of the Salems as the bastion of stability and support he wanted me to be. I read and reread the letter and was almost convinced by the learned exposition I had composed. With hope in my heart, I sent the letter airmail, and with dread in my mind I feared the response.

I was used to checking my mail twice a day for a letter from home. Now I avoided it. No news was good news. This was a terrible feeling. Father wrote beautiful letters, indeed literary ones, full of praise and exhortations. Praise and exhortations were very familiar to me. To my father, I was his winning horse. His more prosperous peers in the village had received advanced schooling and attained high positions. He had not had the means to achieve these things for himself, but with the little he had, he was determined to overtake all of them. He nurtured me just like a racehorse. If he was destined not to run the race himself, he would do so vicariously, not just once with Elie, but six times with his six sons – Elie, Fuad, Antoun, Fawzi, Philip and Kamal. His daughter Milia was the eldest, and in the eye of the patriarch destined for marriage after high school, not for the hippodrome.

My apprehensions were fully justified. Instead of a letter, there came a telegram. I believe that was the first and last technological leap ever taken by my dad. Father did not mince words. He calculated the worst and proceeded upwards from its dismal abyss.

If you are married get a divorce right now. Divorce in the US is easy. This is no time to interrupt your studies and get married and establish a home. Your home is here in Lebanon. We did not send you to the US to get married and settle there but to study. I have written to Lebanon's ambassador asking him to help you. Malik is a good man, a close relative. In America he is in my place. If you need a lawyer, he will get you one.

I must admit, I was not surprised. I rushed to her apartment and Phyllis and I read the telegram and tried to find a guiding light in it. Phyllis was not as disappointed as I expected her to be. She began to decode it as follows: 'Clearly your father has your best interests in mind. His perspective is different from mine, and perhaps yours. Note that he did not say you cannot marry an American. He said you cannot marry now while you are still a student. He is a wise man, a caring father. Some fathers, I know, do not care, and definitely would not take such a stand. I respect him for that and I love him. Fine, marriage must wait, and let it be in Lebanon and with his approval. Elie, you have one bit of good news, and it is going to make him happy.' Phyllis had seen the next critical move in the game of her life. 'Send your father a telegram. Tell him this: I am not married. I do not intend to marry in the US. When I finish my graduate work, I will return to Lebanon, and I will convince you that Phyllis will be a good wife. If we receive no parental approval, there will be no marriage.' Indeed, now feeling victorious with a proposal intended to endear her to my family, she wrote the telegram herself. I only signed it.

The telegram produced a long loving letter to me and a shy salutation to Phyllis. No mention of divorce, no lawyer, no ambassadorial intervention. Just the standard concluding paragraph – study, study, study. The Washingon–Bterram correspondence matured us both and put us on a rational course. We would definitely get married. We knew our love to be absolute and unquestionable. Phyllis would transfer to a steady job in the Department of State, not in its Foreign Service branch. She already had captivated a foreigner, and that was enough Foreign Service. I would complete my PhD in the summer of 1953 and we would sail to Lebanon to get married there. Meanwhile I planned to work hard on my thesis, to finish my papers and my studies. Phyllis would support my work by helping with research, typing papers, verifying texts and checking footnotes. The game was on.

Attention now centred on the School of Advanced International Studies at the Johns Hopkins University where I was one of three PhD candidates. The school was established in the late 1940s by a group of professors who broke away from the Fletcher School of Diplomacy at Tufts University with the view to founding an élite school concentrating on specific regional studies – Europe, the Soviet Union, the Middle East, Africa, South-East Asia, China, Japan. This was a new departure to serve a new need identified from the lessons of the Second World War. America, now a World Imperium, needed area specialists, not only generalists in international law and diplomacy. The school had one hundred students, each specializing in one of the areas above.

I came to SAIS exactly as I came to Cincinnati. A girl in my class, a tall bright blonde, told me she was going to SAIS. She extolled its virtues. I thought it sounded great and decided that I too would go there. Thus my two most important academic decisions were taken on personal grounds – and I have absolutely no regrets.

I started communicating with the SAIS registrar, Jane Holebrook. 'Dear Mr Holebrook,' I wrote.

'Dear Miss Elie Salem,' she wrote back.

When I arrived at SAIS I went straight to the registrar. I was quite surprised to see, behind a sign that read 'Jane Holebrook', a beautiful blonde woman.

'Don't say,' she exclaimed, equally surprised, 'that you're Elie Salem?'

'But, yes, I am,' I replied. 'Don't say that you're Jane Holebrook?'

'But of course I am.' And we stared in wonder across the cultural divide.

At SAIS Phyllis knew that I was studying politics, specifically the politics of the Islamic world. My PhD thesis was on the Khawarij, a fundamentalist sect in early Islam. My favourite courses were reading courses. I agreed with my professor to read five books at a time and write a critical report on each of them. Most of my professors were unique characters, good scholars, greatly political and often intensely partisan. One of them, Paul M.A. Lineberger, stood out especially. He taught psychological warfare. At weekends, Lineberger told us, the Air Force would fly him to Korea, and from the cockpit of a plane or helicopter he would scream at the North

Korean soldiers. His intent was to demoralize them. In class he always singled me out for dialogue. I was the only Arab, and it must have intrigued his psychologist's mind to play me against the Jews. He loved to shock me in both word and deed. One day, he just looked at me, gouged out his right eye and threw it on the table. I went light-headed and almost fainted. Lineberger was delighted. For long I had suspected that it was a glass eye, but it still gave me a *frisson* of horror when he banged it a few times on the table to demonstrate the fact.

Lineberger taught Chinese and, at his urging, I enrolled in Chinese-language classes. As I failed correctly to pronounce every sound he threw at me, he kicked me out as a hopeless student. I really did not mind; I had enough on my plate as a Middle Easterner to venture beyond our increasingly turbulent region. But I must admit, I miss Lineberger. Although we parted academically, we continued to be friends for years. He and his wife had no children but kept twenty cats. They lived as if the animals were an integral part of the Lineberger nuclear family. Each cat had its own name and was given quality time in conversation, attention and abundant affection. Lineberger had a huge ego and insisted that I consult with him on every academic move I made, even though he was no longer my teacher. Before I took my oral exams I showed him a massive book on international affairs. 'What do you think of this book, sir?' I asked him seriously.

He weighed it carefully in his two hands, turned to the index, looked under L, and when to his frustration found no Lineberger, 'Useless,' he said. 'Don't waste your time on this book. The sonofabitch has never even heard of me. Well, I haven't heard of him either. Forget this guy.'

At SAIS, like at Cincy, I did well. A fellow SAIS student was Helmut Sonnenfelt, who became well known in later years as an aide to Henry Kissinger. Helmut came to me one day and said with a smile, 'I believe you are Elie Salem?'

'Yes, that's me,' I replied.

'You got higher grades than I did,' he mused. 'This is a historic reversal of fortune, an Arab doing better than a Jew.' When he laughed at his own remark, I joined in the laughter, perhaps even a bit more heartily.

And my high grades had other consequences. The dean, Philip

Thayer, was a man I came to admire enormously. He called me to his office one day to discuss my standing in the school.

'Your grades are good,' he said, 'and for that, you deserve a hefty scholarship. We provide substantial support for anyone who excels, and you are excelling.'

As I understood it, a scholarship was a sort of charity given by the rich to the poor, by the strong to the weak. So I thanked him politely and proudly refused the offer. 'My father,' I said, 'can pay my fees and my lodging. Thank God I am not needy. The scholarship should be given to those who need it.'

'Well, Salem,' he said, deeply puzzled. 'I never heard such reasoning before, not in America, certainly not in New England – strange, strange indeed.'

When I told Phyllis about Thayer's offer, she was exasperated, indeed furious. She knew that my father was not rich. He was frugal, but certainly not rich. And after my fiasco with Jamshad, I needed every penny. A loss of two thousand five hundred dollars is a budgetary catastrophe that changes the balance, no matter what the explanations are. Phyllis finally convinced me by appealing to my ego.

'This is a reward, stupid,' she explained to me. 'Not charity. It is a sign of recognition, you can list it on your CV as an accomplishment.'

But it was too late, Thayer had bestowed the scholarship on someone else. The next year, the dean hinted that another scholarship might be available for my last semester in 1953. I immediately accepted it, to the satisfaction of Phyllis and the delight of a father counting his pennies.

2

By 1953, Phyllis had two jobs: one was at the Department of State and the other was looking after me. The first job was easy for her, and so she concentrated much of her enormous energy on the second and much more difficult one. She counselled me and helped in my research. She typed reports. She was always by my side. Until we met, Phyllis had known nothing of Islam or the Arab World and now she became deeply immersed in Arab history, culture and philosophy. She read extensively and I supplemented her growing knowledge with extended discussion. She espoused the Arab cause with the conviction and passion of her Arab sweet-heart. She argued valiantly and articulately with those of her friends, whether on the right or the left, who disagreed with her. Phyllis and I were nationalists, fiercely supportive of the Arab cause and strongly anti-Zionist.

America in the 1940s and the 1950s embraced the persecuted Jews of Europe. The Nazis and the Fascists espoused a form of racial nationalism that was nurtured on fear, prejudice and hate. When Jewish scientists, intellectuals, artists and musicians fled the Old World by the thousands, their primary destination was the United States. The Jews, who in the liberal European age enjoyed equality and attained high positions, were now hounded by the Nazis in Germany and the Fascists in Italy. Many sought refuge in Palestine when a Jewish homeland was promised them by Britain as the mandatory power.

In the United States, universities welcomed the Jewish stars in physics, mathematics, social sciences, philosophy. Their entry into the land of the free and the home of the brave was not always rosy. There were American racists who thought of the Jews as an inferior race. There were religious types who accused Jews of crucifying Christ. The anti-semitism that I occasionally encountered in the United States shocked me. As a semite, I am akin to the Jew and so I have always empathized with the Jews as a minority with a tragic history in Europe. As Christians in the Arab World, we too have

56

encountered brutality and exclusion. I was clearly pro-Jewish and anti-Zionist without the slightest doubt and without the slightest confusion.

I admired in particular Jewish achievements in the eighteenth and nineteenth centuries in all the academic disciplines. I was therefore not surprised that in the post-Hilter era, Jewish luminaries occupied high positions in top American universities. It appeared to me that all the rising figures in philosophy, history, literature, political theory, physics, chemistry and biology were Jews. The Zionist movement motivated many Jews to seek posts that put them close to the decision-making process in Washington. Many sought – and won – influential university positions. It was common in 1950s' America for top government posts to be offered to scholars from leading universities. US presidents often tapped the universities for talent, recruiting leading scholars and thinkers as counsellors, as secretaries in the cabinet, as under-secretaries and assistant secretaries, as heads of the hundreds of centres, bureaus and authorities that fall under the umbrella of the Federal Government. Everywhere in the capital, it seemed that Jewish scholars were winning positions of influence in leading universities and in the Federal Government.

As a young, emotional and passionate spokesman for the Arab cause, I was quite visible. Washington was a vibrant centre of free speech and insightful, probing dialogue on important international issues, including the Palestinian situation. The United Nations voted for partition of Palestine in 1947 and Britain as the mandatory power supervised the evacuation in 1948. Jewish forces, highly motivated and mobilized by the Zionist Organization, fought well and occupied by force far more of Palestine than was allocated to them by the UN resolution. The situation was complicated by the Holocaust, which had caused Jews to flee Europe in every direction. Jews of the Diaspora had been drawn to Palestine throughout recorded history, ever since biblical times. Now that a Jewish state was established, Zionist leaders were committed to bringing all the Jews of the world into Palestine. In despair, and sceptical of European assurances, thousands of Jews threw themselves into Palestine and into the cause of the Jewish State in a way that would completely transform the region. Zionist leaders understood that an enemy would help to unify and focus their movement, and they zeroed in on the Arabs. By the time I was at SAIS, the prevailing philosophy seemed to rely on a central guiding principle: Jews are good; Arabs are bad. This was the Washington attitude that I faced, often feeling like a young embattled Lebanese warrior.

It so happened that my German teacher was a pretty Jewish brunette in her early thirties. Lisa Stevens and her husband had fled Austria after the war, seeking a new life in the United States. Mr Stevens was given a government job, while his wife found work as a German-language instructor at SAIS. Lisa's knowledge of Palestine and of the Arabs was distorted and simplistic, a Walt Disney cartoon representation of the complexity of the situation in Palestine. She struggled to deal with what seemed to her a cata-clysmic reality – that she was face to face with an Arab, that he was her student and that she had to be with him for an hour and more each day. She was the quintessential Zionist, I the absolute opposite.

Her first tendency was to try to establish that I must be inhumane and barbarous.

'Elie, are you really an Arab?' Lisa asked me incredulously.

'Yes,' I said, 'you know I am.'

'Why are you killing Jews?' she demanded. 'We poor Jews had such a bad deal with Hitler and Mussolini, and now you want to drive us into the sea?'

I was appalled! Where could one begin with such an attitude, with such ignorant beliefs? How was I to put her right on the facts without screaming, without tearing my hair? My strong reaction clearly shocked the innocent beauty from Vienna. She initially looked upon me as a specimen and she was fascinated. I was Arab, vehemently anti-Zionist, and yet she saw that I was quite normal, rather nice in fact. Thus began a classic love-hate relationship. I tried in vain to Arabize her, and she tried in vain to Zionize me.

Lisa Stevens took me under her wing as a special project. She wanted me to pass my PhD language exams with distinction and offered private lessons. Many times the lesson required me to memorize the poetry of the great German-Jewish poet Heinrich Heine. The poems she chose were a romanticized and not too subtle parallel of our own relationship. The Gentile maiden was madly in love with a daring handsome knight. She tells him he is great and of perfect racial purity. But the knight answers that he is the son of a greatly beloved rabbi in Saragossa, and thus deflates her Gentile belief in white supremacy. Often, while engaged in private language lessons, Lisa would allow her hand to lie close to mine and allow her shiny black hair to caress my cheeks as she stared deep into my eyes. To my own surprise, I behaved well. I even managed to play dummy on the occasions when she let her hand fall upon my lap and immediately excused herself for her clumsiness. I pretended not to notice and also tried to remain objective when she told me of her troubles at home.

'My husband and I went through hell,' confided Lisa, 'but we made it together to the Free World. And now he is going his own way, and I am going my own way. I love you, Elie. I am much older, so we can never be married. But we can be friends. You can come to my apartment for a drink.'

'No, it would be better if I didn't,' I was firm.

'I know,' Lisa sighed. 'You love Phyllis and she has such kind eyes. I understand. But let us be friends, then, if not lovers.'

I greatly admired this spirited woman and cried a lot when she suddenly died a few years later. I spent many hours talking with Lisa, and with her husband. My long conversations with the Stevenses revealed to me the unfathomable chasm between Arabs and Jews. How close they are, and yet how incomprehensibly distant! They are both semitic peoples from the East, both wandered the same plains and deserts between Aden and Babylon. Islam, like Judaism, is fiercely monotheistic; it appropriates the prophets and reveres Moses. Indeed, the Koran has much in common with Old Testament; it is spiritual and mundane, peaceful and violent, revealed and historical. Muhammad was furious with the Jews because they did not recognize him as the Prophet. Contemporary Arabs are furious at the Jews for selecting the Arab-Islamic country of Palestine to make their own. It is vehement Arab-Islamic opposition to Zionist policy that has rendered them more or less anti-Jewish.

Jewish nationalism battled Arab nationalism, thus creating enmities at personal and national levels. Though extremely close in faith they became extremely distant in politics. Arabs felt that Judaism had been hijacked by Zionism, and Jews felt that Islam had been hijacked by rampant Arab nationalism. Jews and Arabs have enormous history to talk about and to explore, and as much political conflict to reason out and to resolve. All of this baggage was carried throughout my relationship with Lisa Stevens. I felt she was way out in left field, and she felt the same about me. We argued a lot, but always with a smile and deep affection.

During this time, Phyllis remained absolutely confident of my single-minded devotion to her. She knew of Lisa's flirtations since I told her everything. Phyllis believed me, and strangely enough loved Lisa, too. Phyllis did not feel threatened by other women, not even Ann from Cincinnati, who was writing to me daily, hoping to maintain a friendship that might grow into something more. Love, however, is absolutist. Love is as much exclusion as it is inclusion. Love excludes all others and the beloved becomes so deeply included in the lover as to constitute the mystical fusion to which the Orthodox Church alludes in its marriage rites. Once I knew that I loved Phyllis, I stopped opening Ann's letters, and I sent them back. This went on for months, and although Phyllis advised me to write in reply and assure Ann of our continuing friendship, I did not do so. I told Phyllis that Elvis expressed my sentiments about the letters from Ann when he sang, 'Return to sender, address unknown, no such number, no such zone.' But Phyllis never really appreciated my musical taste and felt that my habit of relating the words of songs to real-life situations was stupid and infantile. While Phyllis was listening intently to Wagner, I was enjoying Rosemary Cloony singing, 'Come on-a my house, my house a-come on.'

In music, I found soul mates among members of my Cincinnati Turkish gang. Intizam, for example, came to sound like a broken record himself as he repeated favourite stanzas again and again: 'Surprising, surprising, but it is not surprising that I am in love with you.'

SAIS ran an exacting graduate programme, and I worked very hard. I earned a good reputation and was intent on keeping it. My grades were a matter of great importance to my family, particularly to the tough, no-nonsense patriarch. On the few occasions that I received a mere B+, my father acted as if that contemptible grade did not even exist. 'Elie gets only As,' he would tell his village audience, even though they hardly knew the difference between an A and an F.

My father Adib was happy that I was doing well, and in the end that was all that mattered. The villagers too were proud of my accomplishments and some wrote me astoundingly eloquent letters of praise. They were in Arabic, of course, and clearly written under the glowing impression created by a proud father. I still have one of those letters that I kept as the archetype of village literature of the 1950s. 'You are a shining star,' the writer enthused. 'You soar so high we can hardly see you. How high do you intend to fly? Let us know so that we may prepare ourselves to better understand you.' The language was so ornate and flowery that it was not easy to render into modern English. Nevertheless, I translated the letter to Phyllis who was soon bursting with laughter. Her laughter signalled caution, however, lest I should believe this praise and allow it to go to my head. She loved me and believed in me, but had no interest in further inflating my already over-sized ego.

Letter-writing is a cultural phenomenon. It is an intimate way of expressing oneself across the separating distance. Phyllis and I compared Adib's letters with Ernie's letters. What a difference – they were truly oceans apart! After months of culture shock, I was becoming more accustomed to America, beginning to see the country for what it was and actually to relish and appreciate the differences between the two worlds. But Phyllis had never experienced my land. She had to accept on faith that it was really possible to bridge the ocean that separated her from my world. Blessed are those who believe and who have not seen. Phyllis was no Doubting Thomas. She just had a simple and absolute faith in me, and believed that what was good for me would also be good for her. It was a positive and secure feeling, but would it prove reliable?

With Phyllis first things always came first. She had the gift of seeing clearly where she was going and the discipline to focus on the path ahead. First step, I must finish my graduate work, second step I must get a job, third step we will get married. The last step was the culmination and needed no steps beyond it. Children, career, achievement and happiness were all inextricably fused into her idea of marriage. For now, she wanted me to finish my thesis, and she wanted to learn enough about my field of study to help me with it. In that way, she would learn about Islam. Her beloved was a Christian but he lived in an Islamic culture and Phyllis understood instinctively that Islam's values, precepts, customs, taboos and mores had strongly influenced my tiny Christian-Arab community. As we worked together, Phyllis taught me more about life than I taught her about the store of ideas that have made and unmade civilizations over the centuries.

My advisor was the Iraqi scholar Majid Khadduri, a professor of Middle Eastern Studies. It was with his guidance that I had chosen to write my thesis on the Khawarij. To accomplish this, I knew I must develop a theoretical framework to serve as my Virgilian guide in writing the paper. It also meant that I must meticulously review all of the historical, political, religious and literary material of early Islam. Muslim literati in the seventh, eighth, ninth and tenth centuries tended to be encyclopedists. Muslim scholars of previous eras wrote as if time itself was of no concern. Their work survived as page after page, volume after volume, with no commas, no full stops, no paragraphs and certainly no tables of contents.

Nineteenth-century orientalists from Europe introduced into these volumes a greater sense of order. Much of the revised material was in the Annexe of the Library of Congress. So intent was I as a young scholar on finishing my thesis in my second year at SAIS, at the early age of twenty-three, that I often lost my own sense of time. The Library Annexe closed at ten p.m. and a guard made sure that all researchers were out before locking the building. The cubicle in which I was closeted was out-of the way, however, and on more than one occasion I missed the deadline and had to spend the night in the company of the books and manuscripts of antiquity.

The first time that I was locked in the library, it was truly regrettable and most embarrassing. When I had not called Phyllis by eleven and midnight came and went with no word, poor Phyllis suspected the worst. Danger always lurked in the Dupont Circle area. Phyllis called the police to report a missing person. The man who had gone missing, Phyllis told the police, was a bit strange, but not dangerous, and was usually seen around the Library of Congress, perhaps in the Annexe.

Shortly after Phyllis's call, to my complete surprise and terror, alarm bells started ringing furiously, lights came on throughout the entire building and policemen seemed to come out from the stacks in hordes.

'Are you Ely Salim?' one officer asked in an accusing tone, as if I had been caught committing a heinous crime.

'No,' I responded meekly. 'I am Elie Salem.'

'Don't be a smart ass,' he responded. 'What the hell are you doing here? Don't you know it is against the law?'

'No, sir, I did not,' I humbly replied. 'I do apologize, and if there is a fine I will gladly pay it.'

'You know, I could arrest you for this stupidity.' The policeman was still agitated. 'You know what trouble you have caused . . . you know . . . you know . . . ' he went on and on. He was thrilled to exercise his power and I had no choice but to endure his tirade.

'OK, buddy,' a higher-ranking officer intervened, 'take your books now and get out. Don't ever do this again.'

'Yes, sir, yes, sir, I will certainly not do it again,' I promised. 'Yes, sir, yes, sir, I am very sorry.'

'Well, OK then.' The officer decided I was harmless enough. 'We'll have a police car take you home.'

'Thank you, sir.' I was grateful, of course, but I was also deeply mortified and completely disconcerted. Suspecting Phyllis of being the one who had called the police, I headed straight to the Dupont apartment and at two-thirty in the morning stormed into the living-room. To my amazement, all five girls were there, anxiously awaiting news. I pretended to be angry, they pretended to be angry, and in this atmosphere of artificial tension we all succumbed to soothing laughter. Phyllis, feeling somewhat guilty but enormously relieved, made me swear in front of her peers that this would never happen again. I did on the condition that she promise, also in front of her peers, that she would never again report me as a missing person. She made the promise. I drank a cup of coffee with them and then walked back to 1906 Florida, a suspicious loner in a rather dangerous neighbourhood.

For the historical record, although I spent many an unintended night in the Annexe, Phyllis never again reported me to the police, and the subsequent sequestered nights were quite calm. I had only to be careful at eight a.m. when the employees arrived. As fellow researchers began to man their desks and cubicles, I barricaded myself in the bathroom for about a half an hour. Then, when the noise level heralded an atmosphere of normalcy, I strolled out and rejoined the other scholars.

That the Library of Congress had the largest collection in the world on the Arab-Islamic world was a matter of great pleasure and surprise to me. There was the Qur'an in numerous translations, despite the fact that pious Muslims do not approve of translation of their book into any other language. The Qur'an was revealed in Arabic to the Arabs. The brilliant and eloquent Arabic language – in rhymed prose that creates an unmatched poetry – is absolutely unique. It is the quality of the language and how it delivers the blessed message that imbues the work with its inimitable spirit. Arabs hold the Qur'an in the highest regard both as a literary work – beyond even the West's regard for the *Iliad*, for example – and as the work of Allah, the one and only God. The Qur'an is seen to be the direct voice of God, not translated through a poet. Indeed Muhammad was identified as an illiterate, thus ensuring that there was no duplicity in the Holy Book and that it came from God alone. The Hadith is a voluminous compendium collected by reliable Islamic scholars that records in infinite detail what Muhammad said, what Muhammad did and what Muhammad approved by his silence. What the Prophet said, did and approved by his silence is the Sunnah, the true path that Muslims must follow to live the good life and hope for paradise.

All the Arabic references I needed were in the Library of Congress. There were endless treatises telling and retelling the facts, stories and mythologies of ancient times. Working on the Khawarij was a joint project between the Bterrami and the Pottstownian. As the names were novel and somewhat difficult for me to master, they must have been nearly impossible for Phyllis. Yet she went into the project with the determination of a general going forth to battle. She studied Arabic, she read translations, and she acquired some acquaintance with the words. She took in the lives of Abu Bakr, Umar, Uthman, Ali – the Orthodox caliphs, the first rulers of the Islamic Ummah after Muhammad. The early caliphs were the ideals – they were good, just and pure. Those who followed – Umayyads, Abbasids, Mamluks and Ottomans – were not quite as good, not as just, nor as pure. Phyllis learned of the collectors of the Hadith and their rigorous methodologies for recording each act or utterance that was actually seen or heard by a reliable companion of the Prophet. Al-Bukhari in his *Al-Jami' as-Sahih* was one of the most reliable.

Phyllis bravely explored with me the works of al-Tabari, Ibn al-Athir, Ibn Abd Rabbu, Ibn Khaldun – great historiographers of their time. The *Muqaddimah* of Ibn Khaldun, translated into English and properly annotated by Franz Rosenthal, was and remains a masterpiece in sociology and in the philosophy of history. We followed with great amusement the rigorous biographer Ibn Khallikan and his opus *Wafyat al-A'yan*, which is an account of the lives of the great ones who have died. The treasures of the Library of Congress seemed boundless. There we found the great jurists of Islam, Abu Hanifah, Malik, al-Shafi'I and al-Hanbali. There were theologians like al-Ghazzali and al-Asha'ri, mystics, better known as Sufis, like al-Hallaj. The works of the great philosophers al-Kindi, al-Farabi and Ibn Rushd (known in the West as Averroes) were available to us. There were doctors of medicine, like Ibn Sina (Avicienne), and mathematicians, like al-Khawarizmi. Phyllis struggled with how to write these names, and the even greater challenge of how to pronounce them. She had great fun with al-Taftazani, al-Qalqashandi, Miskawayh, al-Shahrastani, al-Asfaryani. She had difficulty in distinguishing between such utterly foreign sounds but she never gave up. I can visualize her lying in bed repeating endlessly names and sounds, struggling with the tongue twisters.

If the names of authors were difficult, even more so were the titles of their books. Among those I presented to Phyllis were *Tilbis Iblis*, *al-Farq bayn al-Firaq, Ihya' ulum al-din, al-Munqiz min al-Dalal* and *Shatharat Ath-Thahab fi Akhbar man Thahab*. Translated into English, this last title is *The Golden Treasures in the Accounts of Those Who Have Departed*. In Arabic most book titles rhymed in accordance with the inimitable style of the Qur'an – for example, *Kitab al-Farq bayn al-Firaq* or *Kitab al-Iqtisad fi al-I'tiqad*. Typing and checking the names of authors and their books was relatively easy for Phyllis as long as I was around; it was harder during the month or so I was travelling throughout the country on a semi-diplomatic, academic assignment, but she continued valiantly.

In the spring of 1953, Princeton University hosted a major conference on Islam. Scholars were invited from all the Islamic countries and about a dozen attended from the Arab World. Attendance at the conference of these Arab notables was intended to be part scholarship, part acculturation and part propaganda. Each visiting academic was given a thirty-day private luxury tour of the States. The Department of State asked my dean to locate an Arab to serve as guide to a certain Shafiq Jabri, a Syrian poet, scholar and dean of the Faculty of Arts at Damascus University. The dean thought of me. He concluded that after three years in America, I must by now be so attuned to American life that I could perform the job admirably. His reasoning was that as a twenty-three-year-old PhD candidate with an American girlfriend, Salem could be assumed to know more of American customs and ways than Jabri. The gentle Syrian dean was eighty years old and looked ninety. He was heavy in body and heavy on his feet. Of the English language, he knew yes, no and 'sank you'.

Jabri had never been outside the Arab World. His scholarship was limited to *Kitab al-Aghani* by al-Asfahani, which was not a very useful credential in the new Walt Disney world that was dawning at the time. Jabri was terrified of everything associated with this trip. He understood nothing of what was expected of him or the culture in which he had landed. Why the US embassy in Damascus had recommended him for this conference was incomprehensible to me. Jabri was far beyond acculturation. However, my dean had selected me to go and I must make the most of the opportunity.

'This is an excellent one-month job for you, Elie,' he told me. 'You will make good money, travel first-class and stay in the best hotels. Although you do not know the specific cities that you will be touring, you will be given reading materials beforehand.'

My dean knew me well by that time and could see that I had reservations about my ability to perform all the tasks associated with this job.

'Elie, don't worry,' he assured me. 'In the kingdom of the blind, the one-eyed man is king.'

When I consulted Phyllis she was enthusiastic, as I expected. 'I only wish I could come with you,' she said. 'What a wonderful learning experience, Elie. It may be as important as the God-damned Khawarij.' I hoped she was right.

'Wow,' she exclaimed as she looked at the itinerary that included New York, Boston, Denver, Chicago, Tucson, San Francisco, Seattle, Los Angeles, El-Paso and Dallas. 'In just thirty days you will visit all these cities . . . ' We knew the separation was going to be difficult, but we both expected to be so busy that time would pass with little pain. Phyllis would be fully immersed in the Khawarij manuscript and its challenging nomenclature, while I would be immersed in what I feared would be a most difficult undertaking. I went to

Princeton to pick up my charge and to start my peregrination. I thought of the famed medieval Islamic traveller and saw myself as a modern Ibn Batutah in a new land.

Jabri turned out to be just as I had been told. He was ancient, gentle, withdrawn, and far too decrepit to move easily. He was still recovering from the shock of travel. The poor man had had to change planes at Rome airport, but he had not been well prepared for the experience. He had been told to go to the Alitalia desk upon his arrival to be given instructions for the next leg of his journey, but when he did so the Bella at the desk regretted that there was to be an hour's delay. The terrified Damascene, alone and disorientated in a strange land and entirely strange setting, chose a seat and sat down. He sat for one hour, two hours, three hours, five hours, seven hours. Sitting is not a difficult occupation for a Damascene of his age. In fact, the act of sitting has an important place for a well-respected elder in our culture. In a coffee house in Beirut, in Damascus, in Cairo, among friends and colleagues, it would not be unusual to sit for several hours. But between flights in a strange airport in the Western World, it was most uncomfortable. Jabri thought after long reflection that perhaps it would be prudent to bother the Bella again and ask about his flight. Jabri summoned up his courage. He approached, he asked about his flight to New York. He thought that between gestures and a smattering of sounds he had expressed his frustrations. He threw in words as they came to him from memory, English words that were familiar internationally – go, sit, yes, no – and names of cities: Damascus, Rome, Washington.

The Bella understood enough to be shocked. 'Oh! You have been sitting there since last night, you poor thing,' she cried. 'Your flight has arrived in New York by now.'

'What do, madame, please?' Jabri enquired.

'I am afraid you must wait five more hours and some Bella at this desk will come to you. This time do not worry, we will come to you.' She realized that in this ancient passenger she might as well have had a piece of luggage for all the ability he had to move by himself.

As a piece of luggage, and a most gentle one, Jabri arrived in Washington. He sat through three days of scholarly dialogue on Islam. The conference was in English and Jabri could neither

understand nor contribute a single thing. Jabri's minimal partici-
pation did not seem to be a great disappointment, however, to the
Department of State that had organized the conference.

At the conclusion of the conference, Jabri was my responsibility. I
was the one who must move the ancient scholar from taxi to train,
from train by taxi to plane, from plane by taxi to hotel, and see that
he performed all the other tasks associated with his grand tour of
the US. In New York, the first leg of our journey together, I faced
the first of many stubborn facts that I was to learn about my charge.
Jabri could not negotiate an escalator. In the metropolitan areas
that we toured, it was no small task to avoid the escalator. Only then
did I realize the importance of the accommodation that buildings
provide for people with disabilities. I tried every possible trick,
including going up and down in front of him several times. But it
was to no avail. The mechanism terrified him. Somehow he fell flat
on his face every time he approached the escalator. Picture a two-
hundred-and-fifty-pound man flat on his face. He was a wretched
sight. Instead of people getting angry with him for blocking their
path to the escalator, they were all very understanding and a bit
amused. It was a great relief when he and I decided that we would
try to navigate no more escalators. Negotiating the stairs in the New
York train station instead was difficult, but at least possible. I did,
however, begin to fear a heart attack. He was breathing quite heavily
and eventually so was I. I was young and strong and the stairs were
no problem, but I was breathing hard in fear lest he collapse on me.

I invited Phyllis to come to New York and help me get started.
She was delighted by the invitation and by the opportunity for us
being together in New York. Jabri was quite taken with Phyllis. He
remarked on how beautiful she was and how kind and intelligent.
Then he confessed to Phyllis through me that he was engaged to a
village girl a few years younger even than Phyllis. But his intended
was ugly, he said, and had no manners and no education. Finally he
said, 'I don't believe I will marry her after all.'

He was beginning to enjoy his status as an honoured guest and
started to indulge himself in some of the wonders he had heard of.

'What is the opera,' Jabri asked us. 'Can we see one?'

'Sure,' responded Phyllis. 'I will get the tickets.'

The three of us went to see *Rigoletto*. It was not easy to manoeuvre
the old fellow up all the stairs and along the narrow spaces between

the rows of seats. But eventually we were settled in our places at the Metropolitan Opera House gazing expectantly at the stage. The curtain rose, the applause thundered and the opera began. Shortly after the first aria, I stole a look at the piece of luggage, and he was sound asleep. When he began to snore loudly, I nudged him. He awoke with a start and asked if the opera was over.

'No,' I replied. 'It has only just begun.'

But Jabri did not like it. 'This is the opera!' he exclaimed in disgust. 'Oh, what a waste of time, let's leave.'

Phyllis and I both tried to explain in gestures and whispers the difficulty of leaving in the middle of the show and that it would disturb the other people. But he insisted. Defeated, greatly embarrassed and with considerable difficulty, we filed out past the hostile stares of the refined New Yorkers.

We took our leave of Phyllis, who had previously worried about Jabri's welfare but who now pitied her beloved the task he had ahead of him. Each new city became a story to relate and justified a telephone call to the Pottstownian.

A volunteer in Denver, for example, was a fine woman who invited us to see her home and get a first-hand sense of how an American family lived. 'Dr Jabri,' she proudly explained as she showed the old man through her home, 'this is the living-room, and this is the kitchen. We call this the dining-room and over here I will show you the master bedroom . . .'

At the mention of the bedroom, the old man became a tiger. 'Elie, she is inviting me to her bedroom,' he said in wondering amazement. 'She wants to sleep with me.'

'You do not understand,' I screamed at him in alarm.

'Oh yes,' Jabri insisted. 'Stay behind in the kitchen and leave me with her alone in her bedroom.'

I was shocked. I was in a panic. I never dreamt he had such life in him, especially not sexual life. I threatened him with hellfire if he so much as touched her, and I stayed right by him, shouting all the time. The venerable lady wanted to know what the fuss in Arabic was all about. There was no way to enlighten her as to the attitude of a traditional Arab to women and bedrooms, the very different architecture, design and usage of homes in the Sunni Muslim world and the many complex associated taboos. I made something up on the spot, ushered my frisky companion out of the door and we escaped from the scene unscathed. I could only hope that the incident would soon be forgotten.

The acculturation plan was to culminate at the end of a month at the University of California in Los Angeles as all the guests to the Princeton conference converged at a luncheon hosted by the president of UCLA. We sat at some five round tables with soft drinks, no wine or hard liquor in sight. The university seemed well advised. A line of well-attired waiters filed in, bearing trays of covered dishes. Beneath turned out to be a course containing corn, mashed potato – and ham. By the time I noticed the ham, strictly prohibited as is all pork by Islam, some of the conferees had already begun to eat.

'Stop!' shouted the innocent guide of Jabri. 'There is a mistake. This dish is pork, it is not intended for you. Waiters, please take these dishes back.'

A shifty Beiruti scholar, who was enjoying the 'forbidden fruit', shouted me down, sanctifying the dish as beef and as such permitted by Islam. As a Christian, I had no trouble with the fatwa, and the ham by default became beef. After all, was I more royal than the king? The famous advice of Talleyrand to his first-year students in the French Foreign Service was that yes, they must defend France, *'mais surtout pas trop du zèle'* (but easy on the passion). My travels with Jabri were fascinating experiences, and I have considered writing about them as a practical illustration of cultural *faux pas* and misunderstandings.

While I was sightseeing from one American city to the next, the Khawarij were following me on a parallel course. In my absence Phyllis had become somewhat overwhelmed with the tasks of verification of names and places. Ever resourceful, she drafted her sweet, adoring and always accommodating mother Dorothy to help with the typing. It was one thing for Phyllis to spell *Wafayat al-Ayan* – a bit tricky perhaps but ultimately successful. It was a completely different thing for Dorothy to spell the words. When I was not babysitting Jabri I was on the phone to Phyllis in Washington and to Dorothy in Philadelphia. Hotel telephones were quite expensive, and to make the calls from public pay-phones was nearly impossible. Once depleted of coins to feed into the insatiable machine, one was rudely cut off.

For lovers' talk the telephone is a most accommodating medium. For that month the telephone was my saviour. The fact that it claimed all the money I was earning as guide and babysitter only added to the pleasure. It was worth every dime. Somehow on the phone I tend to speak with my heart. I dig deep into my being and express feelings that are clean and pure. The phone crowds out all images that intervene in face-to-face encounters. It concentrates the mind. The Khawarij were the excuse for the calls. After quickly dispensing with them, however, Phyllis and I talked at length of the love that bound us, and of the joy of being together again soon.

Phyllis was as much my teacher as I was hers. She steered me through the treacherous currents of life and I guided her into the only realm I knew or was allowed by my family background to know – namely the academic. I gave her books to read. I discussed the books with her. I provided historical connections to the cold facts and accounts that she had accumulated in her high school. Phyllis was a voracious reader. Until we met, she mostly read books recommended by her friends or through the Best Books lists of the leading American newspapers. During our joint project, we had to discard such books or lay them aside for more leisurely times. For now, we were building our intellectual infrastructure. Our love life was set against a continuing search for the truth to be found in history and for the reality to be found in ourselves.

We studied the great civilizations of the Near East, the great thinkers of Athens and Rome, the dawn of Christianity and the emergence of Islam, the medieval world, and how the creative energy of the Renaissance arose from these influences. The more we delved into fundamental issues, the more we were inspired to dig deeper still. For example, one of the readings in my post-doctoral methodology course was the *Symposium*, the famous Dialogue of Plato. Once I read it, I could hardly wait to pass the book on to Phyllis, who also read it immediately. I gave her a few days alone with the classic philosophical debate before suggesting that we meet for dinner to further explore the ideas together. We would glean from the *Symposium*, as we did from so many historical and philosophical texts, the fundamental truths that we perceived to be ours.

Plato's *Symposium* presents a series of ideas and theories through the device of a banquet that goes on late into the night. Those who attend the banquet discuss their ideas of the beautiful and the true. The reader must consider contradictory thoughts expressed by various characters and determine what is true and, perhaps most importantly, how to arrive at truth. Phyllis and I talked of making our life together just such a banquet – an opportunity to exact as much from being as was within our power.

In our discussion of the structure of the *Symposium* and the fact that Plato set the discourse in the context of a banquet, Phyllis recalled a line from the popular play *Auntie Mame*, then a Broadway hit. The colourful and bold central character Mame famously reminds her nephew not to settle for less than all that life has to offer. 'Life is a banquet,' Mame tells the boy, 'and most poor suckers are starving to death!' Phyllis and I were determined not to starve at life's banquet. We were both conscious of language and yearned to realize its possibilities for joining two people. We were eager to articulate concepts and ideas, not merely as abstractions, but more importantly as constitutive elements in the making of the people that we were intent on becoming, both individually and together.

I must admit that when I completed my studies in the summer of 1953, and particularly after I passed my comprehensive PhD exam, I became acutely aware of the yawning depth of my ignorance. 'A comprehensive PhD with distinction in ignorance' is how I characterized my degree to Phyllis. She worried that I was simply afraid to leave school, and that I wanted to remain a graduate student and researcher as long as possible. And she may not have been totally wrong. It is a dreadful leap from the library to the market place. Although I completed the requirements for the degree in September 1953, I opted to stay till February 1954 to work in the Lebanese embassy and to await the mid-year award ceremony. My parents wanted a degree they could frame and hang in the salon for all to see. A simple letter stating that their son had completed all the requirements for the PhD would not do.

Father had no doubt where he stood on diplomas. He wanted his sons to carry final degrees from the best universities. He expected to see degrees in medicine, law and engineering. They must necessarily be big, colourful diplomas with which he could decorate the wall of his salon in Bterram. No other picture was allowed on that wall. He regarded them as evidence of the return on his investments. In this, he succeeded. Over time, our village home became a gallery of diplomas. Father had a field-day with my two medical brothers. They had dozens of diplomas, certificates from every post-doctoral programme that they attended. Although father understood that these certificates were not actual degrees, he never felt duty bound to explain the difference to the villagers. They were all *Shihadat*, or testimonials. Between impact and truth he chose impact.

My job-description as research assistant to the Lebanese ambassador Dr Charles Malik included everything that the permanent staff of the embassy could not do. I researched the content of the ambassador's speeches attacking Communism and exalting the fundamental values of Western civilization. Malik was a great orator, the star of the General Assembly of the United Nations and a much sought-after speaker at important political and academic occasions. I also worked on his extensive library. Publishing houses sent him hundreds of books that required classification and letters of acknowledgement to the donors. This was an ideal job for me. It was the practical application of my skills, almost a continuation of school.

Although I studied politics and Arab-Islamic civilization, my first love was history, philosophy and the philosophy of history. In this realm Malik was the ideal advisor. Under his guidance I realized I had to spend at least two years reading and digesting major books of which I had only read parts, often for exam purposes. As I worked my way through Malik's library, it was most rewarding. The more I dug into the legacy, the greater my appetite to dig some more. When the French say '*l'appetit vient en mangeant*' (appetite comes with eating) they are entirely right. This dictum is even more true in matters of the mind. The engaged and inquisitive mind is dazzling, revealing secrets and opening horizons. One must admire Socrates, that ugly man of Athens who walked the *agora*, the market place, pestering unsuspecting strangers, engaging them in discourse. His questions always penetrated beyond the familiar and prevailing opinion in search of the true, the beautiful, the just. Fortunately for mankind, this great teacher had a disciple. Socrates taught Plato and Plato taught Aristotle. Aristotle schooled young Alexander, and as Alexander the Great, the conqueror schooled the East, learning a great deal in return.

Malik had studied under Alfred North Whitehead at Harvard and under Martin Heidegger at Tubingen. Whitehead was a renowned mathematician philosopher who collaborated with Bertrand Russell on the *Principia Mathematica*. Heidegger was an unparalleled existentialist, fully immersed in *Dasein*, the distinctly human mode of existence. I loved and admired these two great thinkers. I also loved and was greatly influenced by Pushkin, Gogol, Dostoyevsky, Nietzsche, Voltaire, Locke, Machiavelli, Ibn al-Tiqataqa, Ibn Khaldun and al Ghazzali. My core philosophy, the very framework from which I moved backwards in history into the Greeks and the ancient river civilizations, was stamped by Christ and the apostle St Paul. From within the same framework, I was moving forward into the temples of Western civilization in which I sought wisdom, peace and intellectual solace.

The history, literature and philosophy that Phyllis and I read were directly or indirectly informed by our religion. As a Lutheran, Phyllis accepted her tradition without question. Her family prayed before dinner and thanked the Lord after dinner. Her faith was as St Paul counselled, 'without how and why'. In my own way I too was religious. I was not unlike that man who, when Christ asked him: 'Do you believe?' answered: 'Lord, I believe, help thou my unbelief.'

I followed Christ and felt at home with St Paul and his blend of the rational and the mystical, which was 'to the Greeks a stumbling block'. Serious lovers crave strong foundations upon which to build a stable relationship. For Phyllis and me, these foundations were precisely the values we learned from Christianity. Our love had a religious dimension through which we felt connected to the true and eternal. We expected to build our life together on the Christian values of love, honesty, truth, faith, simplicity and care for ourselves and for others. As I tell this at the cynical dawn of the twenty-first century, I realize that it may sound odd or even corny. And yet, within the context of the mid-twentieth century, when we were dedicating ourselves to rebuilding a world that had been laid waste by hatred and years of war, I must state it now as we experienced it then.

Between 1951 and 1954 Phyllis read deeply and widely and reflected on her reading; thus she was influenced by dozens of major books that were unfamiliar to her family, friends and roommates. She stood apart, an uncertified intellect, preparing for her life as a wife and mother and also as a teacher and model for others.

Upon receipt of the prized diploma in February 1954, I was

74

urged by Phyllis to return to Lebanon, get a suitable job and only then to send for her. We had both had enough of Washington, enough of post-doctoral works in the embassy, and were ready to move full steam ahead. We had been talking and planning for two years. I had such big dreams. I had an expansive ego and made no apologies for that fact. When I was preparing to leave my high school in Tripoli, the student paper asked all of us graduates what our plans were, what we most wanted to be. Nearly everyone answered conventionally that they wanted to be a doctor, an engineer, a successful lawyer, a renowned teacher. Not I. I said, 'I want to achieve what curiosity alone will not attain.' I won first prize for this inspired response. Phyllis loved the story and wondered if I had meant the comment humorously or seriously.

'Well,' I told her, 'let's return to Lebanon and see what the future has in store for us. I have been away for almost four years.'

We were a very close family, and all of my relatives were eager for my return. For some time now they had feared the gravitational pull of America, the land of unbounded promise, would prove too strong for me to resist. Phyllis and I had made several more trips to Pottstown and her family had become increasingly comfortable with me – most of their anxieties and reservations had been allayed. The Sells blessed our intention to marry. When I went to say my goodbyes there were hugs and kisses and tears all around. The Lutherans are affectionate in their own way. On the train back to Washington, Phyllis confided that all of her family trusted me except Grammy, Dorothy's mother. Phyllis overheard Grammy tell her daughter, 'Well, this is the last we will ever see of him.' Fortunately, she lived long enough to see me again and again, and to hugely enjoy her visits in later years to our home in Arlington, Virginia – at that time a green hilly suburb of Washington DC.

My return was a great relief to my family. Now I was once again in their bosom. I had two plans, first to find a good job, and second to write formally to Phyllis to ask her to come to Lebanon and marry me. My father also had two plans – to ensure I found a highly paid job and to marry me to a wealthy Lebanese woman. He felt that he knew Phyllis from my constant stream of stories and descriptions of her. He understood that she was a great girl – but her family had no money. Father believed that his prize was worth a very high price. In his view, a woman with wealth would set his son straight and would help the family. Arranged marriages are very practical. They are often brilliant compromises. An old man with position and wealth can expect to marry a beautiful and young girl. A promising youth with an advanced education should equally expect to marry a beautiful and rich woman. Father had compiled a secret list of three or four candidates – all from north Lebanon, Greek Orthodox like us, all beautiful and all rich. I had only one candidate and she was far away. For months he paraded me around the social circuit and for months I resisted. I carried with me several pictures of Phyllis and these I proudly exhibited on every occasion.

My father was an exceptionally proud and confident man. His son possessed a PhD, and therefore a bright and promising future. He saw me as highly marketable and expected to do well in the marriage arrangements. Each Sunday he required me to dress up and accompany him on visits that had been previously arranged with the family of a potential bride. I would arrive utterly un-concerned to meet the well-dressed, beautifully groomed and impeccably raised bride-to-be. Although the parents made subtle reference to the hefty dowry that awaited, such comments did not register with me. In one case my father must have urged the father of the really quite lovely young woman to be specific and frank with me. He certainly was.

'You marry my daughter,' he promised me, 'and you will not need to work for the rest of your life. There is enough to keep you and her and your children in fine style.'

'Great,' answered my father, his eyes pleading with me. 'It is a magnanimous offer, isn't it, Elie?'

But I would not be moved. 'I am sure,' I told her father, 'that your lovely daughter will attract the finest husband. She is pretty, she is rich, and I am sure she will find every happiness.'

As silence reigned, I bade them goodbye and left, followed by a defeated and I believe somewhat humiliated father. Father was a supremely practical man. Had he known Phyllis, he may not have bothered with the traditional ritual. But he did not. America was far away, and my father was worried that his prize horse would be tempted to marry Phyllis and live in America. This he could not endure. Adib needed his son by his side here in Lebanon. Father had worked so hard to educate me. It was critical to him that I get a good job to contribute to the income and to the prestige of the family. Father had been through some extraordinarily rough times.

Adib was in his teens when starvation killed half of his village. During the First World War the Ottoman soldiers were brutal to the Christians of Lebanon. Food was rare for everyone, and the Orthodox of the Kurah region where my grandparents lived were especially deprived. Villagers lived on the little they could forage from the land, walking as far as ten miles to Tripoli to pick lemons that were spoiling on the trees. Many died of exhaustion and starvation on the walk to Tripoli. It was common for those who were able to escape overseas. My grandfather, the one whose name I carry, was one who was able to escape. Grandfather Elie boarded a ship in Tripoli and travelled to Argentina, where he toiled strenuously. He walked from town to town, selling goods as he procured them, and the little he managed to earn and save he sent to his family in Bterram. His wife, my grandmother Helena, stayed at home and waited faithfully for the return of the voyager. Helena had had many children, but only two survived. Families lived in wretched conditions with poor infant care; because of the cramped sleeping accommodation infants were often smothered in their sleep. The two survivors were my father Adib and my aunt Jaleeli.

Lebanese villagers, before the rush of globalization and Westernization, were prepared to live as their forebears did. They expected to till the land, harvest the olives, tend the grapevines and subsist on a meagre income. The economy was based on barter rather than cash. Families ate what they produced and preserved any surplus for the winter months. At the end of the nineteenth century, this began to change somewhat. As village people learned of emigration, a few daring souls ventured to Australia, the west coast of Africa and into the Americas. My father chose not to emigrate although his father had done so.

Schooling, when it existed in our village, was only at the elementary level. Boys were needed in the fields to help their fathers and grandfathers. Girls were rarely sent to school at all. They were bred for marriage, child-rearing and home-management. Father had two years of schooling in language, mathematics and the rudiments of literature, primarily Arabic poetry. Mother fared a bit better.

Her family, claiming a higher social status, broke with tradition and sent her to a boarding school in Tripoli near by, just long enough to prepare her for a good marriage.

Though he had only a little schooling and perhaps because he had so little else, Adib possessed enormous pride and courage. My father was a brilliant man, dynamic, a born leader, and radically different from all the villagers of his time. He taught himself law and accounting, and in competition with bona-fide lawyers, he took first place in the exam for notary public, and won that job for the Kurah District. The job was a petty and provincial one, and would likely have remained so if anyone else had held the post. But Adib made it into a high position, a centre of gravity and a real force in local government. When he learned of his father's death in Argentina, Adib made the journey to South America to collect the savings that his toiling parent had accumulated. And then my father proceeded to use his inheritance well. He bought land, he lent money, he worked hard at his job and he soon became a strong, reputable and beloved leader in our region. Somehow, he even managed to teach himself English and French.

His language skills were put to many uses and his authority was seldom questioned. A story is often told of the day when a local villager received a telegram informing him that his brother Hanna had passed away in the United States. The villager brought the telegram to the village square where a backgammon game was in progress, and where translation – village style – could be had free of charge.

'Passed away,' one neighbour offered, 'means he has gone to a far place.'

'But what place?' asked the brother. 'He often left Allentown to go to California and that is pretty far. They have never before sent a letter much less a telegram.'

'Passed away,' volunteered another, 'means crossing the ocean. Perhaps there was not enough work in Allentown, Pennsylvania, so your brother left for Sydney, Australia.'

This seemed a convincing argument, and the brother was re-assured.

Then my father arrived. 'Passed away,' Adib pronounced with authority, 'means Hanna has died. Don't waste your time, just ring the church bell and let the village know the sad news.'

In a very few minutes the bell was ringing and next day the village held Hanna's funeral.

Our region was known as al-Kurah and consisted of some forty Greek Orthodox villages. In 1927, Adib married Lamya from the Malik family. Though they enjoyed the title of Sheikh, granted by the Ottomans in the late nineteenth century, the Maliks were as poor as the Salems or the Sirhans or any of the other eight families in the village. The Sheikh title encouraged the Maliks to show off, which drove my proud father into violent opposition. The Maliks lacked my father's ambition and industry and were always trying to put him down. Although conservative in most aspects of life, his opinion of the Maliks made a rebel out of him. 'The title of Sheikh is bogus,' he would protest. 'It was bought with money from the Ottoman rulers.'

Adib loved Lamya, though he kept his distance from her family. He was always kind to her seven brothers and three sisters, even though he believed them to be below average in intelligence and scoffed at their desire to emigrate to Australia. He accused them of being lazy, outmoded and superficial. He lauded hard work, individual values and determination to succeed. He believed in education as the only way to get villagers out of poverty and a moribund way of life. He spoke of education as a passionate missionary speaks of his faith. His impact on me and my peer group was profound.

3

The Maliks were my mother's family, and for them there was just one clear purpose in life. They wanted only to emigrate to Australia, open a dry-goods store and make money. This had probably been inspired by the central ambition of my grandfather Sheikh Salim, whose life would be fulfilled if he were able to receive a regular supply of money from his children in Australia, buy fine clothes and eat well. He was actually a poor man, but somehow managed to look grand. He used his position to look down upon the villagers – including us. As a sheikh he expected that any visitor to his house would naturally bring an offering – a few eggs, the village cheese we called *shankleesh*, a bowl of yoghurt, or some other small delicacy. You could expect to get scolded for coming empty-handed.

The sheikh's eldest son did ultimately make the trip to Sydney. The poor boy arrived, exhausted and unemployed, to find a telegram waiting for him from his father. 'Send money' was all it said. 'What money!' was the son's incredulous response. But after a few months, the boy began to send modest amounts to his father. And as often as Sheikh Salim collected the small cheque in Beirut, he would spend most of it on the way to the village.

My father however was more fortunate. Thanks to the inheritance from grandpa in Buenos Aires, and due as well to his basic intelligence and boundless ambition, Adib was able to secure enough income to live comparatively well. In our village in the al-Kurah region that meant he had an olive grove. We ate olives at all meals, we cooked with olive oil, and we sold most of the oil we produced. Although it was only a few hundred gallons each year, by no means an industrial output, our oil income provided a modest sufficiency for the family. In addition, Adib had a regular income from serving as notary public. He lent money to the needy for interest. This was an important function in between the two world wars, as banking had not really made its way into our rural areas. He sent his children to school and always urged them onward to college. He lent money at times without interest to parents intent on educating their children. Education, he lectured, was our pass-port to good jobs, to regular incomes and to upward mobility in the Lebanese system. Father believed in frugality in living, but when it came to education he spent generously.

To bring the first advanced degree home to a rural family of such limited means had significance far beyond my expectation. My father framed the document immediately, and hung it in the most prominent place in our salon. Adib was a master at public relations and had boasted of his son long before my studies were complete. Each time I passed an exam in America father pro-claimed it as a victory, highly exaggerating its importance. Villagers accept myths eagerly, often as readily as they accept facts. Adib was a sturdy, reliable official with quasi-governmental credentials, a great weaver of tales and myths, many of them concerning his son. Now that I had returned, villagers from all over al-Kurah came to congratulate him, and to see this young man whose praises they had heard sung for so long.

Adib was clearly the big man, the wise man of Bterram, a village of about one thousand residents, as we no longer counted the thousands who had emigrated to Australia, Canada, the US, Latin America and West Africa. Looking back now from the dawn of the twenty-first century, the village of Bterram is utterly transformed from what it once was. The radio, the cinema, television, education and improved communications have put an end to virtually all of the village customs and traditions that had been practised for centuries.

But at that time, in the mid 1950s, the villagers still lived off the land. Olive oil suffused our food as well as our social lives. Every evening, neighbours gathered in our house. The conversation was invariably about the olives. Do we have a good crop! Do we plough tomorrow? Whose bulls are we employing for ploughing? How much is the gallon selling for? Should we sell now, or wait for better prices! Have you heard of the new disease that has hit the olive trees in Bterram, also in other villages!

Each family in the village owned olive trees, grapevines and orchards of figs, apples, oranges, pomegranates, almonds and walnuts. Like olive groves, vineyards had to be tilled, trimmed, fertilized and discussed. Grapes were second only to olives in importance. In summer we harvested and ate grapes fresh at breakfast, lunch and dinner. We made wine and arak, our national drink, from them. We dried the grapes and in a simple old-fashioned process transformed them into raisins. I recall walking to school with pockets full of raisins. I dug into them all day long. Now that the village has modernized, I am the only one who still makes raisins. Everyone still makes arak.

The fig tree ranked next to the grape in Bterram. Figs were delicious fresh, and even better when they were preserved and steamed. In winter, our dried figs and raisins made an excellent dessert, and as long as they lasted we had no need for others.

Evenings were for conversation as there were no media distractions to disrupt the family circle. Conversation centred on what we had and what we knew – olives, grapes, figs. Not more than two or three hundred words were needed to engage volubly in evening discourse. For variety, my father would introduce poetry. He would recite from memory the poems of pre-Islamic times. Often he gestured and took on the characters as he acted the meaning and the lessons hidden in the narrative rhythms. As we grew older we discovered that our father's choice of poetry was quite selective. He was actually teaching us lessons in life, lecturing us vicariously through a poet from antiquity. He must have instinctively understood and mastered the art of subliminal suggestion. It eventually dawned on us that he was reciting only those lines that exalted hard work, courage, the importance of wealth, power and glory, and the discerning ability to take advantage of every opportunity. One particular couplet, which he drummed into our subconscious until it became an integral part of who we were, ran like this:

> Should the wind blow your way,
> Grasp the opportunity before it goes away.

To my father life was a battle; he was a maverick who saw no middle ground. A person's fate was either to win or to lose. The villagers revered my dad. They came for visits to seek his counsel and to talk. Adib loved visitors and greatly enjoyed talking. And though we, his family, may have regarded his talks as lectures, the villagers held him in such high esteem that they were gratified by his speeches and came back for more.

The village was one. When a child was born the church bell rang. All the villagers descended upon the new parents and everyone offered heartfelt congratulations. When couples were married the church bells rang. All the villagers congregated at the home of the bridegroom so that everyone could dance and sing and eat and drink together. They made the wedding. And when one of their number died the church bell rang once more. All the villagers sadly made their way to the house of the deceased to cry, to console, to carry the casket on their shoulders, first to the church service, then from the church to the final burial place.

And Bterram honoured the lesser occasions together as well. Even if the village volley-ball team was playing a team from another village, the church bell rang. The villagers gathered to accompany their team to the neighbouring village for the match. God help the villagers on the way back if the Bterram team should win. There would be celebrations and challenges that didn't always end well.

When in September 1950 I left Beirut for New York I travelled by ship. My neighbours from the village filled a few buses to accompany me to the Beirut docks to send me off properly. They came in droves to wish me well. More than a few found it an appropriate occasion to recite poems especially composed for the occasion. Copious tears were shed as I said my goodbyes and ascended the gangway. Aboard ship I looked back at the people onshore waving handkerchiefs and offering advice to their loved ones, now on their way to new climes. And I was struck with amazement by how much people had to say at the very moment when they had to shout to be heard. Though I had to concentrate hard, I knew it was important to separate those words meant for me from those flung from shore to others on board.

Father shouting, 'Good luck, Elie, study hard.'

Mother counterbalancing, 'Take care, do not catch cold.'

Her feminine advice, I knew, always irritated her irascible spouse. 'Who cares,' he would be thinking, 'whether you take care or not, whether you are hot or cold.' To my father this was not the issue, not the issue at all, and it irked him to have his masculine counsel countervailed.

I recall now his letters to me in Cincinnati, and how he reluctantly allowed my mother to add a line or two, even though he regarded Lamya's guidance as pure marshmallow. She would write, 'Beloved Elie, the most important thing is your health, eat well, get plenty of rest.' Her counsel on transport was most intriguing, and must have amused her pragmatic husband. 'Elie,' my mother wrote, 'as for trains, buses and taxis, please do not take them unless "we" know the conductor and the driver.'

On reading such advice my father must have breathed a sigh of despair. 'Let women talk,' he would confide to his sons. 'They know nothing.' For how could we possibly know from our distant village the people out there driving taxis and conducting trains? Womentalk!

And so it must have been for centuries. I believed that Bterram had been much the same for thousands of years. The Phoenician god Ashmon had his temple in our village for two thousand years before the Triumphant Church relegated him to the dustbin of history. The temple, now a buried and forgotten ruin, hides meekly in the shadow of our church. Indeed, tradition in Bterram must have had its roots in prehistoric times.

Phyllis knew a lot about the village since, God knows, I told her all I knew. Phyllis listened without judgement as I told her how my simple and highly traditional grandmother, Helena, actually ate the first excretions of my baby brothers. I told Phyllis that when I demanded of Helena, 'Why are you eating shit?' she answered sweetly and calmly without hesitation, as if voicing the wisdom of the ancients, 'That they may live, my love.'

I concluded, rightly or wrongly, that early man in Bterram, like the animals in the midst of which he lived, ate the faeces of their babies as protection against predators. I related the positive and the negative to Phyllis without truly being certain which was which. Was the primitive bad? Was the modern good? And the modern, I had to admit, was creeping slowly into Bterram. Change seems to occur mostly in the wake of great wars, and the Second World War brought virtually the whole world through Bterram.

Somehow the Kurah district was a staging ground for Allied troops to rest, to train, to manoeuvre, and then to ship off to new fronts in Africa and Southern Europe. All these soldiers were part of the British and Free French Expeditionary Force in the Middle East. Between 1939 and 1945, between my ninth and fifteenth years, Bterram was a virtual United Nations. Thousands of soldiers filled the village and the neighbouring fields. They lived in tents and hastily built barracks. Poles, Hungarians, Czechoslovakians,

French, British, Moroccans, Algerians, Tunisians, Greeks, Indians, Australians – soldiers of almost every nationality brought into our village their own languages, their own food and their own customs. From British and French empires not yet on their way to dissolution came a multiplicity of colours, headgear and dances.

Walking to school we zigzagged among tanks, lorries and horse-drawn cannons. Planes flew overhead, often dropping supplies for the troops. I witnessed one air engagement between British and German warplanes, and raced to the scene where the German plane fell. There was no pilot when I arrived.

In imitation of the armies around me, I recruited an army of my own. Encouraged by foreign officers with time on their hands I assembled a small regiment and held manoeuvres just like the army. For several months we patrolled our territory until, tragically, I lost one of my prized soldiers when he stepped on a mine. His family and friends could hardly collect enough pieces to give him a decent burial. My father put an end to it immediately and I was no longer allowed to exercise my military fancies. The cautious patriarch brought down the Lebanese flag that had proudly fluttered over the leader's tent.

Villagers who had never seen a plane before could now hear the rumble from afar, look up and see hundred of planes in close formation. From time to time they could witness a lively dogfight, and then run to the olive groves to give aid to fallen pilots.

Change had already been coming from all directions. In the 1930s water arrived in pipes underground. It was soon followed by electricity. The older folks, like Helena, branded the new as a miracle. But a miracle ordained. 'Live long and you will see plenty,' she announced. Electricity was truly miraculous. 'This is what He wishes. He knows best. Thanks to Him we are alive and we witness new things. We lived for years in candlelight, then came the gas-light, but electricity – this is truly something.' The wonder of electricity crowded our conversation for a while, supplanting even the olives, the grapes and the figs. Without actually knowing a thing about it, father explained to the villagers how electricity worked and they were suitably impressed. Adib knows it all, they agreed. When huge rolls of electric wires were brought to the entrance of the village, neighbours came out in force to witness this new miracle from the West. As the electricians raised the poles and stretched the wires, Bterramis stretched with them, accompanying the wires step by step for miles.

When the war came, the radio made its triumphant entry. We were thrilled and all marvelled at this great invention. All of us, that is, except my grandmother Helena, who was certain there was a small man sitting inside and wanted nothing to do with the thing. The radio was quite large, a massive piece of furniture that lent some credibility to her argument. When we pressed her to come and look inside it, she refused. When we tried to drag her towards the radio by force she resisted with the force of a regiment. Helena certainly was stubborn, and I regaled Phyllis with stories of my grandmother's eccentricities.

During the war the French forces required householders in the village to provide billets for officers. My father came to his beloved mother Helena and explained to her, 'Dear mother, this is wartime; we could all live or we could all die, we could even be humiliated. As you know our house is small and the French army wants to lodge an officer with us. This means, mother, we have to provide him with room, food and service. To avoid having to do this, mother, I need your help.'

'Mine?' answered Helena, already suspicious of her ingenious son.

'Yes, yours, mother. I need you to pretend that you are sick with a contagious disease. Armies, mother, are terrified of contagious diseases. I want you to get into bed at once and pretend you are sick.'

'Sick?' Helena replied. 'I feel fit and well, I am not sick at all.'

'Yes, I know,' continued her impatient son, 'and thank God you are in excellent health. I am only asking you to pretend.'

'Pretend?' queried Helena. 'How can I pretend? I am not sick at all. *What littleness of mind* to ask that of me.'

What littleness of mind was her answer to every question she could not grasp. Poor Adib, who in the world could literally move mountains, was utterly unable to persuade his mother to act sick. She only repeated, '*What littleness of mind!*'

My father could be heard cursing the day he was born and banging every object that came his way. Poor Adib, poor Helena.

Helena left the village once to go to Buenos Aires, presumably to help her husband. She was totally useless there, and her husband could hardly wait to send her back to the village. She was primitive and stubborn. When her husband stopped a rural train to get on, she refused.

'But why?' pleaded the husband.

'Because there are people in it,' she answered. 'How can I get in? *What littleness of mind.*' And so they walked and walked to the next town.

I recall as a child watching Helena wash baby clothes. It seemed she was always at it. She put the clothes in a bowl filled with hot water then squatted over the bowl and washed by rubbing the clothes with her hands. She squeezed them to get as much water out as possible. She performed this ritual on the roof two or three times every day. Our house was on the way to the bakery and all of the women of the village carried their dough in pans on their heads to bake in the communal ovens. The dough would be flattened by hand and rolled into thin circular pieces and baked into bread. When finished, the sheets of bread looked like exotic napkins. Indeed Protestant missionaries presented with Lebanese bread thought they were napkins and proceeded to lay them on their laps to the great amusement of the villagers. Our neighbours learned to be cautious when passing as Helena tended to empty her bowl from the roof.

I became accustomed to hearing a woman scream, 'Damn you, Helena, you've ruined my dough. You will pay for it.'

Unfazed, Helena always answered with absolute certainty, 'Heed not the water, it is only baby-clothes water.'

'Yes,' shouted the victim, 'Baby shit, baby urine!'

Helena would proceed with her work murmuring, 'What littleness of mind.'

And sometimes she was right to be dismissive. There was an occasion, for example, when a rumour spread in the village that God was planning to punish us. Therefore the ocean, some ten miles from our village, would overflow and overwhelm Bterram. The village priest ordered everyone to spend the night on their roof. The village was nine hundred feet above sea level. Houses ranged across high hills, but some were in valleys between the hills. A flood was itself improbable, and the remedy was ridiculous. If the ocean were to reach Bterram, some houses would be under water, and some not, depending on their elevation. Nevertheless, most of the villagers spent their nights on their rooftops. Two who certainly did not were my father – on grounds of reason, and his mother – on grounds of 'what littleness of mind'. If God wants to reclaim my soul, He will do so just as well in the house as on the roof,' she told us.

There was no logic to her position, only mood. She resisted all reason. Helena spoke in a prose rarely spoken by anyone else. For every event she had a proverb. She had memorized and appropriated all types of proverbs from the Bible and village folklore. She had a gift for applyng just the right phrase to situations as they emerged. Her proverbs often rhymed, which made them easy to remember. Perhaps because she was so simple and so unique I often find that I resort to her proverbs and anecdotes to this day. And she predicted it would be so.

'Wait and see,' she told me once. 'Simple as I am you will remember what I said as you get older and you will say, "May God bless her soul." '

Indeed, Phyllis cherished my Helena stories, many of which I included in my daily letters from Bterram to Washington. I was describing events in the village not to discourage Phyllis, but to prepare her for her coming adventure.

Bterram was different, and a far cry from Muhammad's tent a few miles from Mecca. She wrote that she greatly enjoyed reading of my visits to potential brides. Phyllis especially appreciated my assurance that the more I saw of others, the more I was convinced that she was the right one for me. But I was haunted by the troubling question of whether I was the right one for her. I consoled myself with the belief that that doubt was normal, and was a sign of my sincere love for Phyllis. For after all, had I not heard that true love exists when you worry more about the beloved and less about yourself?

The more I wrote to Phyllis about my father and his ambitious plans, his fears for the future, his possible disappointments, the more she liked him. Of the two of us, Phyllis was the practical partner, destined to appreciate practical parents like mine. In letters you assure, you reassure, and you assure again and again. I began to see love communication like an evening in Bterram. All you needed were a few words, a few sentences repeated endlessly.

But in addition to loving words, the calculating woman, the custodian of the feminine impulse of nesting, caring and stabilizing, had some other things on her mind as she waited on the far side of the globe. My practical Phyllis wanted to know about my search for a job. How was it going? Where would it be? What type of work would it be? She was ready to come and only waiting for me to say the word. Her loving persistence focused my attention. I was inclined to let matters go their own way. I was enjoying the village after my long absence. Beirut held no special attraction for me. I was a villager through and through, despite the PhD. But the facts of life in our household ordained that if there were no job there would be no marriage.

After dozens of attempts, Adib finally ran out of brides and had to give in to my fancy. He wondered about my choice of an American wife, and feared that because our backgrounds were so different it could not possibly work out. I believed I knew his thoughts. I saw that from his perspective my desire to marry Phyllis was hugely impractical and that such extreme love was an expression of weakness. I later learned, however, that the Tiger was softening during this time. He actually confessed to Phyllis years later that he had opened all of her letters, read them carefully, and resealed the envelopes before he gave them to me. He became certain, he told her later, that Phyllis loved me so much that he had no right to stand in our way. Phyllis reassured him that she was not angry that he had opened her letters. In fact, she claimed she might easily do the same with any letters sent by women to her sons. Phyllis and Adib shared the opinion that the boys might require such close supervision because they were likely to be, like their father, a bit emotional and a bit immature.

Before I could bring my future bride home, however, I had to find a job. As a graduate of the American higher-educational system I had two choices – American companies operating in Lebanon or the American University of Beirut (AUB). Father favoured the prospects of an American company, believing they would command a higher salary. I had one brief disastrous interview and did not like the atmosphere at all. I rejected the brash attitude of the potential employer and found his office somewhat distasteful and the prospect of sales and marketing work dull and inconsequential.

This left AUB. Equipped with a PhD from a prestigious American university, I presented myself to Cecil Hourani, chairman of the

Political Science Department. I believed this department to be my only option. Dr Hourani was very respectful and appreciative of my academic credentials. However, there was no vacancy in my field, which was political philosophy with a concentration on Arab-Islamic civilization. Hourani filled this post himself. He mused that there was a colleague whose position I could have if only the fellow would resign, as he had threatened to do for the past three years. Hourani wanted to help. He advised me to see Professor Fred Bent, the chairman of a department called Public Administration, a new field which, Hourani advised me, was the closest I would get to Political Science at present.

I went to see Professor Bent feeling desperate to please and to accommodate whatever demands the Public Administration Department might make. Bent was surprisingly young, quite pleasant and most friendly. He explained to me that public administration was the practical side of political philosophy. His new department would be concerned with how to translate ideas into efficient institutions serving the public weal.

In the 1950s the United States divided the world into three – the Free World under the leadership of Washington, the Soviet Union under the leadership of Moscow, and the underdeveloped world. American writers had experimented with labels to designate each division: the United States and Western Europe comprised the First World, the Soviets the Second World, and that left all of us mortals in Africa and Asia to populate the Third World. The word 'third' as the last amongst three was eventually found to be condescending, and a bit insulting. In time they came to dwell on 'underdeveloped' as the descriptive term, but once again the label was shrugged off as demeaning. Finally, they opted to cheat a little and to flatter us by describing our condition as 'developing', seeking to convey that we were moving actively from underdevelopment to modernity by a process – a dynamic one.

The truth that I saw was that the First World was 'developing' much faster than those of us in the old forgotten world. The discipline of 'public administration' was meant to be one of the academic vehicles to help us struggling post-colonials make the transition from backwardness to advancement – whatever that meant and whatever it took. Irrespective of what scepticism I may have felt for this new discipline, I showed enthusiasm. I convinced

Bent that I would prepare strenuously for the job, that I would give it top priority, if only he would give me a chance. I even confided in him that without a job I could not marry. I told him of Phyllis, his own compatriot, who was eagerly awaiting the result of this interview. Fred Bent was the son of a Protestant minister and he wore his morality openly and warmly. I could see that he felt he was under great moral pressure. And I could see that he liked me.

'OK,' he said, 'I am willing to take a chance. But before I decide, I want you to go right now to the bookstore facing the main gate. Buy a booklet entitled *Teach Yourself Public Administration*. If you read it carefully and you come back to me and tell me that you are truly interested and capable of teaching such a discipline, I will seriously consider you for the vacant position.'

I did exactly as I was told, and devoured the booklet in no time. Then I read it again. Much of it was common-sense political science. Bent and his colleague John C. Adams were political scientists like me who had changed gear to accommodate the emerging needs of the post-war world. Like a groom responding to the priest's question, 'Would you, Salem, take on this duty and do your best to uphold it and promote it?' I looked confidently at the son of the venerable Protestant minister and said, 'I do.' Fred Bent presented me with a contract immediately. I signed it and raced to the post office. 'Phyllis,' I wrote, 'I will be teaching at the university. Pack your bags.'

As ready as Phyllis was, she had no money to buy the airline ticket. What she had saved, she spent on a wedding dress. 'And, Elie, this dress will certainly amaze your impressionable villagers!' But I had no money either. There was no choice but to ask my father to send her the money. In international politics, dad painted with a broad brush. To him America was the master of the world. Americans were all rich. Lebanon was a small insignificant country on the world stage. The Lebanese were poor. Does one expect the weak to help the strong, the poor to send money to the rich? Materially, I said, Phyllis was poor, but intellectually she was rich. For the penny you give her now, you will earn thousands in return. He smiled, half-believing, half-suspecting, but he put the extra money on his first son, his first horse in the race of life.

The story that Bterram was sending money to Washington reverberated through the village. It was a big joke. The villagers made no moral judgements about the arrangement, but made great use of the news for interesting village gossip.

'Can you imagine?' the word went around. 'Lebanon is rendering money to America.'

'No,' I corrected whenever I had the chance. 'My father is sending ticket money to my future wife.' Of course, it made no difference. This is the way it is in life. Rumour smothers the facts.

But once again, thanks to my father's generosity, we went ahead with our plans. It was 1954 and I suggested a gradual journey to Phyllis. 'You can come in stages, like the heavenly one in Hölderlin's poems. First fly to Rome, stay overnight to acclimatize yourself and see the ruins of a great empire. From Rome come on to Beirut, a nice Mediterranean town that has developed a few notches above its surroundings. And then, to be tested by the backward march of history, you can head to the village. After a week or two, if you survive the ordeal, and if you still feel that you can make it, we will get married on the 20th of June. Think of Betty and Muhammad.'

Phyllis's response was as fast as it was certain. 'I am no Betty and you are no Muhammad.' She had no doubt about the outcome of the battle that lay ahead. Failure was simply not a word in her vocabulary. So she returned to Melrose Park and to Pottstown and broke the news to her family. The Sells were actually excited that the little girl who had left home to join the Foreign Service was instead planning to marry her foreigner. There was adventure in the story, perhaps new horizons. Ernie and Dorothy spoke of visiting Lebanon. They looked it up on the map, and found it was near Israel and not far from the Nile. Only the suspicious Grammy Mary remained dubious. Mary doubted the intentions of the foreigner. Even though after a few visits she had come to like him as a person, she continued to mistrust him as a member of some alien culture.

Despite the doubts, and buoyed up by the hopes, Phyllis took the plane to Rome, where one of her Washington room-mates was now working in the American embassy. She came with one suitcase and a huge bundle containing her wedding dress. Wherever she went in Rome, Phyllis kept that bundle by her side. It was her passport to a new life. Rome was beautiful, she told me later, but the men were terrible. They chased her, they called her *bella, bella,* and they talked to her ceaselessly and incomprehensibly. This is how Italian men are with American women, advised her former room-mate. They talk a lot, but they do no harm.

Except for my immediate family we had told no one of Phyllis's arrival. Our friend Norman Burns had been tremendously helpful for the last two years, allowing Phyllis to move from one Foreign Service programme to another while she waited for her marriage proposal. Norman was now living in Beirut, heading an American governmental office in charge of development aid to Lebanon and Jordan. When his wife Connie learned of Phyllis's arrival she insisted that Phyllis stay with her for a week. Connie would introduce Phyllis to Lebanese life, food and water. It was an ideal arrangement to which I readily agreed. And so, when father, mother and I met Phyllis at the airport, we immediately drove her to the Burnses' elegant apartment in Ras Beirut. Connie greeted Phyllis with great affection, bestowing kisses and hugs in warm welcome. But the strong-willed Connie did not for a moment forget her duty and told Phyllis to eat nothing, to drink nothing until she had taken paregoric.

'And what is that?' enquired my father.

'It's a medicine,' replied Connie, 'and every American travelling to Lebanon should take it three times a day. I have a bottle here.'

'I will buy five,' said my father, 'to cover her needs for the coming months.'

Father was always ready to come to the rescue, and not to spare a penny in this regard. Once, when mother complained of a urinary infection, her doctor advised her to eat plenty of water-melon. Father bought an entire truckload of melons, and to our embarrassment our rooms were filled with melons for weeks. It took at least a year before any of us could even look at melons again. And when during the Second World War villagers feared that wheat would become scarce, father bought some twenty sacks of wheat on the black market. As hoarding wheat was illegal, he was inspired to improvise the storage of so many sacks of wheat. He ordered us to replace all of the mattresses on our beds with wheat sacks and to cover them with sheets. For months we slept on the most awful mattresses ever devised by man.

But on this occasion, Connie assured my father that she had brought plenty of paregoric with her. After a short visit with the Burnses, we bid Phyllis goodbye, knowing we were leaving her in good hands. As father, mother and I took the elevator down, I was surprised to find that mother was sobbing and even the Tiger had tears flowing down his cheeks.

'What is the matter?' I asked anxiously. 'You don't like her?'

'Like her?' father answered for his speechless wife. 'We love her. She is an angel, she is so sweet and loving. We have never met anyone like her. Congratulations, Elie. You have made a great choice, my son.'

This was an enormous relief. The values that my family espoused, Phyllis espoused as well, and with strong conviction. This was evident from the first few words they exchanged. My father was not one to waste time in small talk. He had closed in immediately on the essentials and found Phyllis fine, quite fine.

We soon developed a pleasant routine. I visited Phyllis daily and we took walks in Ras Beirut. With Connie's permission, and with a store of paregoric at our disposal, we sampled the exotic and exquisite restaurants of Beirut. We determined that we would leave for the village on Sunday. Phyllis assumed that she and I would hire a taxi and we would unobtrusively enter the tiny village which perched proudly just north of the historic cedar trees of biblical fame.

But the villagers had other plans. Once the Bterramis were alerted to the arrival of the first American woman in its fold, everyone wanted to be involved. The church bell would ring triumphantly, they decided, and buses would carry the immediate family, and also the extended family, the friends, the well-wishers. Many recalled how just four years before the village had travelled by the busload to send off its son to the land beyond the seas.

The patriarch put an end to such plans. 'No buses,' Adib decreed. He had a princess on the point of joining his household and buses would not make the right impression. This time my father was determined that we would assemble an impressive entourage. We would travel by automobile. 'Buses,' he said, 'are fine in Homs, in Hama, in Bombay or in Bangladesh. But we, we have advanced beyond that.' Father was not one to allow mere facts to alter his theories. I was reminded of von Mises who, when told that his theories were not supported by the facts, replied, 'Too bad for the facts.'

Just as Adib had previously exaggerated my talents, he now

embellished the beauty, the brilliance and the humility of the woman who carried the passport of the strongest power on earth. With Phyllis by his side, father felt that he had allied himself with the superpower itself. So he talked, so he behaved and so he believed. As her arrival approached, the greater became his exaltation of America as a military power, as an industrial nation, as the liberator of the Third World. And the villagers took their cue from him. The plans for the reception of the American bride became more grandiose with each passing day. Everyone in the village who owned a car wanted to join the grand cavalcade.

Sami Sirhan had recently returned from Haiti where he had worked for thirty years and earned a respectable sum of money. At the age of fifty-five he decided to return to his home, marry a beautiful young girl and settle for the rest of his life in the village of his birth. As part of his plan, he bought a car to help him make the best impression on the marriageable young women of the town. And it was not just any car – Sami had bought the latest model, a white Buick convertible. Sami was not a handsome man, nor educated, but he owned a beautiful and refined car. The entire Kurah had learned of Sami's return and his wish to marry. He would drive to one village after the next and park the Buick in the village square. He would then stand right next to it, always keeping a hand on its sleek shiny surface. This was his statement. Sami and the car were one. It was clear that by agreeing to marriage a woman would attain both the Buick and Sami; a prospect entertained by many a simple and needy woman, eager to possess the Buick and tolerate Sami. As the plans took shape for the grand calvacade, Sami came to my father's house to find me.

'Elie,' Sami shouted for all to hear, 'I will not allow Phyllis to enter Bterram except in the Buick with the top down. This is not subject to discussion. I love you and I love your family and I am sure I will love the bride. Furthermore, I insist that I will be her driver.'

At the thought of Sami driving, a cloud of fear hovered over all of us and settled on my father's expressive face. Sami's driving skills were brand new and stuck in first gear. It seems that when Sami bought the Buick he was given brief instructions and he had never found the need to progress beyond those fundamentals. The dealer told Sami that it was easy to drive. He must simply make sure that the car was in neutral, put the key in the ignition, turn the key and the motor would start. Move the gear lever into first gear and the car would move forward. Well, that was exactly what Sami did. He drove the car only in first gear. People could hear him coming from afar as the car, perpetually in first gear, made a racket calculated to alert all mortals in the neighbourhood. More experienced drivers, pained by the abuse of such a beautiful machine, often stopped him and told Sami to shift gear. Some volunteered to drive him home before he burned up the transmission of his new, spectacular toy. Our Haitian was now known as 'Gear One Sami' and was not anyone's choice to lead a bridal procession.

After much intense negotiation, a compromise was reached. Sami would ride in the car in the front passenger seat, but someone else would drive. To this, my father agreed, wisely accepting the fact that it would be impossible to take Sami out of the Buick or the Buick out of Sami. The procession had become a matter of civic pride in which the entire village had a stake. Negotiations continued in order to determine who would join in and who would stay behind at the house to serve as the welcoming and cheering crowd. The motorcade looked likely to swell to some fifty cars with five people clamouring to ride in each – more than two hundred and fifty villagers going to greet the bride. Questions arose about how to get this motorized flotilla together, where to park the cars, how to keep the procession orderly, and most importantly how to ensure that the Buick with its special occupants would maintain its proper place at the head of the parade. These questions raised other questions of logistics, and father embraced all the questions, brooded over them, and worried. The capacity to worry was an integral dimension of his being, and he revelled in solving all of the problems that were arising.

The Burnses lived in an apartment building in crowded Ras Beirut. It was essential to anticipate how far the parade would reach and plan how to keep track of all of the cars and ensure they stayed grouped together. When they are excited, and they are often excited, Lebanese drivers do not comply with the norms of etiquette. They will often insist on seizing the right-of-way and some will race to be at the head of all other traffic. Many an accident has taken place through playing this 'upmanship' game. It is a deadly serious game, and instinctive. Once in Beirut traffic, instinct could easily take over and the stately procession become a drag race. It was therefore agreed that the escort would wait outside Beirut in an orderly column. Only four cars carrying the members of the immediate family, including of course the prized Buick, would proceed to the neighbourhood of the Burnses *sanctum sanctorum*.

On the allotted Sunday and with fear and trembling the caravan moved. On such occasions the dread of mishap battles for ascendancy with the joy of the event. In this case, there was no contest. Joy was clearly triumphant. Everyone was eager to please and to make this historic operation – a first in the history of Bterram; a first in the annals of bridal receptions – memorable for its perfection. In Beirut, the Burnses, who were very good friends, insisted on joining the entourage. Norman relished special occasions and he would not miss this one. As a top government official he had a car complete with driver and guards. He also had assistants whom he invited along to share the unique experience.

Connie was adamant that Phyllis could not go alone. 'Phyllis needs all the Americans we can mobilize to be by her side to minimize the culture shock,' she explained for all to hear. She turned to Phyllis with a vehemence born of extreme concern and anxiety and continued, 'Elie's experience in Cincinnati was nearly overwhelming, remember? You had better be prepared for a far greater culture shock in Bterram, or however you pronounce this prehistoric name.'

'But no, there can be no problem,' intervened my father. 'We love her, we love her very, very much.'

'This is exactly the problem,' responded sharp, shrewd Connie. 'Too much love may inconvenience her at this stage. You Lebanese tend to overdo it.'

But we soon assembled our little detachment and proceeded to meet the armada, moored at the very entrance of the capital. We had secured a part of the road vacant enough to accommodate our numbers, and headed there to organize the motorcade for the hour-and-a-half drive to Bterram. Father had gone before us, and when we arrived with the Burnses at the meeting place, the nervous Tiger was running from one car to the other ordering, streamlining and shouting. He had become as Patton in the European theatre of war. Instead of tanks lined against the enemy, my father had cars and the enemy to him was anarchy, confusion and the tendency to break ranks and go it alone.

In this valiant battle he was assisted by his trusty lieutenants Ibrahim Srour, the head of Bterram's municipality, Salim Younes, the secretary of the municipality, and Father Mikhail, my father's first cousin and the priest of the village. Together they constituted the quartet. They made all the decisions for the village. Father was clearly the leader. He spoke *ex cathedra* on all issues and they listened to him. The prophet of Arabia mobilized his followers by revelations from Allah, father by sheer intellectual exertion, by infallible logical deduction. The quartet worked splendidly together as they launched the rolling armada from the command car, placed strategically ahead of the Buick. The order was given, and we moved slowly forward.

Sami, in the front seat, was looking at us and at the Buick with deep satisfaction. Naturally Phyllis and I, the king and queen ensconced on the throne of the back seat of the Buick, were too happy, too enamoured, too young to care about the battle that father was conducting to keep the troops in order. From a quick glance at my mother, I discerned that all was as it should be, for naturally enough she was in tears. Lamya may not have been an expressive speaker, but with her eyes, with her copious tears, she spoke most eloquently. For my mother, tears of joy came far more readily than tears of sorrow.

The procession was spectacular! Father intended it to be impressive and he succeeded magnificently. We may be a tiny country, he reasoned, but see how we are able to impress the Great Imperium. In describing the anarchic conditions surrounding the launching of the Spanish Armada, its famous commander Salvadore De Madeira wrote in his diary: 'And thus we sail against England in the confident belief in a miracle.' And thus our procession, conceived in Lebanese anarchy, moved from Beirut, through village after village, in the confident belief that something would go wrong along the way – except for a miracle. And to our collective surprise, the miracle occurred. The rolling armada arrived in the village precisely as planned.

It is customary for a calvacade such as ours to blare its car horns all the way and as loudly as possible. If a Lebanese family celebrates, all families close by must be included and they are naturally inclined to celebrate as well. We are people who gravitate towards the mass. So it was no surprise that villagers along our route raced to their balconies and rooftops, clapping and shouting good wishes.

Despite the joyous clamour, we learned later that Connie had spent the entire trip with a sombre and worried expression on her face. She felt the weight of history on her shoulders. She knew that she represented the Imperium in this place, and took very seriously her responsibility to protect her charge. 'Phyllis,' she would shout, her head out of the car window, 'hold on tight, tell the driver to slow down.' She was thinking, but could not say, how strange this all was. She wanted to assure Phyllis that this too would pass, and that America was not far behind. What Connie could not under-stand was that Phyllis had been my disciple for the last two years, and in many ways was better acquainted with Lebanese customs than Connie the diplomat. The diplomat sees relationships ex-ternally. But Phyllis, through her relationship with me, saw them internally and very personally. Which is not to say that Phyllis had fully internalized the village customs or that she was yet completely at home with them. Nothing could have prepared either Phyllis or Connie for the bridal rites of entering a small Lebanese village.

And so we arrived at the outskirts of Bterram. The procession came slowly to a halt and the cars disgorged their occupants. Phyllis and I, in compliance with the force of social gravity, descended from our throne, greeted by the wide encouraging smile of Sami, into the arms of Lamya, under the protective shield of Connie. Connie focused only on Phyllis, she cared only for Phyllis, and she truly worried about the sanity and security of her innocent young charge in this seemingly wild, emotional and completely alien hamlet. The villagers who had been assigned to remain at home to await the bridal procession's return from Beirut were already gathered to meet Phyllis at the village entrance.

The noise was deafening. Through an utter cacophony of auto-mobile horns blaring, music playing, women dancing, men singing and young boys and girls scurrying back and forth shrieking with excitement, Phyllis walked with me the few hundred metres from the meeting place to our house. As we moved slowly, Connie clutched Phyllis for dear life, and we were pelted from all sides with rice, wheat, bonbons and roses. The harder the tokens were thrown, the greater the indication of affection.

Connie was distraught. She strove mightily to shield Phyllis, with no idea what on earth these Third World natives thought they were doing. Rather than acknowledge the gestures in the spirit they were offered, rather than accept them with the gratitude expected, Connie shouted and pleaded for peace. In the midst of such a clamorous expression of joyous welcome, however, Connie's protestations were lost. Fortunately no one listened. The assembled crowd continued their pelting to the riotous amusement of all. Old women, many of them close relatives and friends of the family, broke ranks to hug the bride and kiss her warmly as the gift of America to our humble village. Many of these women knew already that Phyllis came from a village not far from Wilkes Barry, Pennsylvania, a town that was more famous to them than New York. Their own husbands had emigrated years before to work in the mines of Wilkes Barry. The husbands had returned with stories that no one entirely believed and with tales of wealth that they all were convinced must be highly exaggerated.

As the women converged, Connie became even more agitated. What terrified her the most was the ululation of these old women. As Connie heard the screeching cacophony, she was frightened by the proximity between the singers and the innocent bride. As the excitement mounted, the men were not to be outdone. They began to break ranks, emerging from the crowd to perform wild dances. Some joined hands to form a circle for the traditional Lebanese *debbke*, complete with exaggerated foot stamping and vociferous exaltations. Several adventurous souls performed a dance called the bee. The dancer who had taken on the role of a victim attacked by bees demonstrated the effects of the bee swarm on his entire body, from the face to the arms, the belly, the legs and feet. The wild, rhythmic contortions of the dancer's body were meant to chase the fictitious bees away. For the uninitiated, it is truly a scary sight. To an onlooker like Connie, who was unaware of the dance and had no idea of the role-playing implications, the dancers seemed possessed, entirely insane. Connie was a Swiss American, a composed and reserved Calvinist, originally from Geneva. She was utterly appalled. She realized that she could exercise no control and finally surrendered to the surrounding anarchy, placing her ultimate trust for herself and her protégée in the hands of the Almighty. Phyllis took it all in and kept a broad smile on her face, hoping against hope for the storm to abate and longing to escape to a closed room with an American magazine and an American book, to find an American pool of serenity.

With some difficulty we climbed the steps to our spacious living-room – the salon. Our house, like most houses in the village, consisted of two nineteenth-century vault constructions. We lived in these vaulted-roof houses till the middle of the 1940s. Then father began to add new rooms on top. With the coming of cement to the village, we now had a new freedom to build on old structures and expand our living space.

Usually, the additions involved a large salon with two bedrooms on either side. Ours was no different. The larger the salon, the greater the prestige. Father, conscious of his image and of his ambition for his children, designed a large salon that could accommodate some fifty people comfortably. We all stormed into the salon, took our seats and began to receive guests, mostly from other villages, friends of my father, the notary public of the Kurah region. Salons are for sitting and talking, and the Lebanese tend to sit and sit and talk and talk at social occasions. The cocktail custom of receiving people standing up and moving about conversing with a drink in hand is a format popular only among the Westernized élite. The more you sit, the more you talk, the more you stare at the bride and congratulate the groom, the better. The more you wait for dinner to be served, the better. The dinner must be the culmination of the ceremony. And as a sign of respect to the guests you delay dinner to show that you really care to spend maximum time with them. The delay, however, took its toll on the American guests. As soon as dinner was served, the Burnses and other American friends from the university and from the embassy were ready to return to Beirut. But Connie was ill at ease about leaving Phyllis alone after the demonstrations of the afternoon. Indeed, she asked Phyllis to return with her American compatriots to the relative safety of Beirut.

Phyllis declined. 'Sooner or later I will have to bite the bullet,' she said.

'But, my God, what a bullet!' marvelled Connie. Her only consolation was her belief that the bridegroom would remain by Phyllis's side, to serve as the hanging bridge between the two cultures. Connie reasoned that because I knew what it meant to be an alien in New York I would surely not leave Phyllis to feel completely alien in Bterram. But Connie was unaware of the arrangement made in good faith between the two lovers. Phyllis had agreed to remain in the village on her own while I was far away in Beirut. Phyllis chose this option herself. She was sure that she would survive the ordeal, determined as she was to marry and live in Lebanon come what may. I had told her in some detail how different daily life was in the village. It was not Muhammad's tent some one hundred miles from Mecca, but clearly quite different from Pottstown, Philadelphia or Washington. I made it easier by emphasizing how much she would be loved and cared for.

Of course, in the context of words romantically declared, and in the spirit of love that binds two people, external difficulties and complexities tend to be pushed aside. The oaths that lovers are prone to take beneath the blinding sun of romantic love may founder on the rocks of reality. I was actually pretty confident that Phyllis would make it, although I knew that she might be shaken a bit psychologically. I did not expect her cultural acclimatization to be as difficult as mine was during my first week in the United States. After all, I had been given absolutely no orientation. However, although she had had plenty of orientation, it turned out to be not quite enough to withstand the day-to-day pressures of what lay ahead. Connie suspected that leaving Phyllis alone in a Lebanese village might change her mind about marrying me and living in Lebanon. Norman was more charitable towards the village lore and Lebanese customs. He liked them.

A central figure in our immediate family was my sister Milia, the first-born child of Adib and Lamya. As she was followed by six boys, my sister always took pride in being the only girl, and the eldest of the brood. She and I were very close. We walked to elementary school together in a village near our own. Milia attended Tripoli Girls' School, while I went to Tripoli Boys' School. Both were run by an American Presbyterian mission. I visited her school often as we grew up. She opted not to go to college, and was now engaged to be married to a villager, Ramez Younes. They were planning their wedding when Phyllis and I announced our intentions. The family determined that we should marry first as the bride from America was already in the village and would be living against tradition in the house of the groom. Separate rooms, of course.

Connie, Norman and their American entourage surrendered their young charge to her destiny and withdrew to the capital. The following day, I too bade goodbye to my bride-to-be and returned to work at AUB.

When I returned a week later, Phyllis was in pieces. I really did not expect her to be so shaken. When we had spoken at length about my home, during our long walks on Connecticut Avenue, Phyllis had seemed truly to understand the differences. She had said that she was ready to accommodate everything provided our love was secure. Although she accepted and indeed had suggested the idea of being left alone as an experiment, she found that she resented my departure to the city. She found that in fact she was not prepared for life in a Lebanese village. She may have envisioned a Mediterranean Pottstown. But Pottstown was not a village. Potts-town was also American. In Pottstown they spoke English, they followed national news, they had a football team, they talked about baseball, they had their familiar food and restaurant chains. Except for a few words of broken English, there was none of that in Bterram. When I arrived in the house, she took me to her room and her complaints spilled out.

The week had seemed a year. Think of the two brothers cited in the context of Einstein's theory of relativity, one travelling with the speed of light and one staying in his place. When the first returns, the earth has made thousands of rotations around the sun, and the brother is no longer there but buried deep in the memory of history. Well, things may not have been quite as radical as that. I did not venture into outer space, and Phyllis was not yet claimed by history's merciless march, but clearly there had been a shift in time and space as Phyllis assailed me with the saga of her week in the village. 'Elie, how could you do this to me?' were her first words. 'You left me here for a week! It has been utterly terrible.'

Nothing I had told her had prepared my American bride for the experience. She spoke between sobs. She cried extravagantly, though with some embarrassment at her need to do so. 'Each day,' Phyllis told me, 'at ten in the morning, I am expected to wear my good clothes, powder my face, redden my lips and just sit until well after noon. The entire village comes by just to look at me. Elie, everyone – young and old – comes by and they stare at me. They touch me, they sing for me. It is sheer hell. By one o'clock I am exhausted. I am allowed to rest only until four. Once again, I must put on my finest clothes and . . . sit! But, Elie, my finest clothes are not fine enough for your family. One day, your mother and sister dragged me to Tripoli and bought me expensive clothes. Look at them! These are expensive clothes, Elie, and while I am sure that they are quite lovely to your family, I think they are hideous!

'But I wanted to do the right thing, so of course, I followed their wishes,' she sobbed, glancing at me to see if I could begin to understand her torment. 'But, God damn it, you have no idea how difficult it is for me to do the right thing in your village. Here I am always on display. Men and women from all over al-Kurah come to see me, and your parents sit there with them exalting my virtues. God damn my virtues! I wish I had none, all I want is some privacy.' The very thought of privacy and the absence of it set her off again. 'Privacy in your house is completely impossible! With three salons, and four bedrooms there is only one tiny non-functional bathroom. You honour it a great deal by even calling it a bathroom. To reach it in the morning, I have to make my way through a dozen visitors already in line to see the American, the future wife of the exalted Elie. It just is unbearable.'

When I meekly suggested that in time she would adjust, she was incensed. 'How can one adjust to shaking some twenty hands before one reaches the bathroom? If that's not bad enough, once finished in the bathroom, I have to retrace my steps through another forest of hands stretched in my direction.

'Elie, do you have any idea what happens all day long? I just sit like an idiot and the women come and cuddle up to me. They touch me, they caress my hands, my arms, my hair. Some actually stroke my skin with their finger, as if to verify my colour. Your mother, gentle Lamya, is the worst offender of all. She just holds my hand and sings what she calls wedding songs to me. To make matters worse, your father sits by her side and in his homespun English translates for me the never-ending songs of Lamya, Sarah, Myriana, Jalilee, Latifi and Zarifi. Elie, it is deadly. From time to time, I excuse myself, I go to my room and I cry and cry. I then wipe my face, summon up enough courage and return to the front. Oscar Wilde may have been right, each one kills the one he loves, some do it with a kiss, some with a knife. Elie, you are killing me with a kiss. When Adib and Lamya see me with swollen eyes, they ask me what is the matter, why are you crying, we love you, we love you too, too much. The more they say it, the more I cry. I cannot explain it. Elie, it is terrible! Please do something.'

I listened with a great deal of sympathy and encouraged her with soothing sounds to pour out her feelings. Not that she needed much encouragement.

'I brought with me a copy of *Time* magazine,' Phyllis continued. 'Although I hate it I have by now read it several times from cover to cover. I get into my room. I cry, I treat *Time* magazine as if it were my life-raft in a turbulent sea. I cry some more. Please get me a new copy of this stupid magazine. Better still, get me a thick book that I can lose myself in.'

I was pleased to have a request that I could gratify to ease her suffering. 'Do you want *War and Peace*?' I asked.

'No, I've read it,' was the curt reply.

'Do you want *The Brothers Karamazov*?' I tried.

'No, I've read it,' she said. 'Get me *Moby Dick*. I read it many years ago, but *Moby Dick* may be most appropriate in my predicament.'

I laughed at that. 'If you are Ahab,' I asked her, 'who is the whale?'

'It's the village, Elie, it's about to devour me,' she lamented. 'Nothing you said prepared me for this torture.'

In a desperate attempt at humour, I asked her, 'But isn't it worse for Betty in Muhammad's tent, a few miles away from Mecca?'

'I am not sure at all,' she replied grimly. 'By God, how do you live in this village, how do you ever earn an income? It seems to me people here sit all day long, and all evening. They just drink coffee, talk, drink coffee, talk – *ad infinitum*. No wonder you are backward or underdeveloped or Third World, as Norman and Connie call you. You sure are different. Do you follow Christ blindly when He says live like the lilies of the field – no worries, no plans, no work, no effort?'

Her verbal outpouring cascaded from one thing to another. For a week Phyllis had stored up grievances to offload on to me. Although she was distraught with her unusual experience, however, she was as determined as ever to proceed with the wedding on the following Sunday. To ease matters for my beloved, and without even consulting her, I asked Connie to come and to spend the night with us in the village. It was a great help.

Norman and some of his embassy friends came the next day to give Phyllis a boost. I got her *Moby Dick*, and she was soon engrossed in it, thoroughly identifying with the valiant Ahab. Plans for the wedding proceeded on schedule. It was to be a purely village wedding, involving all the Bterramis, our friends in al-Kurah and the few American friends from AUB and from the embassy. Unlike the weddings of the rich and famous, there would be only one priest, the village priest, our relative Father Mikhail. I would prepare an English version of the wedding ceremony for Phyllis to follow. She was already too deep into the unknown, she had no desire for more. My cousin Khalil Salem was to read a simultaneous translation.

The last three days before the marriage ceremony I spent by her side in the village. We took walks in the narrow village alleys and I introduced her to virtually everyone around. Of course, she knew the immediate family quite well by now. My sister Milia and Ramez Younis, some twenty years her senior, were good enough to postpone their wedding for a few months to accommodate and legitimize the American arrival in the Salem clan. With nothing but a rudimentary education at the village elementary school, Ramez, like all his peers, was not qualified for any real job. He owned land, he worked it, he owned a donkey and he lorded it over the hired labour who came for seasonal work in the olive groves. He called himself a landlord and acted like one. Except for a brief spell as head guard at a British-owned fuel company in Tripoli, he had never held any paid job, although he spent his entire life looking for one. He spoke English with an Australian accent, learned from contact with the Australian contingent deployed in Bterram by the British military command in the 1940s.

I showed Phyllis the house of my grandparents on the Malik side. The house was now deserted and in dilapidated condition as all of the children of Sheikh Salim, except my mother, were in Australia. There was no love lost between my father and the Maliks, perhaps because as sheikhs they looked down upon him. Father, proud of his achievements, did not tolerate their condescension and frequently needled my mother about her brothers and sisters in Sydney, especially regarding the myths mother weaved about her relatives. 'We have no evidence of their prosperity,' father would insist, 'and as we have no evidence they must be paupers.'

In each quarter of the village I pointed to a home or two and gave Phyllis an account of the lives of the families who lived there. This was serious acculturation prior to commitment. Phyllis, like all women, wanted to know more about my relations with the opposite sex. Whom had I loved in the village? Was there someone I still loved? She wanted to know all about how I learned of love and sex and romance. Although we must have alluded to this subject many times previously when strolling around Connecticut Avenue, this subject is inexhaustible for many young lovers.

'OK, I understand you philandered in Beirut,' Phyllis allowed, 'and in Kentucky. But there must have been other occasions as well.' Who? when? where? she wanted to know. 'Tell me, now before we are married,' she insisted, 'and all your sins will be forgiven.'

I was amazed, and continue to be, that women have no compunction about pumping a man for the last dregs of information about his romantic life without revealing anything of importance about their own. In this respect, women are superior to men. They must be entrusted by nature with the secret of survival. They learn much and reveal little.

But I did my best to answer her questions. I told her again how I grew up in a rural society, reaching puberty in the early 1940s. In those days, and indeed to this day in Lebanon's rural villages, there was no sexual education at all. If you raised this subject at home or at school you were likely to get a pretty good beating from your father, your mother or your teacher. Sex was taboo. Smoking was taboo. A song I heard in an American musical pretty much summed up my early life. According to one verse of the song:

> Folks are dumb where I come from,
> They ain't got no learning,
> But they are as happy as can be
> A-doing what comes naturally.

'We did what came naturally,' I told Phyllis.

'What do you mean,' she insisted, 'you did what came naturally?'

'Well, let's see.' I searched for a way to explain. 'In America you went to mixed schools. Boys and girls were encouraged to go out together. This was not the case with us at all. Naturally you could look at a girl from a distance and say to yourself, "Wow, this girl is pretty! I wish I could touch her, hug her, kiss her." You could wish all you liked, but the chance of realizing your wish was zero, almost zero. At least, it was with us in the villages.'

Phyllis nodded, waiting for me to continue.

'There was this beautiful girl I liked. My dream was to kiss her. When somehow I got her alone in my grandfather Sheikh Salim's house, I stole a quick kiss on the lips. So superficial, a fraction of a second.'

Phyllis looked suspicious, but it was the complete truth.

'Guess what happened?' I challenged Phyllis.

'What?'

'The girl, who could not have been more than thirteen, asked me to sit down and consider. Well, I had acted impulsively. Just the idea that I had something to consider made me feel in a bit of a panic. She told me that the previous week a suitor had come to her father and asked to marry her. She told her father she would like to think it over. As she was thinking it over, it turned out, this young girl decided she was in love with me. She looked me straight in the eye and said, "Tell me now you will marry me, and my father will send this suitor away." '

I glanced at Phyllis to see what she was making of this story. 'Well,' I continued, 'I could not believe my ears. This girl wanted marriage, at once. I urged her to go home and tell her father nothing about me. The idea of getting married at that age was to me completely out of the question. But we had kissed. Kissed, barely touched, a fleeting theft by two terrified kids. She walked away disappointed that day, and I learned not to play with fire.'

By the time I was twelve or thirteen, Sheikh Salim's house was empty as all its occupants had either died or emigrated. I had the great notion to use the abandoned house as a hunting ground. I failed miserably. I had to laugh at my foolishness as I told Phyllis about another childhood attempt at romance in that house. In the 1940s, with thousands of soldiers in our Kurah region, gypsies came from near and far to follow the troops and try to earn a living. Women gypsies often went from house to house begging for money, oil, soap, and whatever the villagers would part with. Their husbands stayed in their tents and drank coffee, and on special occasions the men provided music – flute and drums. They played at weddings, at parties, at any gatherings in the evenings in the makeshift bars that mushroomed throughout the region. Gypsy women ranging in age from about ten to sixty beguiled the villagers with well-rehearsed prayers soliciting the Almighty to give them health, to prolong their lives, to ensure the safe return of their husbands and sons from distant lands.

My childhood friend Rudolph and I were wise enough not to bother the child gypsies but rather to try our luck with the older ones, hoping to claim a quick embrace and to see where it might lead. One day we actually managed to entice one inside the abandoned Malik house. We tried to fondle and hug the unsuspecting female, but she managed to escape with her dignity intact. The woman must have spread the word as no other gypsies fell for our trap, but we were frankly relieved as we were saved from adventures that we were not equipped to handle.

In Beirut prostitution was legal. As kids in our mid teens, we would walk the streets of the red-light district in packs of five for safety and moral support. We walked those streets out of curiosity and a sense of adventure, but were far too terrified actually to go inside a brothel. While attending the university, we invited one of the most innocent of our colleagues to come with us on an excursion to the district. We told him there were fine women there who wove cloth and sold it. We told him that our visit would be part of our social-science fieldwork. The innocent victim was easily persuaded. We took him to the finest house where the women, noticing how obviously shy and inexperienced he was, paid him special attention. One of them finally made her move. 'Hey, lover,' she invited our young friend, 'come with me.'

Puzzled he asked her, 'Come where?'

'To my bedroom of course,' she replied.

Still he was mystified. 'Why?'

'So that you can sleep with me,' the exasperated woman said impatiently, 'you sonofabitch. What do you think you are doing here?'

'Me?' he answered. 'I am working on a social-science report.'

'Then go and report on your fucking mother,' answered the highly cultured female as her sisters erupted in gales of laughter. Our friend was deeply offended. In mock anger we stormed out in his wake.

Phyllis chuckled as I recounted these awkward tales of youthful exploration. Somehow, as lovers, we enjoyed confessing to each other. Perhaps we wanted to close old chapters as we opened this new one. Someone like me, who loved to talk, probably confessed more. And in the light of the major commitment we were making for our future, my sins were a minor issue indeed. Nevertheless, I had a final vice to confess before our wedding day.

'What now!' Phyllis thought maybe she had heard enough. 'Save me, Lord.'

'Smoking.'

She knew I did not smoke now.

'Did you smoke?' she asked me uncertainly.

'No, there is a saying in Arabic, *Kul mahjub marghub*,' I made a story of it. 'What is hidden is desired.'

Phyllis loved to memorize Arabic sayings that rhymed, and she soon memorized this one.

'Naturally, smoking was not allowed in our house,' I continued. 'Come to think of it nothing was allowed except studying. Just in case we might forget, father always reminded us that life was a battle. "If you are not a wolf you are eaten by the wolves," he would repeat regularly and often. This may be the reason why I loved to venture where I was not allowed to tread.'

As I confessed, the plot was simple, but the implementation was difficult, or so it seemed to me. Cigarettes were abundant. Many people smoked, and almost all houses, except ours, offered cigarettes on a tray, the tray exhibiting no less than ten or fifteen packets of the finest American brands. My first cigarette was one I lifted from a tray at a neighbour's house. I sneaked home and found a packet of matches before walking another half-mile into the olive groves. I sat beneath a tree and looked all around to be certain I was all alone. With my heart pounding I sniffed the cigarette, deeply savouring the tobacco's aroma. Finally, I lifted the match and lit it up. In the privacy of an olive forest I was committing a forbidden act that hurt no one. And it was a thrilling and delicious experience precisely because it was forbidden and because it hurt no one.

People then did not associate smoking with disease. But in my family smoking was regarded as a cheap form of showing off, and as something that decent people simply did not do. I only puffed a bit, barely inhaling. And I slipped away to indulge in this purloined pleasure only a very few times, but they were great times. I remembered the feelings so clearly as I confessed to Phyllis.

'When I tried to inhale I coughed and coughed,' I told her, 'and my eyes watered. It was terrible.'

'It served you right,' reprimanded my Protestant friend, who by the way was a heavy smoker. What Phyllis objected to was my doing things behind my parents' backs. I think she was also disconcerted that I was revealing new sides to my character, telling her things I had not confessed before. As an eager storyteller, I always told whatever I thought was of interest or of importance to the situation. But Phyllis's appetite to dig into my person, into my entire background, was insatiable; she needed no situation. I took it as a sign of intelligence. Confessions are as a rule good for the soul. They tend to clear the air. There is usually nothing to be ashamed of. Augustine tried all the pleasures of the world, confessed them, and became a saint. I am not aiming that high.

Phyllis was a simple, practical, straightforward girl. There was no nonsense about her, and she wanted her wedding to reflect her sensible nature. My father fully agreed with her. Ahhh, but my mother, a Malik, was a *sheikha* and wanted an ostentatious affair. Poor mother, she didn't ever really have a hope of getting her wish. Father listened to her, nodded, pretended to hear and simulated obedience. Then he proceeded to do just as he wanted. He took great relish in quoting the Arab Prophet: 'Consult your wives, and do the opposite.' 'A wise man,' father approvingly labelled the ingenious Muhammad.

Lebanese brides pride themselves on how much time they take to get ready – the hairdresser, the powdering, the dressing, the total involvement of her girlfriends. A bride in Lebanon may spend a month or more shopping and at least twenty-four hours arraying herself. A full day prior to the wedding ceremony, the bride is the centre of attention, and is eventually turned out like an exquisite doll. The hairdresser must give the bride's hair an original look. The girlfriends rally to her side and become experts, painting the bride's face, eyes, fingernails, toenails.

Phyllis readied herself in what seemed like about five minutes. She wore the beautiful and simple wedding dress that she had carried with her all the way from Philadelphia. She paid the normal amount of attention to her face and lovely hair. And she was utterly stunning in her serene beauty and simplicity. Her calm demeanour shone like a steady beacon amidst the hustle and bustle of the large noisy crowd approaching our house. The entire village turned out, of course, and many from the villages around us. It was truly a Kurah wedding – a regional celebration. Norman Burns had asked to be my best man and I was delighted to accept his kind offer. My sister Milia was thrilled to be designated maid of honour. Milia and Phyllis had become great friends. We were not surprised to see the American contingent arrive early with Connie in the lead. Connie was more nervous, I believe, even than my mother. Connie and Norman had no children, and it seemed to me that she had virtually adopted Phyllis. Connie ran back and forth, aimlessly, getting nowhere since she was in totally unfamiliar terrain.

The wedding party walked some three hundred metres to the church, with the church bell ringing out. We were actually 'galloping', as we express it in Arabic, as a sign of joy. Phyllis and I were holding hands with my mother on my left and my sister on the right of Phyllis. Great crowds of villagers walked behind us. Two things bothered Phyllis and she asked me to explain as we moved up the hill to our historic church. Why was Milia dressed in black? Phyllis wondered. And why was my mother sobbing?

Why indeed! I explained to the best of my ability that black is formal dress. Milia must have chosen this colour as the most appropriate, the most fashionable. 'No, my darling,' I reassured Phyllis, 'my sister is not mourning for her brother, lost through her marriage to Phyllis.'

'Are you sure?' My bride was a bit sceptical.

'Yes, I am. Absolutely,' I reaffirmed. 'As to my mother's sobbing, this is the most natural thing in the world. My mother is extremely happy, and happiness always brings forth her tears.'

'Are you sure she is not unhappy because you did not marry her relative?' Phyllis asked. 'You know, the rich one?'

Hard as it was for me to believe she would plague herself with such doubts even now, I knew it was my role to clear those doubts away. 'Yes, I am sure.'

Meanwhile, the Tiger was racing ahead to make sure the reception at the church entrance was entirely to his liking. As he looked back at the huge crowd a large smile of satisfaction spread across his face. His proud beaming countenance more than made up for the tears of my mother. The assembled company was festive and joyous. A pasha from a neighbouring village surrounded by his own villagers was conspicuous for his tarboosh, for his Ottoman moustache and for his elegant white suit. In front of us, a short skinny woman, nervous as a hornet and carrying a large tray of all sorts of symbolic grains – wheat, barley, rice – and bread and candles, danced and sang with an intensity bordering on frenzy. She was my godmother Zarifi. Immediately, behind us walked her funny and sharp-tongued sister Latifi. Latifi and Zarifi were born in Mexico, and their Arabic was not perfect. They were close relatives whose parents had left the village ages before and established a business in Mexico City. Their fortunes made, the parents returned to the village to ensure that the daughters married in the village and settled in their ancestral home. They did, and both women were miserably unhappy with their boorish husbands.

But on this day, they were having the time of their lives. Latifi kept poking me, and joking aloud. 'Elie, I have a feeling you and Phyllis got married in the US, and this wedding is for our benefit.'

'No, Aunt Latifi,' I promised her in all sincerity.

But she would have none of it. 'Yes, Elie, you devil you, I know you too well,' Latifi declared with a grin. 'And I love your wife.'

Latifi never stopped talking, and I never ceased translating to Phyllis, who greatly enjoyed the old woman's cynicism and wit.

Only a few of the huge crowd were able to enter the little church. The church was hot, the June heat intensified by the sheer number of bodies pressed together in the small space. Phyllis's wedding attire called for a thin attractive veil. A woman behind Phyllis, I suspect Aunt Latifi, kept sneaking her hand beneath the veil to dry the face of the perspiring bride. After a few attempts, Phyllis gave her attendant an unceremonial kick that ended the intervention and allowed the sweat to flow naturally.

Wedding rites of the Orthodox Church are most colourful and magnificent. The bride and groom are crowned before being joined for all time 'in glory and dignity'. Much of the *credenda* and *miranda* of the Byzantine Empire are enshrined in the ceremony. This centuries-old script is chanted by the priest to proclaim the man to be the head of the wife, as Christ is the 'head of the Church'. This is somewhat softened but not counteracted by the latter part of the script – 'and the man shall love his wife, and the wife shall obey her husband'. During this recitation, I stole a look at Phyllis. My bride had an enigmatic smile that I knew very well. The smile spoke clearly, as if to say, 'Elie your sins are forgiven.'

The priest chanted and my cousin Khalil Salem translated. Phyllis always claimed that to her Khalil seemed silent at that part of the ceremony in which the bride was salvaged from the clutches of Lutheranism and hurled into the warm loving bosom of Orthodoxy. As best man, Norman Burns was himself quite nervous. The priest graciously invited Norman to recite the Lord's Prayer in English if he would prefer.

'What else,' Burns said, 'I know no other language.' He looked at me then in panic and whispered, 'which prayer?!'

'Our Father,' I began for him, 'who . . .'

'OK, OK, I got it,' answered Norman, and he proceeded with unwarranted certainty as follows: 'Our Father, who art in heaven, hallowed be thy name, thy kingdom come, thy will be done on earth as it is in heaven, Amen.'

The priest looked at me puzzled. This Lord's Prayer sounded too short. So it seemed to me, too, and to the few Americans who were looking at each other with surprise, and perhaps with a tinge of embarrassment. Norman himself must have felt that he had taken some liberty with the Almighty as he was perspiring profusely. When we returned to the house, Norman was furious. He realized he had cut the Lord short, and as representative of the greatest power on earth, this did not sit well with him. He wanted the tape, he wanted to record it again in full, but he was told that what is done is done. To make up for his lapse, he spent a full day writing and rewriting a lengthy essay on the wedding of an American girl to a Lebanese boy in a small village in the vicinity of the Cedars of Lebanon, whose praise the Holy Bible sang. We learned later that Norman's famous epistle was so admired by the Department of State that it was mailed to all United States embassies in the Middle East, and printed in full in the *Department of State Newsletter*.

After the church ceremony we returned home. The American contingent surrounded Phyllis and showered her with praise for her serenity and for her courage. After two weeks in the village Phyllis felt that she had endured enough. She was ready to move to Beirut and away from collective scrutiny. My bride craved privacy, spoken English, American food and bourbon on the rocks.

Through the Bents, the fine couple who came to my aid by

employing me in the Public Administration Department, Phyllis had found a small apartment that we rented for one week from a British lady who was on vacation. As we had not arranged for a taxi on our wedding day, pragmatic Phyllis had made another arrangement. Back in the US, Dean Jabri had been that ancient cross that I had borne on a tour around the country. Now the old man was in Bterram for the wedding and Phyllis had arranged for us to ride in his rented car as far as Beirut, leaving Jabri to continue his drive to Damascus. As the celebrations gradually waned, we stole away with the venerable dean to freedom in the famous Mediterranean town. As we left Bterram in Jabri's car, I reminded Phyllis that we would return to the village on the next weekend as custom required.

'No, we will not!' She was adamant. 'We need time together you and me, with each other not with the whole clan. I have served my time with them.'

Recalling the priest's instructions that 'the man is the boss of the woman', I attempted to establish my authority by insisting on our return. I succeeded only in infuriating my beloved and found myself in my first family quarrel. Dean Jabri, already a reserved Damascene, was now transformed into an Egyptian sphinx. He gazed mysteriously at far horizons, distancing himself from the raging conflict in the back seat. We arrived in Beirut at around ten o'clock, exhausted and strained to the very limit. We heaved ourselves sullenly up six flights of stairs to our one-week hideout. We had been instructed that a maid would be there to give us the key. We rang the bell expecting her but, lo and behold, we were greeted instead by a raucous group of ten men playing cards and drinking profusely.

Assuming we were in the wrong place, I wondered what we were to do. But no, they turned out to be friends of the woman tenant who was now on vacation. Phyllis assured me that the card players had been alerted, they were expecting us and would soon leave. About an hour later, they finally took their drunken leave. Another surprise awaited us when we made our way to the bedroom. The Britisher, whom we met later, turned out to be shorter than Phyllis and five times her size. Unfortunately for the honeymooners, the tenant's bed, ours for the night, had been custom made for her size – quite short in length and generous in width. And it was clearly the territory of the three cats who occupied it as we walked in. The room was filthy, with cockroaches roaming unperturbed on the bed, in the bed, under the bed and around it.

'Doesn't Bterram look good to you now?' I said in a desperate attempt at humour. It did not, however, make either of us laugh.

But Phyllis fell in love with Beirut, despite the misery of that first night. Here was a cosmopolitan city with universities, embassies, business corporations, restaurants, shops of all types. She easily fit in with the American community and soon found an outlet for her managerial qualities. She was hired as executive secretary in the office of the Ford Foundation. The fact that her yearly earnings of two thousand eight hundred dollars was two hundred dollars more than my salary was good for her ego, irrespective of who was the 'boss' of whom. We moved into a three-bedroom roof apartment that she found on Shuran Street by the sea. The apartment building had no heat or air-conditioning, but it did have an elevator, though it was rarely operational. It was common for apartment buildings in Beirut to employ a concierge – a combination house-guard and general caretaker. Ours was a Syrian called Nawaf whose proudest possession was a hammer. It was his means of solving almost any problem that arose in the building.

'Nawaf the window does not close,' and Nawaf would race up with his hammer.

'Nawaf the chimney is smoking,' and Nawaf raced up with his hammer.

'Nawaf the radio is not working,' and sure enough there was Nawaf with the hammer.

The hammer to Nawaf was like the Buick to Sami, his proud contact with the technological age.

The very week that we moved into our apartment, father paid us his first visit. Another father might have informed his son before-hand of his intention to visit and what time he would arrive and other details. Not my father. Going to Beirut for him was a big operation, a serious business. He woke up long before sunrise and he knocked at our door just as the sun was poking its head above Lebanon's mountain range. Our maid at the time was Myriana, the simplest and the most primitive villager ever encountered. She had a world view in tune with that of my grandmother Helena. Myriana deferred to my father of course and let him in immediately. He walked straight into our bedroom. While we pretended to continue to sleep, my father opened the drawers one by one. He inspected the contents with raised eyebrows, and then retired to our living-room to wait for us. He made plenty of deliberate noise to ensure that we heard him. We allowed a bit of time to pass before we got up to greet him. We found the patriarch pacing back and forth, with his hands clutched firmly behind his back.

'Dad,' I spoke for my wife, 'why did you open the drawers?'

'Because I wanted to know what you have, what you own, and amazingly you own very little.' He was indignant. 'Poor Phyllis, she has nothing.'

'I have all that I need,' volunteered my wife with dignity.

'Phyllis,' interjected my father, 'I love you too much, too too much, and I want to give you something, a diamond ring, a gold chain, a bracelet.'

'What for?' queried the pragmatic American. 'What I need are pots and pans.'

This did it. The Tiger, already enchanted by Phyllis's grace and charm, now fell in love with her practicality and humility.

'Pot and pans,' he repeated with admiration. 'This is a wife. This is a homemaker, no phony show-off here.'

Phyllis could not have said or done anything to endear herself more to my father. From that day on he was her devoted foreign minister, her propagandist, her true admirer. All the praise he had previously reserved for his first-born son, and with a hefty dose of exaggeration, he now reserved for his first daughter-in-law.

To my great satisfaction and relief, I could now take a back seat and let Phyllis bear the burden of publicity. The fact that Phyllis was earning a good salary only added to his appreciation. He admired Phyllis for her character and respected her as a citizen of a superpower.

Strategic considerations affected all of my father's relationships as I learned early in my marriage. I made the mistake just once, under the pressure of proving myself to be 'head' of the household, of slapping Phyllis lightly, even a bit hesitantly, on her face. Once I had done so, I was thoroughly shocked by my own act, and stood nailed in my place, lost in panicked thought. Phyllis's reaction was one of immediate violence and disbelief. As a citizen of a country with missiles, she raced to her closets and launched all her missiles at me in the form of shoes and slippers. The domestic missiles were armed with the worst curses she had learned from me, both in English and Arabic. The Arabic left greater damage upon impact. At the first opportunity Phyllis told her bosom friend the patriarch about my shocking behaviour. Father assumed the role of apt conciliator, and took me to his study for a lecture on geopolitics.

'Elie, at best we have gendarmes on horseback,' he seriously counselled me. 'At minimum she has the Sixth Fleet. Don't you ever forget that.'

'Never,' I assured him, and I meant it.

After some weeks in Beirut we decided to return to Bterram, now that festivities were over and we could be with the family. We arrived unannounced, although that made no difference to the archaic way our house operated. We were received most warmly. Phyllis was overwhelmed by the love and adoration she generated in the Salem family. Mother was always smiling, always at ease, and never in control. She dropped everything to prepare for lunch.

As soon as we arrived, mother raced downstairs, caught a cockerel and dragged the poor creature squawking and fluttering to be slaughtered in the kitchen. As was her custom, she immediately plunged the dead bird into hot water, the better to defeather it. Mother's home footwear consisted of extremely uncomfortable wooden clogs called *qibkab*. Her kitchen was a small mezzanine above the dining-room. Her stove was a Primus, which she left on all the time to be ready for whatever the constant cycle of domestic activities required of her – to heat water, to cook, to prepare coffee and so on. As mother raced up and down preparing the meal, with no help offered or expected, my brother Fuad decided he needed a cup of coffee, and told her so.

'Of course,' said mother, 'may you bury me. Coffee in a second.' She stopped the cooking frenzy and concentrated on Fouad's coffee.

About this time my brother Antoun shouted at mother that he needed a shirt to be ironed.

'Of course, may you bury me,' was the immediate response of my mother. In a second, she served Fuad his coffee and then dashed into the next room to iron Antoun's shirt. Her boys attended to, mother raced up to the mezzanine to her all-purpose Primus. Just a few minutes later she proudly announced that lunch was ready – it was chicken.

Phyllis whispered to me. 'Elie, I cannot possibly eat a chicken that was only a few minutes ago crowing to high heaven.'

'Yes, you can,' I counselled. 'You represent a superpower, you cannot exhibit weakness in front of your admirers.'

We all ate the chicken and enjoyed it, or so it seemed. Mother, too busy to eat, and claiming as she so often did that she had already eaten, started to clear the table. Phyllis immediately rose to help, but mother adamantly refused. 'No, not you,' mother entreated her daughter-in-law. 'You just sit.'

Phyllis was never one to be easily discouraged, especially not when determined to right a wrong. From her first day in Bterram she felt it was wrong that no one, not my father, not my sister, not my brothers, ever thought of lending a hand to my mother. What was worse, Phyllis reasoned, was that mother did not expect them to. Phyllis was amazed that Milia did not help much around the house. It was true Milia was pampered and felt housework was menial. This attitude drove Phyllis crazy, and my wife tried hard to instil some element of the Protestant work ethic into my sister, but with little success.

My father was really the only one who understood Phyllis and divined that she was trying to do no less than change our family ways. Dad amazed us all that evening. He carried his dish from the table and with a jovial victorious smile on his face looked right at Phyllis and shouted, 'Look, Phyllis!' as he walked towards the kitchen. The family all stood up and cheered. Phyllis had scored her first victory. From that moment on Milia could no longer sit still like a guest, nor could any of us, especially if there were no guests to see the degrading democratization now permeating our household.

Anxious to acclimatize as soon as possible, Phyllis tried all our village dishes, and with paregoric by her side, she managed with no major problems. She once again tried arak, our national alcoholic drink but found it too like paregoric to enjoy at first. After several weeks, however, arak became her preferred drink. And once she had accepted it, Phyllis never would have lunch, whether the food was Lebanese, European or American, without a good glass of arak. She drank it from a large cocktail glass, with one third arak, one third water and one third ice, and in that order. Many a Lebanese who preferred whiskey to arak were shamed in the presence of the

American to forgo their whiskey in favour of arak as she did. To ensure quality, we set up a still and made our own, which Phyllis pronounced to be the best. And the best it was.

The very presence of an intelligent, inquisitive American in our midst changed the nature of our local discourse. More than two or three hundred words were now needed to cover subjects beyond olives, grapes, figs, ploughing, planting and the weather. Villagers who had met the American briefly during her time in purgatory now came for long visits in the late morning, in the late afternoon, and in the evening. They wanted to know all about Philadelphia and especially how close it was to Wilkes Barry. 'Does Phyllis know Salim and Salwa in Wilkes Barry?' someone would ask. 'Has she met Hanna Ya'coub in San Francisco?' might be the question of another. Or, 'Surely you know Adibi Sarkis in Baltimore.' Our neighbours wanted to know where these towns actually were. Were they all in New York? If not, why do the emigrants all say they are going to New York?

'How do you like Lebanon, Phyllis? What is so different about it?' 'Would you consider living in the village? If yes, why? If not, why not?' Phyllis concluded that Bterramis were far more curious than the Pottstownians. The latter do not ask such questions about other lands because they have no frame of reference. But Bterramis are all over the US, and especially in towns in Pennsylvania such as Allentown (pronounced by them Alinton), Wilkes Barry (pronounced Wiksbiri) and Pittsburgh (pronounced Bitbur).

Being with my new wife walking in the village and driving in the Kurah brought to life incidents that we had talked about together in Washington. In Sheikh Salim's house, I showed Phyllis how I had waited with gun in hand to shoot Shakib Malik. When I was thirteen years old, the British arrested my father, accusing him of being pro-Nazi. It was 1943. The British troops were stationed throughout al-Kurah and particularly in my village, Bterram. British officers were naturally influential. If you wanted something done, a British officer was the one to open the door for you. At that time, father thought his in-laws the Maliks were boastful and vacuous show-offs and he didn't care who knew his opinion. One Malik found an opportunity for revenge. British officers visited Shakib Malik's house frequently, as Shakib spoke some English and had three pretty upper-bourgeois sisters. The girls managed to converse with the officers, half in English and half in French. As they got to be friendly, Shakib took an officer aside and whispered in his ear, 'Watch out. Adib Salem, the smart guy, is a German spy.'

During the hysteria of wartime, a rumour could easily be mistaken for the truth. We began to notice a British motorcyclist stop often near our house, pretending to fix his bike. Shortly after that, a few British officers came to our house, arrested my father and imprisoned him. We heard frequent reports that this or that prisoner had been executed and were terrified this would be father's fate.

At thirteen years of age I was boiling in fury. The honour of my family was at stake. Everyone in the village suspected that Shakib was the villain. They all knew that my father was non-political. If pro anyone, he was pro British as he wanted very much for the Allies to win. Our house was filled with posters that the British distributed showing off their bombers, their destroyers, their aircraft carriers. Acting on impulse I helped myself to money hidden by mother in her closet, and with the help of Farid, a classmate, I bought a pistol in a nearby village. I practised shooting it at times when soldiers deployed in our village were on manoeuvres.

A distant cousin, Aziz Salem, knew of my plot and I was encouraged by his obvious amusement. After practising my technique, one day I waited for the traitorous Shakib on the very spot I now walked with Phyllis. I showed her the exact place on the steps where I had lain in wait, facing the path that Shakib usually took to reach his house. Sure enough, I saw the scoundrel coming closer, and I began to aim as precisely as I could. At this very moment Aziz passed by, saw me with the gun and saw Shakib approaching unconcerned. Aziz realized that my amusing fiction was about to translate itself into tragic fact. He screamed at me to stop and yelled to Shakib to duck. Aziz, some five years older than I was, was an incorrigible gambler, and it was my good fortune that he gambled right that time. In the right gamble, everybody wins.

When Phyllis heard this story she wanted to meet Aziz to thank him for his good judgement. We paid a visit and Aziz received us royally. He was somewhat aghast, however, to learn that I had told my wife this story.

'Oh,' I said, 'I tell her everything.'

Aziz opened his eyes wide and took my arm, edging me slowly

away. 'I hope you did not tell her what I taught you,' he murmured.

'I'm not sure I did,' I smiled. 'Why don't I tell her now?'

Aziz panicked and proceeded to close his eyes and shut his ears as I told story after story about my cousin and his role as our guide in sexual matters. When Aziz realized that Phyllis was amused and not offended at all, he asked her if she too had done terrible things when she was young.

'Oh yes,' answered the bride and happily proceeded to tell him how she and her girlfriends used to hitchhike without their parents' knowledge from Pottstown to the Jersey shore some two hours away, and there they would smoke and drink beer. Before they returned home they would eat mouthfuls of mint and parsley to hide the evidence.

'This is terrible?' scoffed Aziz. 'It is not terrible at all!' He had clearly hoped for something entirely more scandalous.

Stealing a leaf from my father's book, I whispered to my cousin, 'Aziz, Phyllis is an American. America is a big and responsible country. Americans, therefore, have secrets they will never tell us.'

Phyllis was delighted by this ingenious disclosure and decided that it was a myth worth perpetuating. And Aziz continued to pester me whenever we met to reveal her American secrets.

'What does Phyllis know about America's intentions in Bterram, Elie?' he would ask me. 'Do they have plans for it? Do they want our oil?'

'But, Aziz,' I would reason, 'we only have olive oil. What America needs is oil, petroleum, fuel to run its machinery, not olive oil.'

'Ah, but you don't know,' he would muse, 'perhaps America has secret plans to extract something from olive oil. This is their big secret. Is Phyllis in on it?' And so from village to village tongues would wag – fiction feeding on fiction. Harmless enough.

4

Phyllis started studying Arabic almost from the moment we met. First, she learned the words of love she needed to speak of her feelings. Then she mastered all of the worst Arabic curses in which I took such pride. By working assiduously on my thesis on early Islam, Phyllis was learning that the norms and concepts of Islam are brilliantly conveyed in the Arabic language and can only be fully understood in the context of the Arab mind. By the time she arrived in Bterram, Phyllis had completed volume one of *Arabic for Foreigners*, a work in five volumes. Volume one was easy and encouraging. The student would proceed to volume two, still not too difficult. Volume three usually introduced classical Arabic and the difficult rules governing its grammar. Phyllis loved volume one and wished ultimately to venture into the more forbidding volumes that followed.

Her ear was perhaps as attuned to the Arabic of volume one as it was to my Bterrami colloquial Arabic, and the concepts were not totally alien. I was by then a talking bore, and she was a most attentive audience. To understand a concept intellectually, however, and to live it in real life are often two very different things. Two events illustrate this point.

My best friend Mu'in, who by 1954 had hardly left the village and its immediate environs, came to congratulate us on our marriage. He kissed and hugged me and then shyly, with some hesitation, shook the bride's hand. As was standard behaviour among friends of the same sex, he took my left hand between his two hands and started caressing it. Recalling the misunderstanding with Elmer, I looked at my bride as if to plead, 'Do not call the police.'

For a moment Phyllis looked somewhat disturbed, although intellectually she fully understood there was no intention there. Nevertheless, she kept shooting me a clear message to disengage without offending my friend. When Mu'in left, she said jokingly, 'When you need caressing, call on yours truly.' By showing what was to him a natural display of regard, Mu'in abused a Western concept and nearly offended a person whom he was eager to please.

After three years in the United States I had appropriated many of that country's values, habits and traditions, both consciously and unconsciously. From the point of view of my peers in Bterram, I was a changed person. Loud music in restaurants drove me mad. Arabic songs seemed long, repetitive and far too slow. Long visits of the sit-down variety, so common in our culture, seemed a waste of precious time and made me exceedingly fidgety. Formality in dress, in speech, in social functions turned me off. Behavioural norms that I once tolerated without question, whether of flattery or exaggeration or dissimulation, were now anathema. Phyllis the puritan, the no-nonsense woman, had made an indelible impact on me.

Depending on the cultural situation, I could mean well and yet cause harm, even inflict pain on those closest to me. A case in point was the visit of the Orthodox Patriarch to our house to congratulate the newly-weds and to bless our home.

The Antiochian Orthodox Patriarch now resides in Damascus and not in Antioch, which was incorporated into Turkey in the wake of frontier arrangements after World War I. How this happened and who the Antiochian Orthodox are do not fit into this narrative. Suffice it to say that we are descendants of the early church established in Antioch by the Apostles Peter and Paul. We follow the principles of Christianity defined in the early ecumenical councils and we are only a few million scattered in Syria, Lebanon, Palestine, Jordan and the New World. The patriarch speaks for his community, and not only in religions matters.

A visit by the Patriarch to our village was a great occasion. Everyone prepared for it and many neighbours assembled to await the arrival of His Beatitude. An advance party was, according to custom, posted on the road to give early warning. Once alerted that his car was approaching, all of us – family and invitees – would race to welcome him as he left the vehicle.

The Patriarch had a *qawwas*, part bodyguard, part road companion, part mystery, whose delicately sculpted persona helped him perform his many tasks. The *qawwas* was usually tall, heavy set, with a large impressive moustache. He dressed in Ottoman style, wearing a highly decorative shirt, a gilded jacket and flowing baggy pants. He also wore a wide belt from which hung an Arabian sword, the curved variety. For the uninitiated it was not clear who was the celebrity we were to welcome – the Patriarch or his colourful *qawwas* whose demeanour was even more impressive than his attire. He looked down at us with a contemptuous sneer. He was haughty, confident, powerful, the sword-bearer. It was obvious he cared for no one but the boss whom he served and from whom he derived his great power. Weighing up the welcoming party with more than a tinge of disdain, he pushed us all aside, turned his back on us and ceremonially opened the door for the Patriarch.

The Patriarch emerged from the car and stood Moses-like before the gathered crowd. To add to the solemnnity of the scene, the *qawwas* drew his exquisitely enchased sword, and with it parted the masses as he walked in front of the Patriarch, opening the way. Clergy had come from the entire Kurah region to pay homage to their leader and they began to chant in unison, wishing him long life. 'Many years, O master. Many years, O master,' the chant was rendered in Arabic, and then, just in case there was a linguistic problem with the Lord, in Greek.

Phyllis greatly enjoyed this ceremony. As an observer, she had no role to worry about. She was actually chanting God knows what with all who were chanting. She was just a happy bystander until my father shoved her forward into the path of His Beatitude: 'This is the American bride, the wife of Elie,' father pronounced. 'Her name is Phyllis.'

The gaze of the Patriarch rested on my bride.

'Phyllis,' father continued, 'kiss the hand of His Beatitude.'

Phyllis froze. I looked at her and saw history unravel, recalling the bloody wars between Lutherans and Catholics, rebels and establishment, Germany and the Vatican. His Beatitude too froze for a moment, recalling the tortuous history of the Church.

Fortunately the Patriarch was a sharp historian as well as a keen psychologist and took a clue from father's description of Phyllis as American. Quickly surmising that she was a Protestant and knowing that Protestants are not inclined to revere clerics, much less kiss their hands, the Patriarch came forward himself and deposited two holy kisses on Phyllis's cheeks.

Thus the Orthodox Patriarch, in a visit to a tiny village in the picturesque Kurah, avoided in his infinite wisdom a major conflict between Protestantism and Orthodoxy as well as between Damascus and Washington. Living in Damascus the Patriarch was accustomed to weigh his words and deeds in the context of the political cantons of Syrian–American relations.

That Phyllis did not rush and kiss the Patriarch's hand was certainly a blow to the Tiger, however. He had given an order and his daughter-in-law had not obeyed. This was painful to a man like my father who cared so much for appearances.

Phyllis had asked me on one of our Connecticut Avenue walks what was the single thing that she should be most careful to guard against when we finally made the move to Lebanon.

I answered without the slightest hesitation, 'Do not ever contradict me in public.'

Over a glass of wine our pact was signed and sealed. She agreed never to contradict me in public, and I would never contradict her in private. By this pact I lived and as a result in many ways I surrendered control. Public statements tended to be ceremonial and non-binding. But not being able to contradict her in private meant total capitulation on my part, in that she had her way about all things relating to the management of our household. A popular joke of the time had a man tell his friends, 'I make all the important decisions about things like where we stand on whether China should join the United Nations or whether Germany should be in the Security Council. My wife handles only minor issues like where we live, what our children should study and how to spend my income.'

Our pact dealt only with oral statements. Kissing the Patriarch's hand was clearly not in the pact, nor was I the one who asked her to do it. Father, however, more assertive than his son, and more conscious of his image, was certainly not accustomed to having his orders disobeyed. 'Kiss his hand' meant that he wanted her to kiss his hand. It did not mean that she could stare into space. It did not mean that she could ignore him. Father was deeply hurt, and was learning the hard way how to relate to this sweet piece of steel that had descended on his household from the New World.

If Phyllis had inadvertently disappointed father with the head of our Church, a more harrowing disappointment was awaiting him still from his prized son. The Patriarch was deeply steeped in Russian literature of the nineteenth century. Orthodox clerics studied in Russia or in Russian theological seminaries in France and in America, where they skipped the Soviet era and delved into Russia's spiritual past. It so happened that I loved Russian literature and was well acquainted through English translation with Pushkin, Gogol, Dostoyevsky, Tolstoy, Soloviev, Turgenev and other Russian literary giants. Like all fresh graduates, full of ideas and full of themselves, I tended to flout my knowledge shamelessly. The Patriarch was pleased with my knowledge of Orthodox writers and theologians, and I was pleasantly surprised by the literary dimension of our distinguished visitor. I mentioned Chichikov's journey through Russia and the Patriarch responded enthusiastically.

'Oh, what a great writer, how sensitive this Gogol was, what a great book is *Dead Souls*.'

'Good for you,' shouted the upstart, giving His Beatitude an encouraging pat on his back. 'How about Soloviev?'

'A great theologian,' agreed the Patriarch. 'Wasn't he the one who wrote, "Where there is death there is hope"?'

'Bravo,' I answered patting him once more on the back. 'What about the greatest novel ever written by a Russian?'

'*The Brothers Karamazov*,' answered the Patriarch without hesitation.

'What a dialogue between Alyosha and Dimitri, between the believer and the secular, the conservative and the rebel,' I enthused.

'The most beautiful dialogue since Plato's,' answered the Patriarch.

I was very happy with this intellectual encounter, and I assumed the Patriarch was too. I glanced quickly at my father, expecting beaming approval, but I saw that he was sweating, obviously furious. He seemed to be sending me strong negative messages, perhaps to cease and desist, but I could not decode them. Father was clearly anxious for the visit to end as something very serious was disturbing him.

When His Beatitude rose to bid us goodbye he hugged me warmly and congratulated my parents upon the spiritual depth of their son. Father, too embarrassed to respond in his usual eloquent flowery language, was uncharacteristically silent. As the Patriarch, guarded by his qawwas, entered the car, and as the final rites of salutations and hand-waving were completed, the Tiger looked at me, and in the presence of all, unleashed his hitherto suppressed anger.

'Elie, you have ruined us,' my father exploded. 'You have greatly embarrassed us with the head of our Church. It is not enough that you were not well dressed for the occasion. It is not enough that you too did not kiss his hand. It is not enough that you argued with him as an equal. It is not enough that you did not show reverence. I am ready to swallow all these insults. But no, you had to go further and do the undoable.'

'Who me?' I asked in genuine surprise.

'Yes you.' My father regarded me furiously. 'You patted the Patriarch on the back. He is not a child to pat him in encouragement. It is not you who is expected to pat in encouragement, it is his privilege. My God, one does not pat the Patriarch!' And father would repeat this exclamation many times, 'My God, one does not pat the Patriarch!'

Father loved talking even more than I did. Now he felt he had a good subject and he was fully in command of it. And thus he continued enjoying his argument although it was presented in anger and disappointment. To conclude his speech he needed a good short statement. He found it. 'Elie, you are too Americanized!' father declared.

Phyllis responded to this with laughter. 'Who Elie? Amercanized! That will be the day.'

A few days later father received a gracious letter from the Patriarch expressing his satisfaction with the visit and his admiration for the groom. Father had been more concerned about my inappropriate familiarity than with the content of the discourse, and was greatly relieved that my 'Americanization' did not seem to have ruffled the holy patriarchal feathers.

Phyllis understood my father well and loved him. He too understood her well and dearly loved her. He would often castigate himself for ever having shown any doubt about her. 'But, of course,' he would add, 'that was before I met her.'

Phyllis worked hard to learn about her new family and more and more about the background of her groom. Phyllis had a natural curiosity, she loved to ask questions and, happily, father loved to answer them. Indeed, he would take her questions as an occasion to lecture on the subject. Whenever the two of them met, a seminar was immediately in session, and the larger the audience the more challenging the discourse. Phyllis was eager to learn, father was eager to indoctrinate. Here was his first daughter-in-law, the wife of his eldest son, obviously intelligent and willing to learn. It was in his nature to try to mould her in the best way that would promote her integration with the family. Though he loved and trusted the bride, he was not sure about American women in general. It is common for people who know of others only by rumour and hearsay to tend to suspect them and to look down upon them, especially in that elusive realm of values. To Adib, the family was sacrosanct, the beginning and the end. If he had any faith at all, it was faith in the family. If he had ambition it was ambition for the family. To father, the family meant himself, Lamya and the seven children. They were everything – one for all, and all for one. In his view, he and Lamya were the means to cultivate the best family possible. Their family duty was to work night and day to educate their children, to prepare the next generation for life, to marry them well, to keep them together, and together to make an indelible impact on Bterram, on al-Kurah, on Lebanon.

Father worked hard on every one of his sons, and he made ambitious plans for them. His daughter would marry. She was not part of the larger game he had in mind. The boys must have careers: Elie would be a medical doctor, Fuad a teacher, Antoun a medical doctor, Fawzi an engineer, Philip a medical doctor, Kamal a lawyer. They were all to have professions. A good profession was a guarantee of income and elevated social position. Amongst the professions, medicine ranked first in his mind, followed by engineering and then by law. Arts and Sciences meant nothing to my father. They did not figure in his background. The educated man, the ideal man was one with a profession, a good position, and a family oriented to achievement.

He loved to hold Phyllis's arm, while she listened admiringly, and talk about his own achievements and his role in building a great family, pressing her arm for emphasis. He would typically go on like this: 'What is the educated man? I am an educated man, although I hardly had two or three years of elementary schooling. I use common sense, I resort to my intelligence and I speak reasonably well on all issues. I could afford to buy a car and drive it to my office in Amyoun, some five kilometres away, but I do not. Instead, I ride a donkey and save money. The money I save is for educating my children to enable them to succeed in life. There is no state, there are no organizations that can help my family. I have to do it myself. I am their guide, and the education I provide them with will be their security. Each of my sons must earn the highest degree in the field of his specialization, and be the best in Lebanon. Take Elie. When he was a child I made sure he studied all the time. Even in summer I sent him to school. All summer long he would ride on the donkey behind me to Amyoun, where my office as the notary public of al-Kurah was. All the way to Amyoun and back to the village, I would ask him arithmetical questions to train his mind; at times, your husband played tricks on me, I would ask and he did not answer. I would look back and find him hanging by his hands from an olive branch we had just passed. I used to go to Amyoun through the olive groves. It is a quieter road and better for the question-and-answer lessons on donkey back. Elie listened to me. This is why he got his PhD at the age of twenty-three. He and his sister walked to school in Aba some three kilometres away. They walked, rain or shine, this is the way to do it.

'Life is tough. You have to be ready for it,' Adib continued. 'Ask me, I know what starvation is. Those who are not well prepared, will starve and die. You in America have a state that will take care of you. Here there is only the family. If Elie is strong, he will help his family. If he is weak, he will be a burden. Elie deviated from the path I set for him, and maybe this was for the best. I knew of Medicine, I had never heard of a field called Political Science. I sent him to the American University of Beirut, the best in the region, to study medicine. By the end of the first semester he announced that he had changed direction and was studying politics. I was totally shocked. Politics? This is the worst thing I could imagine! Look at the Lebanese politicians, was this what he wanted? I called my friends to a meeting with Elie. Mikhail the priest, Ibrahim the head of the municipality, Salim the secretary of the municipality, we all convened to counsel my son. They used to call us the quartet. Salim played the role of prosecutor, asking Elie most gently several questions that I may have asked more rudely. We wanted to gain Elie back, not to alienate him. You know your husband could be opinionated.'

The smile on Phyllis's face was tacit encouragement to proceed with the narrative, not that he could stop once his course was set.

'"What is Political Science?" asked Salim gently.

'Elie answered pedantically.

' "What degree does one earn in it?" Salim continued.

' "A PhD," my son replied.

' "What does one do with a PhD?"

'Elie described to Salim how one could be a professor at AUB, could be a political analyst, could get a government job. As his father, I was impatient and intervened, "But a doctor is better. Medicine provides a secure income, a stable life."

'That inquisition,' smiled father, amused at the recollection now that the event had become history, 'continued for two hours, and Elie did not budge. Salim finally said that Elie seemed adamant. The priest concurred and supported the young man. Ibrahim went along with them, and I could only declare a consensus supporting my prodigal son in his wild chase after a liberal-arts education, in a field leading God knew where.'

Father related his narrative with great satisfaction to the mes-merized bride. She had always admired him, even before she met him. I had translated all of his letters so that she could better understand him and his attitude towards me. She thought it wonder-ful how a villager with no real schooling could express himself so eloquently and so wisely. Phyllis often agreed with the wise man and seemed to learn from him. First, she learned about him from hearsay, and now she saw him, not through a glass darkly, as the Gospel puts it, but face to face.

Phyllis, knowing that my father had no real knowledge of her country and could not therefore ask probing questions about her family, volunteered to tell him. To our surprise, father turned out to be a good listener, but only when Phyllis was speaking. Such was his respect for her, and for the American Imperium, that he thought he could actually learn from her. She told him all about her family, how as poor emigrants from Germany in the eighteenth century they came to the United States to earn a living, like the Bterramis who now emigrate throughout the world. Her family settled in Pottstown and simply never left.

Her father Ernie was the first one to venture some fifty miles away to Melrose Park, a suburb of Philadelphia. The Sells remained Pottstownians. Phyllis told Adib that her grandparents spoke English poorly and with a heavy German accent, and here Phyllis imitated some of their talk. She pronounced these sounds in a funny exaggerated way that delighted us. With a little encouragement, she turned out to be a good mimic. We laughed as she repeated some of her grandparents' phrases. 'They would say, "Outen ze light," for, "Turn out the light,"' she mimicked. ' "Wat ze doing hier?" ' for, "What are you doing here?" "Stop dis Ganaouk," for, "Enough of that." "I am nearly Gobut," for, "I am exhausted." "You such dummkup," for, "You are stupid." '

Unlike Adib, Phyllis's family did not believe in higher education. In her family, once you reached adulthood, you got married, you got a job, you worked in the post office, on the railway, in a store. 'I was the first to leave the Philadelphia area when I went to work in Washington,' she told Adib. 'And look where that first step has brought me – to Bterram, to Lebanon, to the Arab World. My parents could not understand Elie, who he was, where he came from, where he was going. Like you they feared the unknown. They were anxious. Do you blame them?'

'No, not at all,' answered father and mother in unison, 'and your family should know that we love them. They should visit Lebanon.'

'They will, I am sure,' said Phyllis. 'My father loves adventure, but my mother may be more resistant. She will not move, will never leave her bridge partners.'

As Phyllis provided details, the Salems were able to ask more questions. Philadelphia and Pottstown were no longer spatial black holes, but lively places with relatives. My sister and brothers all spoke school English and were eager to practise it. To their delight Phyllis was a good and patient teacher. Kamal was the youngest and most talkative and with him Phyllis made a pact. Teach me Arabic and I will teach you English. The bride got the best of the pact as Kamal never stopped talking, and never gave her the chance to teach him.

Life in Beirut in the mid 1950s was in many ways idyllic. Beirut was rapidly becoming a tourist attraction for the newly enriched Arabs of the Peninsula and the Gulf. Americans working in the oil industry either lived in Beirut or frequented it for rest and recreation. Major musical companies from Europe toured regularly, holding concerts that attracted the growing middle class in Beirut, Damascus and Amman. Culturally, Beirut was the capital of the Arab World. The freedom manifested in Beirut provided an outlet for the more traditional societies around the city. Centuries of interaction between the Lebanese, especially Christian Lebanese, and the Europeans generated a liberal, democratic, open ethos in Lebanon. Beirut had good foreign universities, excellent hospitals, first-class high schools, dozens of publishing houses, a multiplicity of political parties, elegant restaurants, and more importantly, a literate intelligent population with a flare for the region and the international arena.

From her two bases at the Ford Foundation and at AUB, Phyllis made many friends with members of the American, British, German and Dutch communities. As busy as we were in the hustle and bustle of an exhilarating town, we never lost sight of our top priority. We wanted to have children, and like the Tiger before us, to give them the highest education possible. When it came to a Mafia-like obsession with family, father and Phyllis were as one in feeling and thought. Perhaps I too felt the same way, but I saw that there was so much passion and energy generated by these two on this subject that it might have been dysfunctional to add my own.

Our first child was born in 1955. Children, wonderful as they are, have something vengeful about them. Not only do they disfigure the slim shape of beautiful maidens, they kick the poor woman from the inside, soliciting attention long before they are born. Children force their mothers to lean like the Tower of Pisa. Children require their mothers to adopt a new walking style resembling the awkward gait of ducks fresh out of water. As children prepare to be born, they narrow the mother's mind, crush her intellect and crowd out any thought except for the immediate primitive concern with her body and its inner workings. Worse still is the effect on her vision. An expectant mother looks at space and time and sees them differently from other mortals.

In the case of Phyllis, the climb to our sixth-floor apartment, in a building with an elevator that seldom worked, was tantamount to the ascent of the highest peak of the Himalayas. Under normal conditions, a husband may refuse a request by his wife or pretend not to notice a signal she sends and still have a hope of survival. With an expectant mother, any lapse in the attention level of the spouse or in his interpretational ability condemns him to the lowest pit in Dante's Hell. Smart enough to survive and to escape the hidden traps lurking in the dark for inattentive husbands, I regarded my wife, despondent in a foreign clime, at the foot of a six-storey staircase, and, like a medieval knight, I took the maiden in my arms and raced up the stairs to our roof apartment. Conscious of my slight frame, Phyllis often chose to stay in the apartment, sending me on errands.

The apartment was a joy in the spring and in summer. In the windy autumn and in the winter, it was draughty and quite cold. Often in the evening I would walk in and call to my wife, wondering where she was. 'Here I am,' she would shout back, 'trying in vain to light the stove.'

Since the stove rarely worked, I would often walk into a smoke-filled room in which my poor wife was scarcely visible. So adjusted was she to the Burnses' Third World, that she did not often complain. I rarely, if ever, heard, 'The elevator does not work,' or, 'The stove does not work,' or, 'The windows do not close properly. The electricity plays hide and seek and the telephone is unaware of its communicative function.' When love prevails, oh how insignificant are all the trappings of modernity. One even wonders whether they sometimes undermine our fundamental values.

Our evenings in 1955 were focused on the imminent new arrival. A boy? Or a girl? A healthy child? Will the baby be considerate enough to arrive during office hours, or, like most babies, when least convenient, between midnight and dawn? Sure enough, just before dawn, Phyllis screamed and we both reacted as if the event was totally unexpected. 'Elie, Elie, rush – my water has broken,' she cried. Rush? What does she mean? What do I do? Yes, I rush, but in what direction, for what purpose? Rush has a meaning if the function indicated is clear and the husband is 'oriented' to execute it properly.

In my village 'rush' was never addressed to the husband, who was generally aloof and unconcerned with the process of delivery. In my childhood, when mother cried rush, father went to the balcony and gazed into the distance. 'Rush' was a cry addressed to the women in the household, to neighbouring women who are generally at attention, fully mobilized for action. This core group of women knew that rush meant hurry up, find a big pot, fill it with water and heat it fast. Women scurried from bedroom to kitchen, from kitchen to bedroom, shouting at each other, Hurry up! Give me a towel! Where is the towel? Hot water. Is it hot yet? All the time my poor mother moaned and groaned as the hot-water ritual was going on at high speed, utterly regardless of her real need. Why hot water was an integral part of the delivery process, I never knew.

It came as no surprise to Phyllis that when she shouted rush I obeyed instantly by going round in circles, slightly offended at her for giving me a role at odds with my nature.

'Elie, rush means get dressed,' she instructed. 'Carry me downstairs, find a car, any car, and take me to the hospital – and I mean now.'

Obedient and efficient once my path was made clear, I executed the command perfectly. At the break of dawn I saw a service truck coming in our direction. I motioned the driver to stop, and urged him to take us to the hospital. Sure, he said, and raced to the American University Hospital (AUH) in time for our firstborn to come into the world decently on a clean bed, in a clean room, with no scurrying women and no water boiling furiously close by.

The coming of the first child inspires a mixture of terror and of joy, of fear and of hope. Here is a child, a human being taking her first breath, screaming to high heaven, and she is handed over to you. 'Congratulations,' the nurse said, addressing me! 'You have a daughter, she is yours, take her.' I was terrified. Who me? How do you carry her, how do you feed her, how do you dress her? Suppose this, suppose that, all these thoughts flooded my mind. I had never been so awed.

Phyllis held her confidently, gave her a breast and the baby immediately started to suckle. Not that the mother is more competent than the father, I mused, it is only instinct. I was proud of my wife, and consoled myself for lacking the instinct. As the child is the fruit of two lovers we took part of my name and part of my beloved's name and called the newborn Elise and softened it to Lisa. While the coming of Lisa was an occasion of great joy, my traditional family received it with polite but subdued praise.

'Nice girl,' they would say, 'may she live, and may the next baby be a boy.' Or, 'Never mind, a girl is as good as a boy, and they say when the first child is a girl she will be followed by boys. You see, next time a boy for sure.' A few will say, 'It no longer makes any difference – look at America.' But father was not one to allow an opportunity to pass without making good use of it. He declared the baby's gender a positive advantage. 'A girl to me equals the whole world,' Adib avowed, 'because she is like Phyllis.' This greatly pleased the mother of the tiny child, knowing that as went Adib so went the tribe.

After a few weeks of rest, Phyllis returned to work at the Ford Foundation, and I resumed my job teaching public administration on a more regular schedule. As it turned out, I did not much like this field. My interest was in political theory, in history, in philosophy and in Arab-Islamic culture in general. And yet, I found myself teaching personnel, budgeting, bureaucracy and administrative law, and thus rapidly losing my intellectual altitude. The AUB job gave me the opportunity to get married, but not to excel in the field of my interest. Professionally, I was restless and I wanted a change.

The Patriarch, whom I had patted on the back to the great embarrassment of my family, must have been praying for me, as he promised he would. A telegram arrived from my favourite dean, Philip Thayer, at the Johns Hopkins School of Advanced International Studies (SAIS) where I had previously studied, offering me a teaching position for five thousand dollars per year. The telegram created quite a stir in the university as the salary offered was twice the sum received then by an assistant professor at AUB. I liked the idea and wondered how Phyllis would react. She was keen and counselled that we accept it for several reasons. 'You are not in the right department here, Elie. What's more, you are taken for granted and will move forward only in accordance with a strict administrative procedure. If you take a position at prestigious SAIS, AUB will look at you differently, and in the future they will offer you a better job. Also, it will be fun to experience living in the US as a family.'

And so, looking ahead to a new beginning, we bundled up our new little bundle and sailed for the New World. Needless to say I was desperately seasick all the way. Phyllis, an excellent sailor, was impervious to the lashing fury of the Atlantic. She did not miss a meal in the grand dining-room. In contrast, I dared a meal once and had to race back to my cabin before the food was served. Fortunately, I could read while I was flat on my back. I did not read *The Gathering Storm* this time, or any other book that the New York police might consider anti-American. With a strong American wife by my side and a baby committed to uttering piercing shrieks, I looked forward to an uneventful entry to the Land of the Free and the Home of the Brave. My seasickness for some two weeks provided Phyllis with a captive babysitter and gave her the chance to enjoy the deck and read her favourite novels in peace.

Upon arrival at SAIS we rented a cheap house – a rambler – in Vienna, Virginia, and started searching for a more permanent abode worthy of my new position. Vienna was then a small community of working people. They were the salt of the earth – hard-working, churchgoing, end-of-the-month complaining. We became friends with a neighbouring couple, the Lapoints. With three children they were truly struggling to make ends meet. For extra income he trained as a paratrooper and received fifty dollars for each jump. This secured the milk for the baby and the cereal for the other two. Mrs Lapoint had her own way of raising children. If they did not like the food she beat them until they did. If they cried, she beat them until they fell asleep from exhaustion. In vain we tried to inculcate Dr Spock into her system. His book, *Baby and Child Care*, was our bible.

The house was very cheap and very small. Once we entertained a burly Lebanese friend. After a few glasses of our home-brewed arak, he tried to stand up and fell flat on his face. The house trembled so violently that for a flash we thought it had collapsed. It seemed a clear sign that it was time to make a move.

We located a quaint farmhouse in Arlington, Virginia, just one mile from Chain Bridge. The owner, Clark Keating, wanted to sell it to another professor like himself. Phyllis fell completely in love with the house. Though it was small, it was quite cosy and elegant, and sat on a spectacular one-acre hill, with some of the oldest trees in the county. Keating learned that we were Lebanese and told us that he had met a Lebanese character while he was studying at Harvard. The character turned out to be none other than Charles Malik, the ambassador we had encountered earlier. One day, Keating told us, he entered Malik's room and asked, 'Hey, Charles, are you Christian?'

Malik, a tall impressive man, stood up, stared Keating in the face and said, 'Keating, my ancestors were Christian when yours were still chasing each other around the woods of Germany.'

'That did it,' Keating laughed. 'Never again did I challenge

Malik, and will not now challenge you, the house is yours – pay what you wish.'

The house was advertised at twenty thousand dollars and we paid that price. We had one thousand dollars and we borrowed one thousand from Phyllis's grandmother Mary. We worked out a mortgage agreement to pay the rest in the long-term future. The house was perfect. The location was ideal, not far from SAIS and yet in an environment that was largely rural.

The flowering shrubs in the garden provided a riot of colour. They had been planted by the Keatings to ensure a generous array of flowers throughout the four seasons and they attracted the attention of all passers-by. Drivers actually slowed when they approached 4414 Dittmar Road to take in the splendour of the old farmhouse and its flowering shrubs.

'This is the place to raise a family,' announced Phyllis.

We were both twenty-seven years old, and Phyllis wanted to raise all our children while we were still young and strong. She had no intention of following her parents' example – two children, a respite of nine years, and then two more. Raising children requires so much time, so much attention, so much physical strength, we thought it best to do it in one short span.

As SAIS is a graduate school, my teaching load was four hours a week. Two hours on Tuesday afternoon and two hours on Thursday afternoon. I spent quite a bit of time at home, to the surprise of the milkman. One day he gathered enough courage to ask, 'Dr Salem you are always home. What kind of work do you do?' I told him I was unemployed. Being kind and helpful, he said he could try to get me a job as a milkman. I said I would be delighted. Within a week he had arranged an appointment for me with his boss which promised a good possibility of a job. I then explained to him the reality, that I was a professor, and professors profess only in the afternoon between three and five.

'Oh!' He considered this new information with a mixture of admiration and doubt. 'Great and how does one become a professor? It sounds like a good job. Does it pay?'

'No,' I answered. 'Not more than a milkman. To become a professor you go to school for one third of your life, and then you start looking for a highly paid job. When you fail to get one, you become a professor.'

Suddenly his job took on greater value in his own eyes. 'It's a pretty good job,' he said, 'and the pay's not bad.'

In the United States, I discovered, a job is largely regarded as a job, not necessarily a social position. You are pretty much what you earn. The fact that you are a professor might impress others in Europe or in the Middle East. In the US, your social status is determined largely by your income. My neighbours, many of them technicians, lived in bigger houses, drove better cars and dressed more expensively than we did. I took comfort from the fact that an academic life provided a clean intellectual atmosphere, and in time would guarantee us financial security for our entire working lifetime.

For the coming few years, we agreed that I would strengthen my academic credentials and Phyllis would tend the nest with as much help as I could provide. Having spent two years in Lebanon with a memorable period in a village surrounded by cows, horses, goats, donkeys and chickens, she found the appropriate name for her new Washington vocation – *qurqa* (mother hen).

The day we moved from our lower-class rambler-house in distant Vienna to the choice location of Arlington was among the happiest in our lives. We realized then what a difference one's surroundings made, and how the setting affected our psychological attitude and coloured our perspective. Beauty, Plato wrote in his *Republic*, is a requisite for thought and an indispensable path to truth. Moving was an important occasion, and in America it seemed that everything that had to be done we must do ourselves. Phyllis and I rented a truck, not the small everyday variety called a pick-up, but a genuine truck. You had to climb a few steps up to get into it. Neither of us had ever driven a vehicle of that size. I must admit that being at the wheel of a thing like that gives you a sense of power. You look down upon mortals in their fragile vehicles, and they look up at you with terror in their eyes. We tried to emulate the truck drivers we saw as we drove the monstrous vehicle, shuttling between Vienna and Arlington, and between Pottstown and Arlington. We furnished the house, with a piece from here, another piece from there. As we assembled the pieces, we noticed a bird busily building a nest in one of our tall trees by collecting a twig here and a twig there. The laws of procreation and survival we learned in school were here applied before our eyes by viewers and viewed alike. Chained to nature we seemed and yet we were not loath to accept the chains and appreciate them.

The entire process of moving to this old farmhouse had the flavour of setting up home in the Garden of Eden. The combination of a good position, a beautiful neighbourhood, our location in the buzzing capital of a great power, gave us a sense that a future favoured by the gods awaited us. Lisa was a passionate, active, outdoor child, who fell in love with the new place. The garden was ideal for children with its well-kept lawn, flowering bushes, fruit trees and gigantic maple and oak trees. The county designated our ancient trees 'historical', and treated them with special care. Arlington is a woody place and the gardens needed lots of care. The autumn is spectacular. The trees turn into a blaze of red, orange and yellow.

Suburban rituals decreed that husbands returned home in the afternoon, tended the lawns, raked the leaves, stuffed them in nylon bags and left them by the road for the garbage truck to collect. Pleased with their labours, my assiduous neighbours sat on their porches and looked askance at my garden. Somehow the more they looked the more the wind blew and raked my lawn effortlessly and dumped all of the leaves from my historical trees on their lawns. Not that I did not want to rake my garden, but the wind, I figured, was doing a fine job.

Of all my neighbours, the most fastidious was a certain McCarthy. His garden was just perfect, too perfect, almost unreal. If his lawn ever turned a bit grey he actually sprayed it with shiny green. Of all the porch-sitters he was the most particular. I could see him staring in our direction, growling, 'Who the hell is this new neighbour? He doesn't even look American, by God! He could be black – if so, down goes the neighbourhood, bang goes the investment.'

I imagined that the neighbourhood mutterings went something like this. 'The new arrival is truly strange. When all others return, he goes to work. All of us Arlingtonians have new cars. This intruder has an old Chevrolet – an eyesore in a neighbourhood as trim as Arlington. His wife is clearly American, normal, beautiful, gentle, blue eyes. The husband is very different, perhaps an alien. He behaves funny, he talks funny, he plays with his daughter funny. He has a loud voice. He laughs uproariously. What is there to laugh about? He even talks to himself.'

Well McCarthy had had enough. He summoned up the courage to pay a visit to another neighbour, a certain Mr Scott. Once or twice McCarthy had seen me talking to Scott and knew that I had invited Scott for a drink. In Arlington, homes were castles that might just as well have had moats around them. Neighbours exchanged shy, polite greetings, but seldom called upon each other, and there was no socializing. They all worked, they returned home, they raked the lawn, they washed their cars, they had dinner, they watched TV, they went to sleep. For McCarthy to decide to walk to Scott's house, some hundred and twenty yards away, there had to have been an important reason. I should emphasize that it was I who took the initiative with Scott. It was therefore portentous when I saw Scott knocking at our door.

Scott made it his business to learn the basics about me, and went on to interpret them to the Cadillac owner whose garden was sheer perfection. 'No,' he explained to his neighbour, 'the guy is not crazy. Unlike us, he works only with books. He speaks English very well, but with a heavy accent. I doubt if he will ever rake the yard. He is a funny type, a professor, you know. He is from Lebanon, he studied in the US and knows a lot about the US. He is a good neighbour, will not bother us, and we need not bother him.' For the five years that we spent at 4414, McCarthy never spoke with me, nor I with him. He eyed me distantly, perhaps respectfully. He may have been wondering if his new neighbour was so damn smart why did he drive a 1947 Chevy that he parked on a slope to start?

Washington is an exciting city, possessed of major universities with world-renowned scholars. My school was among the best and it had its share of stars. Georgetown and George Washington had serious scholars in history, theology and philosophy. Unlike New York, Washington in the 1950s was really more of a grand town than a metropolis. Scholars, artists, and members of government usually lived in suburbs like ours and commuted to work. In America in those days intellectuals were not especially well regarded. They were labelled eggheads by the populace. One of the reasons that Adlai Stevenson lost the presidential election to General Dwight D. Eisenhower was because he was labelled an egghead. The more he explained in his brilliant learned style the more eggs he collected on his head.

In Arlington there lived a group of Lebanese merchants who had emigrated decades back and opened shops in fashionable George-town. They spoke their own version of English. Judging from their sumptuous homes, language was not a hindrance in their trade. Their wives dressed to kill, each competing with the others in displaying their gold and diamonds – tangible statements of success. The community embraced and loved us and we loved them in return. Yet they never could make sense of how simple and poor our furniture was, how simple and unassuming Phyllis was – no gold, no diamonds. What was incomprehensible to them was not only that she did not have these things, but that she did not seem to desire them.

Amine, who came from a village near mine, was always fighting with his wife Muriel. She was born in the US of Syrian parents. She criticized him often in public and he responded by shouting at her and cursing the moment he met her. He was most eloquent in cursing her father, mother, grandfather and great-grandfather. At formal dinners in embassies she would stare at Amine and remind him in a firm threatening voice to remember to chew with his mouth closed. Not only would Amine continue to chew with his mouth open, but he would now shout at her, sputtering food and wine all over the table, attracting more attention than Muriel had bargained for.

While most of the inhabitants of the Arlington neighbourhood were technicians, there were a few artists, singers, musicians and painters. If we academics were of limited means, the artists were even more so. But they were such a pleasure to know. They needed little beyond their art, and in this sense, they were much like the academics. Many of these artists became our friends. Soon our warm home became the centre of activities of a most exciting cultural and political character.

Jim McLaughlin was the curator of a top private museum in DC, the Phillips Gallery of Art, a great painter in his own right and our neighbour. His wife Nancy was a free spirit of great brilliance and an accomplished performer on the viola. There was Bob White and his wife. Bob played the violin in the National Symphony Orchestra; she sang opera. There was Russ Holt, press secretary of Washington State senator Scoop Jackson, and later a major player in the John F. Kennedy presidential campaign. There were professors, senators, members of the House of Representatives, top officials in the

White House, in the Department of State and in the Department of Defense. To all of these and many other friends, our house became the informal meeting place. We offered them authentic Lebanese food, and Phyllis was the dynamic hostess who made them all feel at home. Two to three times a week, these friends gathered at our house, under a large tree in good weather, by the fireside in winter, simply to have a good time intellectually and politically. Washingtonians drank well, and bourbon was their favourite drink. It became ours because it was good and relatively cheap.

In Washington I had a major problem. As professor of Middle East Studies in the most visible and credible graduate school, I was carefully watched by the Israeli embassy. The embassy was efficient and watched over the interests of its country with the eye of a lynx. An embassy official visited me in my office and invited me to a private dinner with the ambassador. I declined. A week later a visiting scholar from Israel called at my office and cordially invited me to visit Israel. I declined. When the embassy gave up on me they sent some of the embassy staff to enrol in my courses. They were good students who worked hard at their studies and some of them excelled.

Israel's ambassador in Washington was Aba Eban. Whenever I made a statement on Palestine, he would call my dean, Philip Thayer, and tell him that what I had said was wrong, was incomplete, was inaccurate, was sheer propaganda. Thayer would then call me and tell me what Eban had said. Eban actually asked my dean not to renew my contract, promising to send an Israeli scholar to fill the Middle East Studies position. The second time Thayer relayed Eban's remarks, I told the dean that I had heard enough. 'Should you relay a third time what Eban has said,' I told him, 'I will resign immediately.'

In fairness to this great puritan dean, he never again mentioned Eban, although I continued to see him quite often having a private lunch with Dean Thayer at the Cosmos Club. The club was the meeting place in DC for intellectuals and top government officials. My dean had lunch there regularly. Thayer was a heavy drinker and he normally drank several vodka martinis for lunch. Quite often he would invite me to have lunch with him. When I returned home at six p.m., some three hours after the Cosmos Club lunch, Phyllis would look at me knowingly.

'You had lunch with the dean,' she would say.

'How did you know?' I wondered.

'Obvious,' Phyllis declared. 'You look smashed.'

When Thayer interviewed a faculty candidate for SAIS, he would invite me and the candidate to the club. As we were seated at the table, Thayer would instruct the waiter, 'Vodka martini for me. Vodka martini for Dr Salem here . . . ' And then he would look at the unsuspecting candidate and ask pleasantly, 'And you, sir, what would you like to have?' If the candidate asked for a Pepsi, or iced tea, or Seven Up or any of the soft drink varieties, Thayer would turn away from the candidate and say, 'Elie, you talk to him.' The candidate in that case had failed the oral, and he was out. Thayer firmly believed that SAIS graduates and SAIS faculty members would be assuming top positions, and that in these positions they must outdrink and outwit all the other sonsofbitches, by which he meant Soviet diplomats and all members of the socialist block.

In drinking with Thayer, even I was a stumbling novice. One day I told myself I would go along and keep pace with him. He ordered one martini, I ordered one; second, third, fourth, and I went along. I was so proud of myself, unaware of what the drinks were already doing to my face, my mind, my knees. We walked the four blocks from the Cosmos Club to 1906 Florida Avenue, our school address. My legs seemed to be walking on their own, my body following behind, and there was a stupid smile on my face over which I had no control. To show bravado, I went ahead and conducted a seminar on Napoleon's invasion of Egypt. Thayer had actually recruited me to teach the course on the nineteenth century to, as he put it, 'get the God-damned French dictator to Egypt and out again before the semester is over'. This was his way of saying that my predecessor was excessively slow, spending all the semester on Napoleon preparing the Expedition to Egypt and thus never getting as far as the nineteenth century. Anyhow, I thought I did rather well, allowing for the four martinis coursing round my system.

My students, biding their time, acted as if everything was normal. At the end of the year, SAIS students staged a play, in which I was the central character. They presented a drunken professor conducting a seminar on Napoleon's Expedition to Egypt. The yearly plays were considered serious political satire centring as they did on the faculty. The theatrics were widely attended by faculty, adminstration and others of local notables. Phyllis and I laughed uproariously at the Salem satire. I looked over at Thayer. He was in his seventh heaven. When the play ended, he went to the platform and thanked the young drunkard for diverting attention from the greater culprit, himself. Thayer received the loudest round of applause from his many admirers among students and faculty.

After a luncheon with Thayer, I was of no use for the many household chores that accumulate in an American family with no extended family support, no maid, and no help from neighbours. Club lunch or not, I was truly a good father, a good aide to my wife. Phyllis bragged that Elie helped at home more than any American husband. It was true. I washed dishes, I carried out the rubbish to the garbage container in the street. I made up bottles for babies, I changed nappies, I told stories to children, I played with them, I helped with the shopping and I mended things at home. I paid little attention to the lawn. I rarely raked leaves during the summer, conspiring with the wind to blow them towards the McCarthys.

For Phyllis to be living in Washington meant a great deal to her Pottstownian family. Americans own cars, they drive everywhere, and they love to sightsee in this expansive land. Our new home gave her parents, her aunts and uncles and her high-school class-mates the opportunity to visit the capital, to see the Washington Monument, the Lincoln Memorial, the White House, Capitol Hill and the blooming cherry trees. Almost every weekend we welcomed visitors. Uncle Walt and his sons loved to go to the National Airport and watch planes take off and land. Aunt Mimi, his wife and Phyllis's aunt, liked to come and cook Pennsylvania Dutch food. Phyllis's father Ernie, the tireless salesman, came frequently with his wife Dorothy.

Ernie loved to sit under one of our historic oak trees, reading a novel and enjoying a good drink. As a Lutheran he was frugal and stubborn. One afternoon, Phyllis called me to come and look at her father, who was crawling across the yard. He seemed unable to stand up. When we approached to ask what was the matter, he confessed that he had made a mistake. He usually made his drink in a tall glass, filling it one third with bourbon, one third water, and one third ice. This time, he mistook the arak bottle for water, and instead of pouring water in the glass, he added the hard Lebanese liquor to his whiskey. When he took the first sip, he realized what he had done. But Ernie was stubborn and frugal, and a principled child of the Depression. He would not knowingly waste anything. So he drank it all, and spent some fifteen hours in bed.

Grammy Mary and Dada came to visit us in Washington too. Grammy came to spoil the children, Dada to wash dishes and to imbibe bourbon. Phyllis followed Dr Spock's book *Baby and Child Care* religiously. This meant I had to read it carefully and also follow it religiously. When you put a baby to sleep for the night, Dr Spock advised us, it will cry for twenty minutes on the first day, and then fall asleep. The next day, it should cry only ten minutes and then fall asleep. By the third day, the baby should cry for only three minutes or so before falling asleep. Our children, like us, complied with Spock faithfully. Dada was soft-hearted and often inebriated. He paced back and forth as he listened to a child cry before sleep. Phyllis caught him one day cursing the parents under his breath: God damn the cruel brutes, letting this lovely angel cry. He thought poorly of our scientific way of raising children, and we teased him by exaggerating our dedication to the method.

Sisters tend to be close, and Phyllis was devoted to Bonnie in spite of the difference in years. Bonnie loved being in the care of the sister who seemed to be leading such an exciting life in the nation's capital. One year, Bonnie came on the train unaccompanied. When I met her at the station, she ran in my direction as soon as she saw me. In an attempt at humour, I walked towards her limping and aping the idiot. Greatly embarrassed, she walked right past me, acting as if she did not know me. She went her own way until in humble defeat I mended my manners.

Arlington was the right place to raise a family. Phyllis got pregnant irrespective of our use of prophylactics and technologies, and all of our four children were born within a period of five years. Lisa was born in Beirut in 1955, Nina was born in Philadelphia in 1957. It was not easy to report to the Tiger that a second daughter had arrived. I emphasized how pretty she was and how like her mother. 'Good,' came the emphatic response, 'now it is the time to have sons.' Always obedient to father's command, we had our first son and named him after the Tiger, Adib. Father sent his first telegram when he suspected I was married when I was still a student, I sent my first telegram when young Adib arrived.

Hurrah! The village celebrated. I always marvelled at how strong and persistent tradition was and how little it was affected by change. Immediately after we had Adib, and we were not yet prepared for a fourth, Phyllis got pregnant once again. We wanted badly to abort the pregnancy. We drove our old car recklessly on bad roads full of holes to no avail. Fortunately, Paul held on, and when years later we confessed in shame how hard we had tried to get rid of him, he seemed to forgive us.

Shortly after we had our fourth child, I overheard Phyllis confiding in her mother on the phone. When wise Dorothy counselled a vasectomy, the decision was made. In the early 1960s vasectomies were popular. Once I began enquiring about it, I learned that quite a few of my acquaintances had undergone the operation. Having failed in all the tricks of avoiding pregnancy, the option was clear. Either I had the vasectomy or fifteen children. Much as Phyllis and I loved children, we did not intend to spend the rest of our lives changing nappies, talking baby-talk and becoming little more than procreation machines.

As a method of birth control, it was at that time much safer for a man to have a vasectomy than for a woman to have her tubes tied. There was much less risk and we learned that it could be done in the doctor's surgery. Once the procedure was complete, we were told, you rest there for an hour, and then you go home, wife driving of course.

It so happened that the day we chose to have the vasectomy, Washington was in the throes of two major events – the inauguration of President John F. Kennedy and the most furious snowstorm in the recent history of DC. With difficulty we reached the doctor. The operation was performed, I rested as instructed, then Phyllis had the impossible task of driving through the blizzard out of Washington to Arlington. The inauguration brought thousands of Democrats from all over the nation to participate in the festivities, many of them from the South, where they were not too agile in snow. Snow piled up over a capital not well equipped for snow-ploughing and snow removal. Roads were blocked. Traffic was diverted, and cars broke down. Men in dinner-jackets, heading to one of the several balls that Kennedy would attend that evening, stood perplexed with their cars stalled. There was simply too much snow and no one was moving. All of the men were out of their cars consulting, cooperating and trying to get their vehicles started.

Meanwhile, the women sat patiently in their luxury interiors awaiting deliverance by their capable husbands. All, of course, except Elie and Phyllis.

Elie sat in pain, clutching his balls, hoping that no one would see him. Phyllis stayed behind the wheel of the motionless old Chevrolet. She maintained that the only car in the US that a dealer had ever sold without starting it was sold to her husband, and with her own father acting as counsellor. Now that same car was stalled in jammed traffic, and the snow was rapidly engulfing it. To add to the agony, we were at least three hours late to relieve the young baby-sitter who was guarding the infant Paul. Phyllis was in panic as the mother of a starving baby, as the wife of a man useless when he was needed the most, and as a driver who had no idea how to get the naturally recalcitrant Chevrolet to start. And even if she managed by some miracle to start the damn thing, could she thread a way through the frozen maze of cars and the crowd of helpless drivers who tended them? Men were scurrying back and forth with what looked to me like doctor's stethoscopes, and several of them glared at me in disgust. What kind of a man is this one sitting unconcerned while we all work to get things moving and his wife sits in frustration behind the steering wheel?

I was torn deep inside. I wanted to scream at all the men-turned-mechanics, 'I just had an operation.' Of course, Phyllis had tremendous sympathy for me. She actually told a few of the men who came to help, 'My husband would have been the first to help but he is just coming from a big operation.' One man apologized for his disgust and wondered aloud what kind of operation? 'A lobotomy,' Phyllis answered, knowing it would amuse me and confuse him. The scurrying men did well, however, and when we were miraculously freed, Phyllis drove like a mother possessed, frantic to feed her starving baby and to release the explosive pressure in her overflowing breasts.

I was reminded, I told Phyllis, of a parallel from the past. 'We owned a she-ass which was my father's method of transport between his home in Bterram and his office in Amyoun. When our donkey had a foal she would move most reluctantly to Amyoun – one leg forward, one leg backwards, as we say in Arabic. On the way back, however, she raced to feed her baby and it took all the power at my father's disposal to hold her back from subsonic speed.' Although

Phyllis could not hide the fact that she liked the story, it was also clear that she disliked the analogy.

Of our many Washingtonian friends the closest were the McLaughlins. They had two daughters who were as devoted to our daughters Lisa and Nina as two human beings could be. Jim McLaughlin painted landscapes, animals and birds. We exhibited a nude of his in our living-room. An American eagle, which he painted with a broad brush, I greatly admired. He knew that. One evening, Jim walked into our house carrying the huge eagle on his stout shoulders. Happy birthday! he said. I was so pleased. As he sipped a glass of bourbon, I wrote him a poem in honour of the eagle. The very next day, the poem was framed and could be seen hanging in the very place the eagle had once hung. Jim, poor like so many great artists, launched a housing project in Virginia's Shenandoah Valley. He built the chalets, Japanese style, by hand, completely by himself. He was physically sturdy and a heavy smoker. We spent good years with the McLaughlins and the artistic community in this spectacular valley.

Phyllis and Nancy, Jim's wife, became very close, and together they arranged exciting cultural–political evenings in our house. The children, all products of the Spock method, would automatically retreat to the basement, which I had fixed up as a playground, when they saw the guests arriving. Phyllis was a voracious reader and was eager to test her ideas, to explore their truth, their relevance and their applicability to our world. Nancy was musical, through and through. She knew everyone who played jazz, who belonged to symphony ochestras, who sang opera. While not a wide reader, she was a brilliant conversationalist, often a non-stop talker. Jim, by contrast, said little in the presence of his wife. Jim depended on Nancy. 'She talks for both of us,' he would volunteer between sips of his ever-present bourbon glass. Jim smoked Gitanes, unfiltered. When I asked why he chose the unfiltered variety, he answered they worked faster. In the Phillips Gallery there hung a painting by Braque. Under the Braque was a comfortable sofa for two. When in town, Phyllis and I would meet under it to wait for Jim and Nancy to join us for lunch in one of the fine Italian restaurants near by.

As our family life and friendships flourished, my career advanced as well. In Washington I was often invited by the media to speak on the Lebanese crisis, on the Palestinian problem and on Arab–American relations. Ezra Taft Benson, who was then Secretary of Agriculture, called me early one morning and told me that I was saying things very different from what they usually heard in the White House. Would I kindly write a memo on the Middle East situation that he could submit to President Dwight D. Eisenhower? As I was working on the memo, I received a call from Milton Eisenhower, the president of Johns Hopkins University, and the brother of Dwight D. Eisenhower, asking me to meet with him and to bring the memo with me. Of course, I agreed.

Since the eruption of the Arab–Israeli conflict in the mid 1940s, Arabs and Israelis disagreed radically on their respective interpretation of history. They even disagreed on basic facts. Arab scholars were utterly certain of their position that Palestine belonged to the Palestinians. Israeli scholars were just as sure that Palestine was their Promised Land and resorted to the Bible for support. The Arabs resorted to two thousand years of history, to demographic facts, to political rights and to the fate of all Arab countries after World War I. Israeli scholars, Zionist writers and Jewish leaders had greater influence in the American media and easier access to decision-makers in Washington than the Arabs did. This was as true in the 1950s as it is at the present time. Accordingly, the tone I introduced, the facts I referred to, the analysis I provided differed from what decision-makers usually heard.

Change of perspective does not necessarily change the course of policy. The world is so diverse and what seems an absolute truth to one side may turn out to be mere opinion as far as the other is concerned. And in the reach of politics as I have experienced it, truth is more often an extension of political–military–material power than it is of moral power.

Dean Thayer was pleased with the governmental attention but was worried about Aba Eban, the ambassador from Israel. President Dwight D. Eisenhower passed the memorandum to the secretary of state and to the Secretary of Defense, hinting there may be some truth in what I was saying.

5

In 1959 I received a social-science grant to travel with my family to Lebanon, Syria, Jordan and Egypt to collect material on courses I was developing for SAIS on the contemporary Middle East. The grant was for one year. We made our base in Beirut. In 1958, Lebanon was in the midst of a bloody, though relatively short, war that led to the landing of American forces on its shores. The war pitted the rightists, who wanted close relations with the US, against the leftists, who opposed this orientation. By the time we reached Beirut, a revolution had toppled the monarchy in Iraq, and a new president, General Fuad Chehab, was installed in Lebanon. Chehab was supported by both the US and Egypt.

While the violence had subsided by the time I arrived with my family in 1959, there remained aggressive groups who now concentrated on robberies. For that year we rented Majid Fakhry's furnished apartment in Ras Beirut. Fakhry was a professor of philosophy at AUB, and like most professors had limited means.

After settling in to the apartment for a week, we were eager to visit the village and went for a three-day visit. When we returned, we found that our apartment had been robbed. The place looked as if a hurricane had hit it. Everything was upside down. The floor was littered with our things and Fahkry's. All the drawers were open and their contents strewn around the rooms. Even the paintings on the wall had been removed, as if someone suspected that a safe might be hiding precious stones behind them. The apartment was in our care but we had no idea what of the contents was valuable and what was not.

'Hurry, call the police,' said Phyllis, and then remembered where we were. 'Oh! I mean go to the police – we know they will never answer a call.'

Dutifully, I went to the police station and told them that our apartment on Hamra Street had been ransacked. The police hardly turned a hair at this information and replied with the observation that it was the fifth robbery reported that day on Hamra Street.

'God damn these bastards whoever they are,' ranted a policeman in angry frustration. 'May Allah curse them and bring ruin and devastation to them, to their sons and grandsons.' The curses were actually a bit juicier than that but are likely to offend and may lose their lustre in translation. I waited for more pearls to fall from his eloquent mouth, but no more were forthcoming.

'Aren't you going to do something?' I asked urgently. 'Aren't you going to investigate?'

'We will, if you want us to,' the policeman replied. 'Give us your name and address and I will send someone to look at the apartment.' He then turned back to his newspaper and proceeded to read.

Defeated, dejected and in despair, I reported back to my wife.

'What!' Phyllis was irate. 'They must come right away or I will raise hell. I will, I will, I will.'

In America, the natural reaction if the police do not respond is to threaten, 'I will call my congressman.' In Lebanon, in the period following the 1958 revolution, the 'I will . . . ' evaporated into thin air.

But to our surprise two policemen did arrive, and they were accompanied by a civilian who I suspected worked as an undercover police agent. To encourage them in the execution of their duty we served coffee, biscuits and coffee again. They asked us very basic questions like who owned the apartment, who we were and when had we assumed the tenancy. Otherwise, they had no questions for us. Instead, the top officer paced back and forth from living-room to bedroom, from bedroom to kitchen, back and forth, followed by the other two. What emerged from this investigation was an eloquent composition in classical Arabic describing in infinite detail the robbery scene. I was taken by his ability to express himself so clearly and by his gift for detail. He dictated, calmly savouring his task, while the other officer listened in awe and the civilian recorded the brilliantly succinct revelations.

'We entered the apartment and were truly shocked. The floor may have rugs, but if rugs exist they cannot be seen. Instead, the floor is covered with pants, jackets, shirts, dresses, underclothes, broken dishes and three shattered pictures. The pictures must have been removed violently in the seach for a hidden safe. No safe is in evidence. In the bedrooms the situation is not only as bad as it is in the living-room, it is worse. Here the closets are flung open, one of the doors has come off its hinges. One closet was completely empty and its contents scattered in the bedroom and in the living-room. The mattress was removed from the bed and knifed in various places. I must deduce that the robbers were looking for money hidden in clothes, in the mattress or in safes. As for the kitchen, the scene is no better than that I have described in the living-room and in the bedrooms. Here dishes were broken and bottles of whiskey were put aside with the intention of taking them if they found nothing better. As they were left behind, I deduce they must have found money, perhaps gold, or precious stones.'

On hearing this deduction, I expected the officer to ask me if we were missing money, gold or precious stones. He did not. In fact he did not seem particularly concerned with our predicament. He was totally absorbed in the description as if he were writing a composition for a baccalaureate exam and expecting a good grade for it. He went on dictating in a perfect state of calm detachment for at least an hour. He sipped coffee. He smoked. He stared into space. He closed his eyes and he dictated. Phyllis was anxiously trying to determine what was going on.

'What is he saying?' she wondered. 'Why is he dictating? When is he going to ask us questions?'

To all of these reasonable queries I could only give non-reasonable answers, hoping the officer would soon conclude his monologue, turn to us and engage us in the normal question-and-answer process that, since the dawn of civilization, has been used to solve problems.

When he finished dictating, however, he instead shook our hands and proceeded to leave with the other two.

'Stop,' I pleaded. 'Aren't you going to do something?'

'In due course,' he replied. 'Please just leave things exactly as they are. Keep the children away, lest they disturb the scene that I have now fully described, and police experts will come tomorrow to complete the investigation.'

The experts did not come the next day. I went to the police station only to be told that they were quite busy but would come tomorrow or the day after tomorrow for sure. They did not come tomorrow or the day after tomorrow for sure. And, for sure, we tried to live in the midst of the chaos for three days to avoid seriously impairing the delicate investigative process.

Finally, the experts arrived. They were in civilian clothes. They were polite and seemingly a cut above the first investigative team. They carried what seemed to me powder, a brush and faded pictures of fingerprints. They proceeded to sprinkle the powder on the drawers, brush the powder gently, look for marks, and move on from one object to another.

'What are you doing?' I asked, curious about their procedure.

'Oh,' answered one expert, 'the government sent the three of us to England to study fingerprint technology. We learned nothing. Or at any rate, nothing that we learned in London applies in Beirut.'

I persisted. 'Are you going to be able to identify the robbers?'

The expert answered in English much to the dismay of Phyllis. 'Who do you think we are, Scotland Yard?' Their open reference to the fact that they were not the equal of the famous English police force meant to Phyllis that they had no confidence in themselves, and that the robbers would not be caught. Phyllis was right. She was almost always right.

The Fakhrys and the Salems went through their respective possessions and it turned out nothing was missing. The unfortunate robbers had hit upon poor professors and must finally have pitied us. In desperation, they were about to take the two bourbon bottles and one Scotch bottle but ultimately decided against even that unkindness. They left the bottles by the door. Had they had time on their hands, they might have written us a note promising aid from a more affluent household.

After this inauspicious beginning, we settled into our home base and headed off for the field-research part of the programme. We were eager to learn about new developments in the Arab World and I wanted to write about them or use them in my teaching. Field research is more interesting than work in a library. It involves travel, interviews with political leaders, intense discussions with intellectuals and journalists.

In Jordan, I had a constructive meeting with the young King Hussein, father of the present incumbent King Abdallah II. Hussein was greatly interested in my work. He spoke quite freely about the problems of Jordan, of Palestine and of the region. He enquired about attitudes in the United States, and he left a very good impression – intelligent, humble, responsible.

Egypt in 1959 was at the height of the Nasser era. The young and charismatic colonel had deposed the monarchy, declared Egypt a republic and put the country on a revolutionary socialist course. Phyllis wanted very much to meet the celebrated Arab leader and his military clique. By 1959 Nasser could do no wrong. He had nationalized the Suez Canal, and with the help of Eisenhower, had thwarted a British–French–Israeli attack on Suez.

To improve his image in the West Nasser invited scholars from Western universities to join him on the visits he made from time to time to major development projects that he was launching throughout Egypt. Phyllis and I were invited to join him on a visit to the neighbourhood of Alexandria where the government was distributing land to the peasants. Nasser confiscated land from the rich and assigned it in small parcels to the erstwhile dispossessed *fellahin*. The reformer in Phyllis greatly approved of the idea. It sounded revolutionary, perhaps promising. It was most exciting for her to meet the rabble-rouser, the anti-American, the new adventurer on the Arab stage. The prospect was more alluring as we had to live for a week in army tents, not far away from the tent of the new Pharaoh in rebel garb.

Herodotus wrote that Egypt was the 'gift of the Nile'. Egyptians teemed along the river's banks cultivating every inch of soil fed by its waters. For six thousand years Egypt was governed by Pharaohs, irrespective of other titles assumed by those who sat on its throne. They were kings, walis, sultans, amirs, khedives, presidents. Whoever governed Egypt was the sun-god, the all-powerful. And since the seventh century when the country was invaded by the armies of Islam, its ruler has held the Koran in one hand and the sword in the other. The Egyptians on the tour with me greeted any mention of Nasser with the exclamation, 'Allah U Akbar' (God is Greater). When it was so exclaimed, Nasser was in effect associated with the deity and so he was regarded.

Nasser was proud of his navy, and in the vicinity of Alexandria he wanted to show it off. Thousands of Egyptians learned of the arrival of the new Pharaoh, and took every possible boat or dinghy that could float to be there ahead of the navy and to parade to welcome the great man. A look at the sea revealed literally thousands of boats, each overflowing with poor peasants, with nothing on but the typical Egyptian *gumbaz*, the white robe that hangs from the shoulders to the floor. In their boats, the peasants sang, they danced over each other, they jubilantly hailed their leader. They whipped themselves up into an absolute frenzy. In vain did the Egyptian admiral try, through a blaring loudspeaker, to thank them and order them to move out of the way so that the navy could begin their manoeuvres. The more he shouted, the more excited they became and danced and sang with renewed fervour. The admiral looked at Nasser in despair and asked what he was to do.

'Give the order to start the manoeuvres,' advised Nasser.

Soon naval vessels of all sizes and shapes ploughed through the waters, creating huge waves that battered the small boats. The greater the assault of the waves, the louder the singing, the faster the swinging and the more joyous the seafaring peasant crowd. Soon, peasants began to fall out of boats.

Nasser looked truly puzzled. The Egyptian masses were here to express their adoration, but here too was the navy, bought from Europe and the Soviet Union to impress the masses. Soon enough he realized that if it was to be people versus the navy, the people must win. He gave orders to stop the manooeuvres. At that moment no one could have been more miserable than the hundred or so naval officers who, in full array, had expected their moment in the sun and were deprived of it by the happy and unruly crowd.

Nasser, a quintessential Egyptian, enjoyed the moment and went back to his newly erected tent, telling one joke after another, needling the commander of his armed forces, Marshal Abd al-Hakim Amer. I took advantage of my presence with the leaders of revolutionary Egypt to inform Nasser of a study done in the US examining the widening gap between Egyptian technology and Israeli technology that predicted disastrous military consequences for Egypt. Nasser referred me to the great marshal who was too far gone on hashish to listen to me and who considered me a young scholarly upstart.

In Egypt, Phyllis and I became tourists, attracted by the fabulous antiquity of this river civilization. With expert guides we went deep into the pyramids where some of the Pharaohs were buried, where their ships were stored to carry them across the mythical river unto the land of eternal light. We stared at the Sphinx who seemed to gaze at distant horizons, impervious to the tide of events in human affairs. Just so must the Sphinx have stared in indifference at Napoleon when he mounted his ambitious expedition to bring modern French ideas to Egypt, the ancient land of the Pharaohs.

For centuries before the rise of Islam, Egypt boasted the greatest library in the world, a library that repeatedly suffered at the hands of conquerors – pagan, Christian and Muslim. The final blow came in the mid-seventh century when Arab conquerors, carrying the message of Islam, occupied Egypt and looked critically at Alexandria's library, the pride and jewel of Egypt.

'What shall we do with this great store of knowledge?' wrote the general to his caliph in Medina.

'Destroy it,' came the answer, 'for if it has knowledge that contradicts Islam we cannot tolerate it, and if it has knowledge that confirms Islam, we have confirmation enough in the Book of Allah.'

And, thus, this great store of the human spirit, like thousands of such stores in man's long and tortuous history, was obliterated at the whim of a conqueror. Successive Islamic regimes in Egypt, however, built magnificent mosques and gorgeous palaces, and in later years they have come to appreciate Egypt's pre-Islamic heritage. The ancient legacy is now exhibited and carefully preserved, on site and in museums, and is the focus of extensive Egyptian tourist policies.

To have a true glimpse of Egypt you must concentrate on the Nile. We took a boat late one evening and just floated down that legendary river. Unlike other rivers, the Nile is silent, enigmatic, deep. It penetrates the barren desert like a beam of light does total darkness. In places, it stretches itself so wide as to become a sea. Indeed, the Egyptians refer to it as al-Bahr (the sea) and regard it with awe and reverence. What the Nile touches, lives. What the Nile does not touch, remains arid, scorched, dead. As the Nile is one and all-powerful, so is the one who rules Egypt, and as the Nile flows from the bosom of the Dark Continent so does the ruler seem to the people to descend as a demi-god from a high and mysterious realm – Allah U Akbar.

The scholar and his wife, now turned tourists, wondered about the vast differences between Egypt and Lebanon. Egypt had one dominating river. Lebanon had a dozen rivulets. Egypt's terrain was flat – plain desert to the east, plain desert to the west. Lebanon was mountainous, two lofty ranges with a tiny horizontal plain in the middle. Egypt was mostly a homogenous Sunni Islamic community. Lebanon was a heterogeneous society, a 'museum of religious survivals' as Arnold Toynbee called it. The Nile unifies. The hills and valleys of Lebanon diversify. Unity versus plurality. Does this prove the power of geography? Does it add more weight to the new theory of geopolitics?

Like all those of my generation, and perhaps like all who study abroad and drink deeply from other cultural wells, Phyllis and I were still debating what to do with our lives. A decision taken early on was to live in Lebanon and give it the best we had. We never deviated from this resolve. But there were many unanswered questions nevertheless. When should we really settle down? How long should we stay in the United States? What position in Lebanon should we seek and when? How should we apportion our care for our respective parents? Phyllis thought I should take advantage of this visit to weigh the opportunities available to me. She knew her opportunities would wait until she had set the children on the right course.

Lebanon in 1959 was undergoing change under President Fuad Chehab, the former general of the army and the conciliation candidate acceptable to all parties after the bloody conflict of 1958. The American ambassador then was Robert McLintock, a powerful figure after the American military intervention. During the 1958 conflict, Charles Malik was Lebanon's Foreign Minister and he and McLintock clashed frequently. Somehow, I became an active emissary, trying to bring the two superegos together. In the process McLintock thought I should stay in Lebanon, and told Phyllis so. Phyllis urged me to consider the options.

One day, the phone rang and a voice asked for Phyllis. It was McLintock. He said he wanted to talk to her to recruit her help in persuading me to stay on. McLintock informed Phyllis that he had scheduled a meeting for me with the reforming President Chehab. He wanted Phyllis to ensure that I would at least consider any position that the president offered me. He felt strongly that young Lebanese scholars working in the United States should now return to their country and lend their support to the new reforming regime of Chehab. The United States approved of Chehab and wanted him to succeed. Knowing that I was related to Charles Malik, McLintock feared that I might let my ego get in the way. He knew that Phyllis was practical and would help me make the right decision.

At the appointed time I arrived at the presidential palace, dressed like a candidate for a government position. The Chehab Palace was then a quaint villa in Jounieh, which amused Muslim leaders. The Muslims often reminded the president that Jounieh was not Beirut, nor Greater Beirut where the president's seat should be according to the Constitution. Chehab was unlike most Lebanese politicians. He was definitely a man of the army. He believed in the law, he was highly ethical and efficient, and he lived like a monk.

His office in Jounieh was smaller than my office as assistant professor at Johns Hopkins. His desk was smaller than my desk, and there were only three spare chairs in his office – one close to him where I sat, and two by the wall. Chehab's wife was French. He was Francophone through and through and had no idea how to deal with an Anglophone like me; a graduate from an American university, and with an American wife to boot. I too had no idea how to talk to a person of his background. He looked at me with some amusement. I stared back like the Sphinx, revealing nothing. He expected me to talk, to ask for a job, to seek something from him. This is what visitors to a president do. I just sat there a bit proud, a bit unconcerned, which may have seemed a bit irreverent to the president. Finally he broke the silence.

'Yes, Dr Salem, what is it you want?' he asked me.

'Nothing,' I answered.

'Then why did you seek an appointment with me?'

'I did not, sir.'

Now he was thoroughly taken aback by this disrespectful, insolent person. He rang a bell, and his aide walked into the bare office. The president asked his assistant how this appointment had been made.

'You recall, sir, that Ambassador McLintock talked to you about Dr Salem,' the aide replied, 'and you expressed interest in seeing him.'

'Oh yes,' muttered the president and turned back to face me.

'Dr Salem,' he said, 'the American Ambassador has told me a great deal about you, that you have made some impact in Washinton DC, and that you are highly educated. I believe that you are the kind of person we need in Lebanon now that we are rebuilding the country along new lines. We want the Lebanese University to be a good university; as good if not better than the private universities now operating in Beirut. I would like you to be one of our professors there.'

He seemed quite pleased with the offer he had just made to me. I could see that he expected acceptance and gratitude as he gave the Anglophone the floor to respond. I thanked him politely for his interest in me. Then I proceeded to acknowledge that the Lebanese University, the only government university in the country, was in bad shape. I professed myself as being glad to help. I delivered my counter offer.

'Mr President, if you offer me the presidency of the Lebanese University,' I suggested, 'if you give me a free hand to make it a real university, I will gladly leave Washington and join your reforming efforts.'

Chehab was shocked, completely aghast at this unthinkable proposition. He looked at me incredulously. 'You must have been out of Lebanon for a long time,' he observed dryly. 'You don't seem to understand the Lebanese game. Are you aware that the Lebanese University is the preserve of the Francophones? Don't you know that it would be easier for me to appoint you foreign minister than to appoint you president of the Lebanese University? You know what the Maronites would say if I were to appoint an Orthodox? Do you know what the Jesuits would do to me? Do you know the French Ambassador would be after me? You know? You know?'

Poor man, I thought he was getting near to being apologetic, while I was actually the one who should have been. I realized then how limited the powers of the Lebanese president were, and how many considerations he had to weigh before he could make any decision.

France had maintained close contacts with the Maronites since medieval times, and enforced them later through the Crusades along educational and commercial lines, culminating in the twentieth century with the French Mandate over my country. France was not about to relinquish its cultural and linguistic hold on Lebanon.

When he heard, McLintock was not unsympathetic to Chehab's position, but I believe he was disappointed that the president had not offered me a role outside the French cultural preserve. Chehab, I reasoned, preferred to get rid of me, as he must have found me a loose cannon on deck. Certainly from the hierarchic point of view he found me a bit offensive.

When I recounted the interview to Phyllis, she quoted to me favourite lines of mine from Robert Frost's 'New Hampshire':

> How, to my sorrow, how have I attained
> A height from which to look down critical
> On mountains? What has given me assurance
> To say what height becomes New Hampshire mountains
> Or any mountains?

She felt my attitude was reminiscent of my immature days, an attitude that often got me into trouble for no good reason. But I was in Lebanon on a research grant anyway, not to seek employment in its government or universities. And research I did. I collected enough material to strengthen my course offerings and to write a book had I been inclined to do so. Unlike most young Jewish professors in Middle East Studies, I did not give much attention to publication in academic journals. Other than having my thesis on the Khawarij published by the Johns Hopkins Press, I did little in the publication realm. I was a good teacher. I enjoyed teaching, and enjoyed the praise lavished on me by the dean, by colleagues, and by external observers who published a report on American higher education saying 'there are still good teachers in America', and went on to praise my teaching style and my creativity in getting ideas across.

When we returned to the US, the country was in the midst of a presidential campaign pitting Democrat John F. Kennedy against the Republican vice-president, Richard M. Nixon. SAIS was divided into two camps, just as sociologists predict will happen with any small group. To the faculty members at SAIS the presidential campaigns provided opportunities to volunteer their expertise to the candidate of their choice. Many entertained the hope of a victory that would offer them positions as secretaries in the cabinet, as assistant secretaries, as under-secretaries, as advisors or as ambassadors to major world capitals. SAIS was definitely in the thick of

Washington politics. The stakes were high for the winners. Most of the faculty already held important consultative positions to top government officials. The Federal Government currently employed a good proportion of SAIS students, and most of the school's graduates sought federal positions.

Phyllis and I had several connections in the Kennedy campaign. As our neighbourhood was home to a number of aides to Democratic senators, and as they were all now mobilized in the Kennedy campaign, and as our good friend Russ Holt was now a member of the campaign team, there was real action there. Our house became the hub of this action. All eight of our active Democratic Party neighbours met at our house in the evening to discuss how Kennedy's campaign had gone during the day, brainstorming on what he should be saying tomorrow, and how to respond to positions taken by Nixon.

Why our house? Perhaps because Phyllis was by nature a catalyst. She provided the right atmosphere, the right drinks and a diversity of Lebanese dishes called *mezza* that were greatly appreciated. The fact that I am Lebanese and accustomed to an open house helped too. The group often contributed to the table, and they all felt that if they were to get together our home was the right place. It was exciting to think up ideas and slogans and to telephone them directly to the aides of the candidate on the campaign trail. It was even more exciting to hear our thoughts or some variation of them proclaimed the next day with such strength and conviction by the candidate.

Writing in retrospect, it is interesting to note that all of us were heavy smokers. During the entire campaign period, Holt was never seen without a cigarette dangling from his mouth. I proclaimed Phyllis the Madame de Staël of Washington politics. It is impossible to describe the utter jubilation of this crowd in our house when Kennedy won the election of 1960. On that evening, more bourbon was drunk and more Lebanese food was consumed than ever before. An atmosphere of near hysteria prevailed, and the sounds of celebration radiated from 4414 throughout the entire neighbourhood.

If Scott and McCarthy had wondered about the new neighbour, now they hated him; the two stuffy men were, it turned out, 'closet' Republicans. One of our closest friends from AUB days was Professor George Grassmuck. George worked for Nixon's speech-writing team, and thought that Nixon was the most intelligent man he had ever met. My dear friend George wondered why we would give our allegiance to Kennedy. I put the blame on my neighbours, and George forgave me my sins. After the Nixon defeat the Grassmucks invited us for dinner and, of course, we went. The evening was a calamity. They were silent, despondent and totally dazed. When we left, Phyllis told me this was no dinner, it was more like a funeral wake. When it comes to passion and excitement, few games generate greater levels than American presidential elections. For the inauguration festivities we were out of circulation because of that small operation thanks to which I suffered such embarrassment in a stalled car and a snowstorm.

The passion generated in our household during the election period led us to review our immediate plans. Were I to stay a few more years in the US, maybe I should apply for American citizenship. If it became necessary for me to relocate due to friction between my immediate superior at SAIS and myself, I would have to consider when and where to go. On the other hand, were we to decide to return to Lebanon, this might be a good time. With a relatively small academic income, and with four children to raise, to educate and to launch, perhaps I should reconsider the business world and get a well-paid job. We sat one evening sipping vodka martinis and planning. Phyllis loved to make plans, to make a list of things to do and options to consider. To stay, Elie must go to a certain office on Constitution Avenue and apply for citizenship; to move to another university, Phyllis must first make a list of the most attractive universities on the East Coast for us to choose from; to apply to business companies operating in the Middle East, Phyllis must first make a list and prepare letters. Fine, now we had the list of options and would take first things first. By now we were on our second martini.

'Elie, you will go early on Monday morning and apply for citizenship.'

'Yes, ma'am.'

On Monday morning at ten a.m. I presented myself at the appropriate building on Constitution Avenue. The information officer directed me to a second-floor waiting-room, which I found to be a complete madhouse. A crowd of people jostled each other to get ahead, to reach the application table and to take a shot at paradise.

Jostling turns me off completely. It is uncivilized, undignified and usually wholly unnecessary.

With patience, I moved an inch at a time until I reached the inside of a hall where a semblance of order prevailed. Order is a relative concept. The crowd inside this hall, though shepherded by two policewomen, was still unruly. A few women, some in front of me, some behind me, were particularly restless. They were constantly pushing and shoving with outstretched necks to get a better look at the Promised Land. The closer I was to the goal – a woman distributing application forms – the more uncertain I became. What was I doing in this crowd? I asked myself. How come I am in line with hundreds of people from all over the world? How could I have waited some two hours under terrible and humiliating conditions just to reach a desk with a fat woman behind it? Well, here I am, and I must do my best.

The woman behind the desk was one who enjoyed her authority and exercised it mercilessly on all members of the huddled masses who had the misfortune to come her way. She screamed constantly. She had the gift of her black race, a strong melodic voice, now raised high in anger.

'Get moving,' she shouted, 'I don't have all day!' 'You don't understand? What don't you understand?' 'It's not my job, I don't care, move or get out!'

The bureaucrat shoved forms at each of us mortals as if she were shoving dirt; judging from the expression on her face, dirt it was. I felt like the *Titanic* heading straight for the iceberg and complete disaster. By the time I reached her, the woman was no iceberg, but a boiling volcano, a black hole that pulverized every object that came its way.

'Here, take this,' she barked at me. 'Fill it in and give it to the man over there. Move! Don't just stand there and stare.'

I have been told that I attract trouble as a flaming candle attracts a moth. Relishing the opportunity of a fight, I barked right back at her, 'I am not staring!'

Wow, this drove her bananas. She was not accustomed to contradiction. The woman shouted, she spluttered, she fumed, and in the midst of the sound and the fury I heard, 'If you do not want to become a citizen, there are thousands behind you who do.'

I had to calculate quickly in order to respond properly to this ultimatum. My inner cool took over; I looked at her kindly and politely, smiling. When I had thoroughly disarmed her, I gently folded the forms, tore them to pieces and walked away. My hope now was to exit the building before some smart policemen chose to arrest me for insulting an officer on duty. When I hit Constitution Avenue, I looked behind and no one was following. I felt independent and free and laughed to my heart's satisfaction.

When I reached 4414 Dittmar, Phyllis was, as expected, in the middle of changing and feeding babies and preparing lunch. Lunches and dinners Phyllis thought of as civilized occasions when a husband and wife sat together at the table in total peace. We would have a glass of wine and a serious conversation about ourselves, about the children, about the future in general. And today was a pivotal day in our life when much hinged on our discussion.

'Well,' she began as we sat down to our lunch. 'You signed the papers? Are you on your way to becoming a citizen?'

'No, I did not,' I answered. 'I tore up the forms after fighting with the woman in charge there.'

Phyllis knew me well. The unpredictable in my behaviour was easily predictable to her. Her mind, intelligent and quick, drew an obvious conclusion. 'Elie, you didn't really want American citizenship. You must have reflected on the pros and cons subconsciously and decided against it. I think you're right. I think the best thing we can do is return and settle in Lebanon where you can fulfil your potential.'

'We should move fast whatever we do,' I told her, 'because we are still as broke as ever, despite the Hopkins salary.'

'Then let's do two things at the same time,' decided Phyllis. 'I will type letters to business firms operating in the Middle East and letters to universities on the East Coast in areas less expensive than here. If we stay until we find a job in Lebanon, let's at least get into a better-paying university in an area cheaper than Washington DC.'

In 1961 personal computers and electric typewriters were unheard of. My poor overworked wife, already a full-time housewife, sat at an old-fashioned typewriter and typed individual letters to sixty-five firms operating in the Middle East. The letters offered my services and listed my qualifications in a professionally prepared curriculum vitae. Once they were mailed, we waited impatiently for responses hoping I would be offered a post in Beirut for a salary triple my academic salary. As the family grew and expenses multiplied, income was becoming an issue. We pondered how we would deal with all the business options we would be offered; 'considering' the ones we liked, 'rejecting' the ones not worthy of our status.

To our shock, and within two to three weeks, we received sixty-four rejections. The responses were polite. They all flattered me, and wondered why a highly qualified person like me should show interest in a job in their corporations. Only one letter held a one-per-cent chance. The writer thanked me for my enquiry, indicated that there was no position open for a person like me, but expressed an interest in meeting me if I ever found myself in New York.

Phyllis was glum. 'Elie, we have sixty-five rejections.'

'No,' I said, 'there is hope in this one letter.'

'No hope,' Phyllis replied. 'Look at the letter, it says if you ever find yourself in New York, we would like to talk to you. They are not inviting you to an interview, they are just letting you down gently.'

I thought she was probably right, but still I wanted to explore the one-per-cent chance.

I went to New York and entered swanky offices, utterly unlike those in universities familiar to the professorial class. I was received royally as per the instructions of top officials in the company. I was grilled for information on the Middle East, on business prospects, on security conditions in the region, then I was thanked for coming and dismissed. I had been duped. At my own expense, I had had my brain picked on the Middle East and got nothing in return. My instinctive antipathy to business was now confirmed and hardened in concrete. I was now liberated from the temptation of making a career in the business world. Freedom dawned on me then as the compulsion to accept what was truly mine. 'Freedom,' wrote St Augustine, 'is the compulsion to accept Christ.' My particular freedom turned out to be the compulsion to accept my fate as an academic, not to fritter away my energies in other directions.

Fortunately, the few letters we sent to universities yielded half a dozen excellent opportunities on the East Coast and in Canada. I decided to accept an offer from Smith College to serve as director of Middle East Studies in a joint programme conducted by Smith, Amherst, Mount Holyoke, and the University of Massachusetts. We bought a station-wagon, converted the back seat into a playground for the children, and drove to Smith. The campus was beautiful, the country lush and peaceful. We found an ideal home on a lovely hill in a spectacular wooded area and fell in love with it. I signed a contract with the president of Smith. I promised to buy the house during our next visit within a week or two.

But miraculous indeed are the workings of the Lord. At this critical juncture, a person from a distant clime re-entered our lives to play a decisive role in our career decision. This person was Norman Burns. He had played a similar role when, as director of the Foreign Service Institute in Washington DC, he had 'saved' Phyllis for me by postponing again and again her assignment to a foreign capital. He was there in Beirut when Phyllis arrived as a bride-to-be and the Burnses took her into their American-type apartment for a period of adjustment before consigning her to her fate in my village. Norman was there at our wedding as my best man, assuring Phyllis that America was not far away, but so nervous he forgot half the Lord's Prayer. And now he was there again, this time as the new president of the American University of Beirut (AUB). This was a post he had always coveted as a way to live in Beirut and there represent America and the American educational system. Upon arrival in Arlington from a short visit to Smith we found the following telegram awaiting us:

> Dear Elie and Phyllis, I have accepted the position of president of the American University of Beirut. I cannot do the job well unless you are here by my side. Pack and come. Cordially, Norman.

Phyllis and I were delighted. To serve at AUB with Norman as president was a golden opportunity. However, I had just signed a contract with Smith. We were about to buy a beautiful home. The children loved the area. On the other hand, Lebanon was always our ultimate objective. Our family was now complete – four children – a number sealed by my vasectomy. Phyllis wanted the children to grow up as Lebanese, to learn Arabic and excel in it as their native language. Identity was important to her.

We wrote to the Burnses expressing our delight at the offer and bemoaning the impasse we found ourselves in. Norman, the battle-tested diplomat, informed me that he would write to the president of Smith explaining to her that my return to Lebanon right now was the greatest contribution Smith could make to a developing country. In a short while I received a call from the President of Smith inviting me for a meeting. Phyllis, the children and I got into the station-wagon and drove to Smith. Burns had done his job well. He had convinced the President that I was indispensable to a developing country on the easternmost shores of the Mediterranean. Norman's friends at the Department of State and his former colleagues at Johns Hopkins, had also been in touch with the now beleaguered president. She came straight to the point. 'You obviously have a good opportunity at home – people there want you. I assume you want to go. I will be pleased to release you from the contract if you will get me a replacement as good as you are.'

Greatly relieved, we went straight to Princeton University asking for a graduate with high credentials in Middle East Studies. We were told about a fine Palestinian called Ibrahim Abu Lughud who was brilliant and had recently received his PhD from Princeton. He was desperately looking for a job. We located Ibrahim. We put the proposal to him and he grabbed the opportunity as manna from heaven. Abu Lughud was happy, I was happy and Smith was happy.

Now began the laborious and exciting process of moving our family, our possessions and our future across the oceans. To sell the house, to desert our garden, our shrubs, our fruit trees and our historic oaks was not easy for us. It was especially hard for Lisa who at seven was very emotionally attached to our home. Indeed, when we left, Lisa spent the whole morning kissing every bush and every plant with tears in her eyes. Departure was relatively easier for Nina, Adib and baby Paul.

In those days, I was a handy person and I had a most impressive array of tools for all jobs and occasions – literally worth thousands of dollars. To my dismay I found out that Phyllis had sold them, practically given them away, to the first comer for ninety dollars. No more sales, we decided, after that. We gave away antique Pennsylvania Dutch chairs and tables on which Ernie and I had worked for years scrubbing, polishing and rubbing. One of these was a rare eighteenth-century piece that our dentist neighbour wanted to buy with the intention of building a house to accommodate it. Instead, it went free to some neighbours who just happened to have the right place for it.

To the Sells, our departure fell like a heavy blow. We had become central to their lives, a window on the wider world for them. They had come to like our Washington friends and were stimulated by new ideas and new contacts. They bragged about Phyllis and me to their homebound relatives and friends in Pottstown and Melrose Park. Ernie got a big kick out of taking me with him on his sales trips, introducing me as doctor, as professor, as a big cheese in Washington. He exhibited me proudly to his Jewish neighbours, who suppressed their Zionist leanings and exalted the humanity of our race.

'Jews, Arabs – what the hell,' exclaimed the Sells' immediate neighbour Mr Paris, 'we are all human beings, and we all got to live in peace.' Mr Paris was always half drunk as the burden of life was too heavy for him to bear. He was never seen without a beer bottle in his hand. I loved Mr Paris, and I was exuberant and open in my love, and he as a Jew, passionate like all semites, responded in kind. The Jews in the Melrose Park area became our close friends. We learned to avoid politics and to dwell on the infinite realm of human relations in which they were deeply interested and eloquently con-versant. Again and again I reflected on the tragic conditions of this mysterious existence. The Bible itself is not very certain about man; a question-mark has hovered over the human race throughout its history. 'Who is man that Thou art mindful of Him and the Son of Man that Thou visitest,' queries the Holy Book. And we can ponder in this context the words of William Shakespeare:

> Man, proud man,
> Drest in a little brief authority,
> Most ignorant of what he's most assured
> His glassy essence, like an angry ape,
> Plays such fantastic tricks before high heaven,
> As make the angels weep.

So deep were Ernie's neighbours in many ways, and yet so shallow and parochial when it came to the politics of Arabs and Jews. We soared high when we talked about universals. We sank low when we delved into the Palestinian problem. On this sensitive subject, laden with myth and passion, both they and I were tied down Prometheus-like in unyielding chains.

The Sells wanted to come with us to Lebanon. Even the Jewish neighbours hoped to visit us in Lebanon if conditions permitted. Bonnie was now in her early teens and was determined to depart with us, to live with us in Beirut and go to college there.

169

6

We decided to go by ship. Despite all we had given away, we still had possessions to move with us. When the family items were all finally packed we had two huge bundles containing mattresses and bedding, kitchen equipment, eighteen trunks and fifteen suitcases. Five of the suitcases belonged to teenage Bonnie. She had an entire suitcase devoted only to her hats, another one for her shoes, one for toiletries and two for her clothes. We took berths on an American ship, the *Constitution*. Its final port on the Mediterranean was Genoa. From there we were to take a Turkish ship to Beirut. As all my travellers carried American citizenship, they did not need a visa for Italy. I was told that I would not require a visa either as I would be in transit.

To avoid another possible travelling crisis and perhaps excruciating embarrassment, I called the Italian embassy in Washington to ensure that this was correct information and asked for the consular officer. 'Sir, I am a Lebanese citizen,' I told him. 'I do not have American citizenship. I am travelling by ship to Beirut in transit through Genoa. Do I need a visa?'

'No, you do not,' he answered immediately, 'because you are a transit passenger.'

'Are you sure?' I insisted.

'Yes, of course,' was his firm reply.

Doubting Thomas that I am, I asked Phyllis to call the Italian embassy again. She did, and got the same answer, albeit more affirmatively. Thus reassured, we arrived at the pier in New York on a stormy, rainy day. Traffic to and from the pier was not only heavy, it was virtually at a standstill. In due course we made it to the ship: Phyllis, her sister, our four children and I as travellers, and the immediate Sell family to help with logistics and bid us goodbye. The seemingly endless store of bundles and trunks were lifted by crane into the hold. We carried the suitcases aboard to be with us in our spacious cabin. Everything was being loaded quite smoothly until I arrived. I was told I could not come aboard, as I needed a visa for Italy.

'No, I don't need one,' I informed them. 'I called the Italian embassy in Washington and was told positively that I do not need a visa.'

The officer was calm and helpful, yet quite adamant. 'Please do not waste your time,' he advised me. 'I cannot permit you on board without a visa.'

'My God what shall I do?' I lamented. 'I have a wife, four children and a guest already on board. It's impossible, there must be a mistake. I cannot be separated from my family, they need my help.'

The very calm officer repeated, 'There is no way I can allow you on board without a visa, Dr Salem.' He was now truly helpful and understanding. 'You have two options. You can let your family go by ship while you go by air and meet them in Genoa.'

Phyllis screamed, 'No. No. We can't go without him. What with four children, my teenage sister and dozens of trunks and suitcases, I could never manage!'

The officer continued just as calmly, as if he had not heard my distraught wife. 'Or,' he went on, 'you may now race to the Italian consulate, which is about forty blocks away. You still have about an hour. I cannot delay a ship with a thousand passengers for the sake of one individual. However, I will call the consulate and I will tell them to be ready for you, to give you priority. If you're lucky, you'll make it. Now, Dr Salem, if you want to be with your family on this ship, just make a dash to the consulate. Here is the address.

It is amazing how much power and determination a human assumes when his back is to the wall. I literally ran as fast as I could. I spotted a taxi but it was full of people. Somehow, in the most emotional language, I pleaded with them to evacuate the taxi and let me have it. The occupants could not believe their ears – what! relinquish their warm place in their taxi and get out into the pouring rain? What was the emergency? I lied that it was a matter of life and death. They got out still looking at me, and at each other in obvious disbelief.

The taxi driver was a black youth who rose happily to the challenge.

'I am in great great hurry,' I told him. 'I want you to drive at full speed to this address. For every red light you go through, you get five dollars. No police will stop us. I am a very important man on a very important mission. Do not ask any questions.'

'You got it, buddy,' yelled the joyous youth, and he drove lawlessly, mentally balancing the money he calculated he was making against the odds of being arrested. Had we been arrested, of course, the consequences would have been disastrous for both of us, but even worse for me.

At the consulate, sure enough an officer was waiting for me. He was polite, but I was furious. How could the embassy mislead me like this! How could I possibly make it back to the ship in this traffic and the torrential rain? The officer was doing his best, but in my anxiety I pushed him to go faster. He threatened not to proceed and called his superior. When that dignitary came to intervene, I apologized, got my visa and leapt into my faithful taxi waiting outside.

We blazed through the streets of New York at high speed, oblivious as to whether the lights were green, yellow or red, oblivious of speed restrictions, oblivious of stares from motorists and threatening hand signals from law-abiding taxis. As we made it to the vicinity of the pier, the traffic was at a total standstill. I must have been some five hundred metres away from the ship.

I had about two hundred dollars in cash in my possession and I gave it all to the grateful driver. I jumped out of the taxi and ran towards the *Constitution* in driving rain. I recall jumping over cars, climbing on others to get across. No obstacle, no etiquette, no decorum, nothing was going to stand in my way. It seemed the kind officer aboard ship had posted a few of his men at fifty-metre intervals. As I made my way along the pier, I heard one shouting to the next, 'Here he is! Dr Salem is going to make it!'

I felt as though I was in a horse race, only in this case I was both the horse and the jockey. When I reached the ship, Phyllis was frantic. The officer had already had most of our trunks unloaded in case I could not make it. My family had made the decision that if I did not return in time, they would not board the ship. I ended my race to a sincerely jubilant reception, made a quick sprint to our cabin and downed a large glass of whiskey.

Did I curse the Italian embassy, did I threaten fire and brimstone, did I promise to strangle the sonofabitch who forced this humiliation on me? Yes, I did, in wild anger. But now all was well, and the anger subsided once the ship began to move. As usual, I became terribly seasick, a horizontal babysitter now for a good-sailor wife and not-too-bad-sailor sister. The children, conscious of my condition, were most cooperative, including one-year-old-in-age but two-year-old-in-wisdom Paul.

After a brief respite at Genoa, we moved to a Turkish ship for the rest of the voyage to Beirut. A day after we left Genoa, Bonnie got sick. She stayed in bed, hoping her trouble, whatever it was, would end shortly. Instead, she became more ill each day. She was running a high fever and could no longer eat or drink anything. The small amounts of liquid that we were able to force down her throat were insignificant compared to the amount of liquid she was losing through heavy perspiration. The ship's doctor was useless. He seemed to know nothing and to care less. 'It's only sunstroke,' he would say.

Bonnie's pulse was getting slower and slower. Phyllis and I were in a panic – the girl was dying slowly. My fear for her life overcame my seasickness and gave me the strength to search among the passengers for a doctor, a nurse, or someone who knew more than this idiot who in Ottoman exaggeration called himself doctor of the ship. We wired Beirut and asked to be met by a doctor from the AUB Hospital, with an ambulance and a medical team competent to handle an emergency that we had no name for. At that point, Phyllis and I calculated the chance that Bonnie would survive to reach Beirut was no more than twenty or thirty per cent.

While we were met at the port in Beirut by family and friends, our arrival was a terribly sombre affair. Bonnie left the ship on a stretcher ahead of us with doctors and nurses by her side. They hurried her into a waiting ambulance that screeched its way through the crowded Beirut streets to the hospital. The girl was diagnosed with a bad case of meningitis and given only a fifty-per-cent chance of survival. Mercifully, she recovered after a month in intensive care and some five months of recuperation at home. What we thought was going to be a joyous adventure for her and us turned into sheer hell. We began to doubt the wisdom of adding another youngster to our already existing band of four, but our love for the extended family and the wish to draw as many of them into our new life as possible outweighed our misgivings.

Phyllis was clearly the most stable element in our family, the voice of authority, the main decision-maker. To Phyllis this move was final. 'We are now in Lebanon to stay,' she declared, 'to raise the children as Lebanese, to prepare them for careers in Lebanon. Elie must now plan for a long-term post here.'

Phyllis intended to enrol in college to finish the education that she had never had a chance to complete in the United States and to plan for a career in Lebanon, in this Third World country which she had literally married. All was clear, vividly clear to her, and the first step was to find a house, a nest. Her goal was to buy a villa worthy of our plans and boundless ambition, a place where we could enjoy Lebanon to the fullest.

Phyllis loved the seashore, but she loved the mountains more. 'Where else,' you could hear her boast to her friends, 'can you find a country where the mountains just sit majestically by the sea? You can be swimming in the sea one minute, and half an hour later you can be skiing on the mountain slopes.' We rented a temporary abode as we scouted the mountain chain from the Shouf region in the south to the Kisirwan region in the north. Phyllis wanted an old house. Magnificent old houses were scattered along the mountain range like fortified castles guarding the lofty peaks from alien raiders. To appreciate the beauty of this mountain chain you must drive slowly through it, or better still go on foot.

The mountainsides were dressed by nature in forests of oak, pine, olive, cedar and shrubs of all varieties. On the forest floor and in the open meadows grew wild flowers, many of them native to Lebanon, stretching their necks, proudly exhibiting their beauty. Charming villages, a kilometre or two apart, some peering from low-lying clouds, some clinging to steep hills, some spread out generously in lush valleys, stretched from Beirut on the sea all the way to the mountain tops, some as high as ten thousand feet. We were most drawn to those villages that were perched around three or four thousand feet, with spectacular views of the Mediterranean. The villages were a perfect Lebanese mix of Christian, Muslim and Druze, a breakaway sect of Islam. The houses displayed the variety of their origins and history. Some wore pyramidal roofs of red brick shaped like the turbans of the Ottomans, the rulers for some four hundred years. Some had flat roofs of either earth or cement. Neighbours vied with neighbours in building large, sturdy vaults of stone, popular in the region since pre-Roman times. The Byzantines built churches and cathedrals with a strong Greco-Roman influence.

The Umayyads and Abbasids converted some of the most spectacular of the cathedrals into mosques. The Crusaders, fighting in a distant land, built fortresses on almost every hilltop. The Ottomans, while not known for their contribution to culture, were great builders. Each government office in even the tiniest village was a work of art, a testimony to the power of the sultan in Istanbul, formerly Constantinople. The villages reflected the art of their conquerors and the houses retained a touch of grandeur. Each successive community made its contribution to the vault architecture in the construction of abodes for amirs, pashas, beys, sheikhs and any others who could afford them.

Mount Lebanon was a museum of nature and a museum of architectural beauty. The scattered villages were as varied as the landscape. Some of the towns were exclusively Druze, or Maronite, or Orthodox, or Islamic. But most of the villages, the absolute majority of them, were home to diverse populations. And in diversity, these communities had lived in harmony for centuries in a rich and healthy interaction. They shared each other's joys and sorrows, they celebrated each other's feasts and holidays. And while there had occurred occasional instances of disruption and violence, these were almost always brought about by external forces.

As Phyllis and I saw more of these old houses, we became increasingly ambitious. Phyllis wanted a mansion, I wanted a castle, and here in Lebanon it actually seemed possible. How to pay for such flights of the imagination did not seem to hold us back. We had sold our 4414 Dittmar dream house and realized a profit of ten thousand dollars, which was a handsome sum in 1962. Father said he would help us, and fathers, as all children assume, can do anything. The greatness of Adib was that he gave us the impression that he was rich enough to fulfil all our needs. He made us feel only the sky was the limit.

We found a great old castle, in need of extensive repair. It belonged to al-Amir Majid Irslan, a Druze chieftain. Phyllis and I had coffee with the amir. He showed us the place. It was huge, a fortress some five hundred years old built of massive stones. The ground floor had most likely been a horse stable and was still intact. The second floor was half destroyed. Some walls stood precariously on the verge of falling down. One hallway seemed perfect, some rooms were almost habitable, others were practically destroyed. A third floor was in ruins, but one could visualize it in its glory. To think that such a treasure belonged to an individual and that he might sell it for a good price was incredible. We could perhaps buy it for thousands of dollars, but it would take millions to restore it. We could not possibly entertain the idea of undertaking a task of such magnitude, even if it had been given to us as a gift.

Another spectacular mansion was offered to us for a reasonable price, but there was a drawback. Her Majesty's government rented it as the summer residence of the British Ambassador. We checked with the lawyers, who informed us that we could certainly buy it, but to evict the tenants we would have to go to court – the Salems versus the British Empire. Unwilling to antagonize an allied nation, once good to me in my student days at AUB, we decided reluctantly not to pursue this house.

Another mansion on a lower hill was closer to the shore. The property had huge vaults, a spacious second floor with forty-foot ceilings, a private chapel, well-kept gardens, and was formerly owned by the papal nuncio who had moved to a higher hill. Catholics seemed to migrate upwards. We could afford to buy the house but could not see a way to afford the repair and maintenance. Phyllis observed that we had champagne taste on a beer budget and it was true.

We found a dream Andalusian-type house with an inner garden. It consisted of some twelve vaults forming a perfect geometric figure. The inner garden was decorated with an Arabian fountain such as the ones you see in Spain at that jewel of Arabic architecture, the Alhambra in Granada. The house seemed almost too beautiful to be real. It was more like a painting – a painting in stone. It was not realistic for us, but it was perfect for one of my friends at AUB. I thought of the professor Sami Makarem, a calligraphist and the son of a prominent Druze sheikh. He was the ideal candidate for this house. I told Sami about it and when we went to see it he fell completely in love with it at once. He bought it, worked hard on the repairs and it is now a beauty to behold.

Next we hired a guide, Khalil Mallat, to show us the area of Ba'bda, Hadath and Hazmieh in the hills immediately above Beirut. One day he took us to view some of the venerable old houses of Ba'bda. There was a substantial vaulted house that was not bad, except that it was on the way to Ba'bda Cemetery, not a good omen we felt. There was a Victorian school with a spectacular view of Beirut and some thirty bedrooms, but it needed too much renovation and we decided it would not do. Walking down from the school, Phyllis saw a grand old house hidden in a pine grove. 'How about this one,' she asked.

'Ah, no,' said Mallat, 'this one is not for sale. This is the house of the first president of Lebanon, Bisharah al-Khuri. It is now owned by rich people who will not sell it. And furthermore it is rented by the director of the Belgian Bank, a certain Mr Van Bisen.'

'Let's at least check with them,' said Phyllis. 'Maybe the rich people will sell it.'

Mallat laughed, 'But there is still Van Bisen.'

'Well,' said Phyllis, 'maybe he will accept a deal, maybe we can take him to court and win.'

Phyllis and I looked at the house from all angles. We fell madly in love with it. The house stood out in Ba'bda, an ancient village in the process of becoming a modern town. In the 1960s in Lebanon, old houses were disappearing fast and in their place new apartment buildings were springing up to accommodate the rapidly growing foreign community. This house stood out as the only one in Ba'bda with nearly two acres of garden around it. The garden was magnificent and included pines, carobs, olives, eucalyptus, figs, walnuts and grapevines. The house was so bundled in its woods, you could hardly see it.

We felt like the Mormon leader Brigham Young who, travelling through the state of Utah, stopped and declared to his followers, 'This is the place.' His place became Salt Lake City, the site of the Mormon temple and the home of a university preparing leaders in the Mormon faith. We were just as certain we had found our place, but we had yet to contact the owners and determine if they would sell and, if they would, whether we had a chance of evicting the tenant. Yes, it turned out the owners would sell. Yes, as new owners with no other home we could legally evict the tenant. The entire process took two years, and we moved into our new dream house in 1964. We bought it for a hundred and ten thousand Lebanese pounds. We had fifty thousand, father gave us forty-five thousand and we borrowed fifteen thousand from the Agricultural Bank. It took us ten years to repay the bank, such was the value of the

Lebanese pound in the 1960s. Our house was on the fault line between Ba'bda town proper and Sibnai, a suburb of Ba'bda. Ba'bda was exclusively Maronite; Sibnai was exclusively Muslim. Most of the residents worked for the municipality of Ba'bda or for the governorate of Mount Lebanon whose capital was Ba'bda.

The Maronites were introspective, provincial and as suspicious of non-Maronite Christians as they were of non-Christians. Many of the Ba'bda women were unmarried, and they paraded with their ubiquitous umbrellas in summer and winter. Phyllis often heard them muttering, 'What a shame this lovely villa has been sold to a Greek Orthodox family.' Although Phyllis took it lightly and laughed it off, our carpenter was also an Orthodox from neighbouring Wadi Shahrour and he took these comments to heart. Whenever he heard a snide remark about the new owners as Orthodox, he would respond, 'And what is wrong with the Orthodox? They are better Christians than you.' The women would scurry away, murmuring and cursing him under their breath.

The people of Sibnai were Sunni Muslims. In 1964 they were still largely Bedouin. While they may have had a few houses, they had many more tents. They owned camels, horses, sheep and goats. They were basically sheep traders bringing their stock from Syria and Turkey. They were exporters too, to Kuwait, Qatar and the United Arab Emirates. While the Ba'bdawis stayed largely aloof from us as newcomers, the Sibnai Arabs welcomed us with proverbial Arab hospitality. The moment we arrived with loaded trucks at our new abode, they came in force to help. They carried refrigerators, washing machines, beds, desks, chairs and suitcases. The whole community turned out – men, women and children. Here were two adjoining towns with radically differing traditions and behaviour patterns. Once the Ba'bda people adjusted to our presence, they became most respectful, but never truly warm and friendly, as the relatively poor people of Sibnai were from the very beginning.

As we were quite different from all of those around us, and as our garden was the most spacious and accommodating, the garden became the playground of a host of children of our children's age. Our kids played baseball, and so the neighbourhood kids learned baseball. Our kids played American football, and so the neighbourhood kids learned to play American football, and play it too in

American English. This was a major victory for the Salems in highly Francophone Ba'bda. Soon our children formed a jazz band and now and then a daring friend from the neighbourhood would join them.

Phyllis's determination to strike roots in Lebanon and make an impact was already felt in Ba'bda. There were conflicts from the start between children raised in our secular household and children raised in the bosom of the Maronite Church. With the Maronites, the Church is the guiding force in their daily lives and ever present in the form of priests, monks and nuns with strong and uniform positions on all religious, social and political issues. In such a milieu myth is strong, miracles are common and the Virgin Mary is the ultimate insurance policy. The sheer number of statues of the Virgin on street corners, in houses, on hills and in meeting places was staggering.

Over the centuries, the Maronites have merged into Lebanon and have fully incorporated Lebanon into their liturgy. They pray to the Virgin Mary as protector of Lebanon. They pray to Christ in His Olympic abode in the Cedars of North Lebanon. While Christ as God is a bit distant, the Virgin as the mother of Jesus is more accessible. Maronite children would proclaim in all seriousness that the Virgin was angry, that her statue was oozing blood, that in disgust with corruption or violence in Lebanon, the Virgin statue had turned away. Our children would contest these tales and say statues did not move. The Maronite kids, with strong conviction, assured our kids that if she was unhappy, the statue of the Virgin would bleed, would turn away, would change the expression on her face. Then the gang of contentious kids would come to us for mediation.

Phyllis was thoroughly Protestant, practical and no-nonsense. She proclaimed such tales to be total rubbish, much to the chagrin and confusion of the Ba'bda believers. They turned to me for another opinion. I tried to break the truth more gently. The Virgin, I said, could get pretty upset if we didn't do things right, but surely she would not convey her message by making her statue move but by a higher and more effective method. I do not know which of us was the more convincing, but the result was triumphant Salem offspring and despondent friends.

Ba'bda in the mid 1960s had a significant German community,

and a smaller British community, but no American community at all. The Germans seemed to me to be Nazi sympathizers who had established roots in Lebanon in trade and technology. As Arabs, we were anti-Zionists. We were careful to distinguish between Zionism and the Jewish faith. Zionism was a secular ideological movement. Judaism was a faith. The Old Testament is the foundation of the New Testament. Phyllis and I admired Jewish culture and bemoaned the fact that Zionism has become the visible political argument of many Jews. Our new German friends in Ba'bda were truly anti-Jewish. To the Ba'bda Germans, Judaism was a red rag that aroused deep passions and fierce animosities. A mention of the word Jew and their eyes would pop, the veins in their necks would swell and their throats would open wide to deliver invective totally unfamiliar in my Arab cultural background.

Only then did we begin to understand the anti-Jewish sentiment still deeply embedded in the German soul. Often Phyllis and I wondered after an evening with a German family in Ba'bda how a nation as culturally advanced as Germany could be so viscerally backward in racial matters. The nation that gave the world the most sophisticated music, the deepest philosophy, the greatest scholarship was found wanting at the level of the most elementary humanity. And to hate the Jews who were as sophisticated in all realms as the Germans was even more surprising. We were strongly and militantly anti-Zionists, but we were pro-Jewish in so far as the Jews were great historians, great philosophers, great musicians, great scientists and thinkers. Far from holding a contradictory position, we felt absolutely clear on where we stood, and we never confused the legacy of a people with the crime of one of its organizations, no matter how effective and extensive that organization was.

As our Arlington home had been the vortex of social and cultural activity at the end of the 1950s, so our Ba'bda House became the vortex of intense socio-cultural activity in the 1960s. By then I was a professor in the best university in Lebanon, a university with a large mix of professors from America, Canada, Britain, Germany, Austria and Australia. Phyllis too was now a student at Beirut College for Women (BCW), a mature student with a network of friends in the faculty.

We were lucky to find upon arrival in Lebanon a maid from a

village near mine. 'Maid' is actually not a word you would use to describe this woman. She was the mother of five grown-up children, a manager, a cook and an accomplished housewife. She functioned as a maid, but for all practical purposes she was a member of our family. She was proud, efficient and great with children. Her name was Salimi. She took the job because she loved Phyllis, she adored the children, and she needed an income. She was a friend and we knew that as we gave her affection and treated her as a member of our family, she would give us her all, and so it was. She literally raised Paul, who was still in pre-school when Phyllis joined BCW as a freshman student.

Phyllis enrolled in college in the way she did everything – with complete dedication. She took to it with a vengeance. This was the chance she never had. She was a great reader and had compiled enormous stores of information but her mass of knowledge had yet to be disciplined and accredited. She it was a brilliant student. She concentrated on literature, philosophy and history. We shared the belief that the liberal arts were the cornerstone of education and the requisite for all specializations. When Phyllis graduated with a BA from BCW, we congratulated Salimi as much as we congratulated Phyllis. Without Salimi, Phyllis's hands would have been tied.

The ease with which Salimi maintained the household, dressed the children, prepared the family dinner and acted the clown to amuse the children was a matter of great joy to us. Salimi was a tough villager. She cooked village food. She spoke village patois, which Phyllis tried to emulate. Salimi cursed freely like a peasant, in complete violation of social constraints. When we had a formal dinner for people who thought highly of themselves, such as diplomats and government officials, we would plead with Salimi to guard her tongue and not to act the wild untamed Salimi she usually was. She would promise to behave, knowing full well she was beyond control. Once we adopted a new method to communicate with her from the dining-room to the kitchen. We got a small bell with a gentle, hardly audible ring. The first time we used it at a formal occasion she came racing into the dining-room faking anger.

'A bell?' she exclaimed. 'What do you think I am, a cow?'

'No, Salimi, we love you,' we responded. 'You are human.'

'Fine then,' she forgave us, 'but use language next time, not bells.'

Her acts of outrage always brought laughter and encouraged her proclivity to the audacious and the profane. Our family tended to attract women who were not typical maids at all. There was Suad. She just walked into our house and declared that she knew who we were, that she respected us and that she needed a job.

'I will kill myself working,' swore Suad, 'and in return all I want is respect for my dignity. Give me my dignity, and I will not give a damn about salary.'

Suad was a tall pretty brunette from Tripoli, from a poor family with no prospects. Somehow she had heard of Beirut, of a better life, of foreigners and their style of living, and she wanted to be part of a Western-run household. She wanted to be taken in as a member of the family, and we were happy to oblige. She shared a room with Lisa and Nina, and she worked hard. In the evenings she dressed up and took part in our social activities, looking beautiful. She was conscious of her dignity and helped out not as a maid but as an effervescent member of the family.

And then there was Marie. She was in a class of her own. Marie was simple and illiterate. My crusading Protestant wife, bent on improving herself and all those with whom she came in touch, wanted me to teach Marie to read and write. I told Phyllis that it was impossible to teach a forty-year-old woman who had never been near a school to read and write.

'It would take a century,' I maintained, 'to teach her how to write and another century to teach her how to read. The project is a non-starter.'

'No, Elie, it is unfair.' Phyllis was determined. 'This woman is deprived because she is illiterate; a whole world is closed to her.'

'I know, Phyllis,' I agreed, 'but there is no way for you to open this world to her through the written word. Try images, try stories, try myths.'

'No, Elie, you must teach her to write.'

Assuming an enthusiasm I did not feel, I called to Marie. 'Marie, bring paper and a pencil.'

'Paper and a pencil?' Marie queried. 'What for?'

'I am going to teach you how to write.'

'But I do not want to learn how to write,' she declared.

'When you write, then you can read.'

'I don't want to read,' Marie avowed. 'I am happy as I am.'

'Marie, you and I have no choice,' I confided to her. 'Phyllis wants it, and you must do it. Bring paper and a pencil.'

And so Marie reluctantly brought paper and a pencil, dropped them on the table and walked away, determined to allow no connection between these writing materials and her future.

'Come back, Marie,' I encouraged her, 'and sit down. Hold the pencil like this.' And I tried to demonstrate.

'I will sit down if I must,' she said, 'but I will not hold the pencil. Why should I hold the pencil?'

'You hold the pencil to make letters,' I told her, 'and then we connect the letters and they become words, and we relate the words to each other and we have a meaningful sentence. We can read it, Marie, and learn what it has to say.'

'I do not want to learn,' she repeated. 'Why are you forcing me to do something I hate?'

'For my sake, please hold the pencil like this,' I persevered.

Marie held the pencil like a knife. If held like that a knife will cut, but held like that a pencil will not write. After a number of half-hearted attempts, Marie held the pencil in a manner approximating the first efforts of primitive man.

'Now, Marie, this is aleph [the letter A], try to draw it yourself.'

'Why should I draw it?' She was getting agitated. 'I can never draw. It is of no use to me.'

'Please, Marie,' I tried to be reassuring, 'just try. It doesn't have to be perfect, just apply the god-damned pencil to the paper.'

Marie tried and drew something resembling the letter. The more I asked her to repeat it, to perfect it, the more nervous she became.

'Great, Marie, we have made progress,' I encouraged her. 'Now let's write B.' I wrote the Arabic B, which is a straight line with a dot under it. 'Please try, Marie.' I was pleading.

'This is very complicated,' she complained. 'I cannot do it. What is this drop under it?'

'This is a dot to distinguish it from other letters that have dots above them.'

Angry, frustrated and in tears, Marie fled to her room and locked the door. Phyllis and I put our ears to the door and tried to listen. Poor Marie was sobbing. She would not come out unless Phyllis promised that reading and writing would not be forced upon her. To my great relief, Phyllis gave her promise.

If Phyllis could not improve Marie's mind, however, she would at least improve her health. It took several weeks to persuade Marie to submit to a medical examination. 'No, no, Marie,' Phyllis entreated, 'I am not asking you to go to a hospital, but to have the exam in your own bedroom. A woman doctor, a friend of ours, Marie, will examine you. You will be alone with her, and if she finds something wrong, the doctor will give you medicine.'

Finally, Marie agreed and on the appointed day the doctor arrived. Marie sought to postpone the examination as long as she could. First, she offered the doctor coffee. The doctor accepted and drank a cup of coffee. Next, Marie offered tea with a piece of cake, which the doctor declined. When next Marie asked the doctor if she would like beer and peanuts, her strategy was uncovered. The doctor gently led Marie to her room.

As the doctor told the story, Marie seemed resigned to the examination until she was asked to uncover her breasts. Under no circumstances, protested Marie, no, no, no way. The doctor asked why she was so protective.

'Because,' answered Marie, 'no one is supposed to see them.'

'Well then, just tell me if you have any soreness, any pain, anything new that was not there before.'

'Yes,' said Marie, 'there is a sore and infected lump, and it has been there for a few months.'

The doctor, calculating quickly, feared a cancerous growth. She begged Marie to allow her to cure it. 'I will not hurt you, but you must just let me see it.'

Cautiously, reluctantly turning her face away, Marie allowed the doctor to see and to confirm a serious cancerous condition. Now it was the job of Phyllis and Elie to persuade Marie to go to the hospital. The dozens of attempts were met with screaming. 'No, no, they will take my breast away. I will never part with my breast.'

'No, Marie, don't worry,' we replied. 'The doctors can cure your cancer. But if you don't accept hospitalization, you will die. You are only forty years old – please go to the hospital and live.'

The frightened woman finally consented, provided they would not remove her breast, no matter how important for her survival removal was. It is said you can take a horse to water but you cannot make it drink. We coaxed Marie inside the hospital; we coaxed her into a private hospital room, we bid her goodbye and returned home. Early next morning the hospital administrator called to say that Marie had been left unguarded for a minute and had run away. They could find her nowhere in the hospital. In a panic Phyllis and I got in a car and raced to her village in the *shouf* where we found her, full of life and joy. She had fooled the hospital and was now sipping coffee and gossiping with her friends. All our attempts to bring Marie back with us to have the operation were met with an adamant refusal. She continued to tell us, 'I will not trade my breasts for the world.'

A few months later we attended her funeral and cried not only for Marie but for the many Maries throughout the world who die in their youth because of fear and ignorance. There may be a beauty in the simple and the primitive, but it comes at a heavy price.

When we returned to Lebanon, the United States with John F. Kennedy as president was set on a course to save the world, or at least to nudge it forward into a universal liberal democratic order. This was the age of the Peace Corps, of young and enthusiastic boys and girls leaving America to help people in Africa, the Middle East, Asia and Latin America to catch up with the capitalist and industrial technological world. These new crusaders taught English and helped natives build schools, introduced new methods in farming and created civic organizations of all types. This was the age of the American Agency for International Development (AID), and my best man Norman Burns, now president of AUB, was the archetype of the AID officer.

Norman was determined to make things happen.

'Elie,' he would muse with me on the porch of his elegant residence, Marquand House, 'is it possible that we will witness in our lifetime the transformation of the Third World into the Second World?'

Always prone to the cynical and the sardonic, I assured him that we were more likely to witness the transformation of the Third World into the Fourth World, not only in our lifetime, but probably within the decade.

'No, no, Elie,' Burns would laugh, 'you are wrong. Progress is linear and the march towards democracy is irreversible.'

'Perhaps,' was my response, 'except in the Middle East.'

In the 1960s the Middle East was fast on its way to trampling over the last vestiges of the democratic institutions that were introduced under British and French mandates. In nearly all cases, they were replaced with authoritarian military regimes. In Egypt, a military coup removed the king and transformed the constitutional order, imposing a dictatorship under the charismatic Colonel Jamal Abd al-Nasir, known to the West as Nasser. In Syria the democratic constitution was abrogated by successive military *coups d'état*. The same was happening in Iraq. Of all the French and British mandates, only Lebanon survived as a democratic state. The Arabian peninsula and the Gulf States were under traditional monarchial rules applying Islamic law and the United States had good relations with their monarchial regimes.

The US needed the Gulf States for oil and for the strategic routes of shipping oil to Europe and to Japan. But the United States was in a reforming mood and was encouraging the monarchial regimes of Arabia to be more modern. AUB was already accommodating United States' interests by helping to modernize Arabia. First AUB had to attract students from those countries, teach them English, and prepare them for new careers. The regimes, though nervous about change coming in the wake of modernization, were willing to reform in small incremental stages. They wanted their subjects to learn English and to gain some training in order to master the technologies and deal effectively with their new oil wealth and with their rapidly expanding relations with the US. The AUB, under Burns, was now fully committed to development, and in Burns's view had an obligation to contribute to that end.

'Elie, it is true you have come here as associate professor of Political Science,' Norman approached me, 'but for my sake, for the sake of AUB, for the sake of regional development, I would like you to make a sacrifice and turn your efforts in a new direction.'

'What direction?' I wondered.

'I would like you, if only for a few years, to serve as director of an orientation programme.'

The orientation programme was created to bring to the AUB about a hundred Saudi students per year. The programme was designed to teach the Saudis English, to strengthen their science skills and to qualify them to enter AUB as regular students.

'This may take a year or two,' Norman said.

'Or five or ten,' I joked grimly.

'No, no, Saudis are intelligent,' Norman insisted. 'They are motivated. They are ready to join the modern world, and, Elie, it is our destiny to help them realize their goal.'

'As a good soldier, I will do it,' I reluctantly agreed. 'I will give it my best, but I won't like it.'

'Thanks,' said Norman. 'Now you're on your own.'

The AUB already had an orientation programme of sorts. It was called Special Form. The programme offered basic English exclusively. Its faculty consisted of twelve instructors. I moved into the Special Form office, and within a month I sent non-renewal letters to all twelve instructors. The president liked that. Salem is on the right track, he thought. The instructors got together and fired off a letter to the dean.

They asked the dean to fire this new director, branding the newcomer as utterly unqualified. He is not a linguist, the letter claimed, nor a native speaker of English. Salem had, unawares, stumbled into the middle of a bitter feud between the president and the dean of the Faculty of Arts and Sciences, Farid Hanania. Whatever the American Burns worked towards, the British-trained dean opposed.

Hanania was originally Palestinian but, after studying in England, had become a British citizen. He practised law in London and was in his 'Britishness' more true-blue than the queen. Hanania came to the support of Special Form only because Burns, through Salem, was transforming it into a broader orientation programme. My four children were in school, my wife was in college and my sister-in-law was also enrolled in college in Beirut. The last thing I needed was to fall into a political trap that would transform this opportunity into a calamity. Now, conscious of the power struggle in the university and fearing for my future in it, I went to Burns and asked him bluntly, 'How secure are you in your position as president?'

'Elie,' Norman answered, 'I am as secure as the USA, and I am not going to allow the dean of your faculty, a fake Britisher at that, to get the upper hand. Stick with me.'

Thus assured, I stuck with Norman Burns. By the end of the year all the instructors were out and a new faculty was installed. The Saudi students were unlike any students we had previously enrolled. They were all married, for one thing, and all seemed to be related to some influential Saudi. Each student arrived with a large entourage that had to be accommodated. They came with the expectation that English would be spoon-fed to them with the least amount of effort on their part. They expected to pass their exams easily and then to join the regular university classes without further delay. After one year, nearly half of them had utterly failed, and the others had only a dim hope that in a year or two they might qualify for the university proper. Saudis, however, could not fail. They could not, we were informed by the Saudi Ambassador, return without a degree or a certificate to show to their families. To return with nothing would represent a loss of face. Such an insult was virtually inconceivable in that tribal society. We were asked to keep them another year and to try again.

'Teaching them,' I said, 'is hopeless.'

Because their results had such personal implications, and as they were all very well connected, the King of Saudi Arabia himself intervened with a solution. The King would send all the scholastic failures with their families to Europe for one year, as a subterfuge. They would then be able to return to Saudi Arabia as if returning from specific missions ordained by His Majesty. This solution was rightly interpreted as reward for failure, and the Saudi students who were doing a bit better now wanted to fail and to be assigned to fictitious missions in Europe. One of the more intelligent of them told me that the King was so wealthy that they felt they were all entitled to a good life, whether they studied or not. And if they were to study, most of them preferred to be in Texas, Florida or California, like so many other Saudis. In those places they were treated in a special way and all of them were allowed to pass, some with honours.

Burns's nation-building effort with Saudi Arabia was not working. I regretted my 'sacrifice', and I urged Burns to let me return to the Political Science Department. The fight between the president and the dean continued. The dean was accused of inciting a strike among the staff that really hurt Burns. Connie, the sweet Calvinist, wanted to kill Hanania if only Christ had just hinted that the aggrieved may resort to such a measure. She confided to me that she was praying for Hanania's death. 'O Devil, get thee behind me,' Connie would pray, 'and push!'

One evening, Phyllis and I joined Norman and Connie in their lovely home for dinner. Phyllis commented to Connie on the progress of the Burnses' beautiful garden and the magnificent view of the Mediterranean. Norman sighed and confided, 'My friends would have trouble believing that the man who lives in this great setting is absolutely the most miserable man in Beirut.'

In a few months the Board of Trustees fired both the president and the dean. Norman did not prove to be as strong as the US and Hanania did not have the Empire behind him when he needed it most. I learned then that academic politics can be just as vicious as state politics and one must play the game right or risk one's future. I played the game right, I taught well, I published extensively, and I was granted tenure.

7

Phyllis, too, was playing her cards right. She received her bachelor's degree in English with distinction from the Beirut College for Women (BCW). She immediately enrolled in the AUB and dedicated herself to earning an MA in Philosophy, as well as another in Comparative Literature. Had there been a PhD programme at AUB, she would have enrolled in it and done brilliantly. Throughout her college education she continued to study Arabic. It seemed to me that her courses always came in four volumes, each of increasing complexity. She would do very well in the first volume, and would continue to do well in the second. She would generally make some progress but begin to flounder in the third. By the final volume, she would become overwhelmed and hopeless. She was not alone in this situation. Many students of Arabic are misled by the classic simplicity of the language. As they advance, however, and encounter the complex and unruly structure, even the most determined are often discouraged. What Phyllis always failed to realize was that she more than compensated for her inability to master the written classical Arabic with her complete mastery of the colloquial.

Phyllis was hired to teach English at AUB and to edit manuscripts for university publications. The challenges at AUB were every bit as exciting, perhaps more so, than those at Hopkins DC. AUB was the home of a most sophisticated professional class. The atmosphere lent itself to dreaming the finest dreams, to striving to excel, to serve and to leave a lasting impact. As our home was a meeting place for colleagues – Lebanese, Arabs, Americans, Europeans – we tended to carry on a running debate about how best to move our region forward. Phyllis, the realist, wanted to galvanize the Salem family first. This lively, socially adept woman had been fired up and wholly engaged by our Arlington experience and our involvement in the Kennedy campaign. She greatly admired the Kennedy model. She also admired the Salem family. She had the highest degree of respect for the head of the

Salem clan, Adib. She found Elie and his brothers no less competent than the Kennedys.

Phyllis conceived the notion that the Salems could join together like the Kennedys and exert a similar influence on their own country. As she became obsessed with this possibility, practical Phyllis set out to achieve it. She focused on the unifying goal. She began with my brother Philip. Though a medical doctor, he was well read, and he and Phyllis got along famously. He was quite a good dialectician, and Phyllis could engage with him for hours; they would agree and, just as often, disagree. I attempted to dissuade my wife from her notion that our family could emulate the Kennedys.

'We have no money,' I argued. 'We do not come from a political family and are not even members of a political party. In fact there is no party in Lebanon that has prestige enough to afford us a national platform. And anyway, we Salem brothers have differing interests.'

My arguments were rejected. 'Nonsense,' Phyllis replied, 'of course you can do it, and we should take the lead.'

And so Phyllis began a tradition of inviting the brothers and their wives to lunches, dinners and to all special occasions as she set out to mould the family to her vision. She succeeded in becoming the dynamic hub of the Salem family and certainly was its proudest flag bearer. The family loved and admired her for her total immersion in their extended family and for undertaking a role not usually assumed by a woman with her background. But she was ultimately frustrated in her ambition to unify the brothers for a specific political goal that would do justice to her political philosophy and to her belief in the latent power of the Salem brothers. We all had different professions and vastly different interests. Our wives too had views different from ours, naturally enough. The political system in Lebanon was far too complex and influenced by strong foreign elements for a local family to dominate without planned external support. Also frustrated was Phyllis's attempt to organize the brothers to work on a commercial or industrial enterprise that would enrich them, solidify them and give them clout in mercantile Lebanon. None of us was, by nature or upbringing, inclined towards business. Adib and Lamya raised us with the strongest emphasis on education and it was this education that determined our future careers.

Our children were all enrolled in Pinewood College, a small elementary and secondary school near Ba'bda. They had been steeped in English while we lived in Washington and initially had trouble mastering Arabic. Not surprisingly, the older children had the most difficulty. But within a year or so they had all adjusted and were progressing through the governmental baccalaureate system. Phyllis was wholly committed to the plan that her children would grow up as Lebanese, and that they would have a clear Lebanese identity. The commitment was strengthened at AUB and given an Arab dimension, as AUB was a regional university. As Lebanese, our children were raised to appreciate Lebanon as an independent sovereign country, part of the Arab World and heir to a rich Arab culture. The fact that we were at AUB enabled them to interact with students from Syria, Iraq, Palestine, Saudi Arabia and the Gulf States, an association that gave them a broader national horizon than their peers in exclusively Lebanese schools.

The AUB itself was an Arab forum reflecting Arab opinions, especially in regard to the Arab–Israeli conflict in the turbulent 1960s. In 1967 Arab–Israeli tension had exploded into an intensive war. Israel defeated Egypt and occupied the Sinai Peninsula. Israelis occupied the remaining part of Palestine, annexed Jerusalem, and declared that city the eternal capital of Israel. Israel defeated Syria and occupied the Golan Heights. In short, 1967 was the year of abject humiliation for the Arabs. Palestinians, formerly dependent on the Arab states to rescue them from the Israelis, now formed their own militias and launched Bedouin-style hit-and-run operations against Israel. Students at AUB were restless, full of life and passion. They could not accept this defeat. Many students threw their lot in with the Palestinian military organizations that were mushrooming in the Palestinian camps in Lebanon, Syria and Jordan.

Phyllis, like almost all Americans on campus, fiercely upheld the Palestinian cause. Our house became a meeting place for Americans who were anxious to distance themselves from the official United States policy in support of Israel and against the Arabs. The ex-patriates wrote reams of letters to their congressmen. They sent multiple memoranda to the US Ambassador and to the ambassadors of European nations in Lebanon, including Britain, France, Italy and Germany. Palestinian students on campus had a national cause to espouse, and they had the major Palestinian military-type organizations behind them. Palestinians on campus were passionately dedicated to their cause, to the exclusion of all other considerations. This stance generally offended the new Lebanese organizations on campus, which felt that the Palestinians were taking over, violating Lebanese law and paying no heed to Lebanese sensitivities.

The Arab–Israeli conflict was raging. Each confrontational event was a cause for a student strike at AUB. The strike would inevitably take an anti-American stance as most students saw America as fully complicit with Israel in denying Palestinians their right to live in their ancestral homes. Strikes were directed against the American president of the university and student demonstrations would march to Marquand House as often as they marched to the American embassy. Protestors carried strident placards: Down with America; Down with Israel; Johnson is a Zionist; Down with the Arab regimes; Down with the Lackeys of Imperialism; Long live Palestine; Palestine is Arab; Jerusalem is Ours. Demonstrators chanted nationalist songs and shouted their slogans, which became increasingly pointed.

Al Fatah, under Yasser Arafat, became the hope of the Palestinians and of the Arab masses. The central goal of the Al Fatah movement was to establish an independent, completely sovereign democratic state on all Palestinian lands. Al Fatah claimed Jerusalem is its capital city, and advocated for citizens legal and equal rights with no racial or religious discrimination. They passionately opposed Zionism and called on all Arab states to support their claims. In Lebanon and Jordan, Al Fatah and its allies were rapidly becoming a state within a state. Under the organization's direction, Palestinian students and their allies at AUB escalated the campus strikes to include the occupation of academic buildings, as if they were enemy territory, and the siege of Marquand House, as if it were the villainous White House.

After 1967, Nasser was in worse shape than Napoleon after Waterloo. The aura of supremacy had passed from his head and hovered instead over that of Yasser Arafat. Between 1967 and 1969 classes were held intermittently. The university was a forum for political debate on the future of Palestine, the fate of the regimes that were responsible for 1967 and the ideology that must now replace the vacuous legacy of Nasser and the Nasserin.

Precisely because AUB emphasized liberal education, AUB faculty and students debated freely on extremely sensitive topics. Everyone had strong opinions and openly exchanged them – about the future of the Arab World, Arab–Israeli relations and Arab–American relations. And because AUB was a private school, its faculty and students were largely free from the restrictions that governments tend to impose on their official educational institutions.

I was asked to be chairman of a university committee in charge of the turbulent student body; perhaps because I was the chairman of the Department of Political Science and Public Administration and my wife was an outspoken and staunch supporter of the Arab cause. The committee was simply called the Student Affairs Committee, abbreviated to SAC. We were unfavourably compared to the Strategic American Command, but that misunderstanding was the least of my problems.

Palestinian students, supported by Arab nationalists, Syrian nationalists, communists, socialists and the many Muslim political organizations that proliferated in that period under the guise of supporting the Palestinian cause, were making academic life at an American university virtually impossible. I sympathized greatly with the Palestinian cause. Indeed, it had been the Salem cause before many of these students were born, but I wanted the university to operate in freedom. Political discussion and activism I completely supported. I could not, however, sanction the disruption of classes, the repeated occupation of buildings or the carrying of weapons on campus.

Phyllis and I invited student leaders to our house in a spirit of collaborative guidance. Like her father, Phyllis was highly principled. She based her decisions and actions not on political expediency, but on what was right. She expected others to do the same. She wanted us to help the students to refine their concepts, to publish pamphlets and even to organize orderly demonstrations on and off campus. Our students, like so many students in universities operating in Lebanon in that period, were the intellectual vanguard of the political parties. They were often at the front, easily mobilized and a potential mass ready for immediate action.

The Student Council of the AUB met in West Hall, the student-activities building. During this time representatives of many of the Palestinian and leftist parties would attend the Student Council meetings as well, even though these parties, especially the communists, thought of AUB as foreign territory, and were determined to undermine it. This coalition zeroed in on the American president of the university and accused him of being an agent of the CIA. The accusation in the mind of impressionable and frustrated youth soon extended to administration and faculty alike, and no one escaped its vituperative sting.

In 1974, the Student Council called for a strike that lasted a month. Led by Palestinians and leftists, students occupied most of the buildings on campus, splattering the walls with nationalist, socialist, anti-imperialist slogans. The 1960s decade was one of student revolution and sexual liberation not only in America and Europe, but also in the Middle East. In Lebanon, the revolution played itself out primarily at AUB. As chairman of SAC, I wanted the students to express their anger, but the strike went too far.

I felt strongly that this was the beginning of a Palestinian-leftist takeover of Beirut. By the end of the 1960s hundreds of thousands of Palestinians were displaced. Angry, frustrated and humiliated, they were tragically disappointed by Arab regimes and were taking over wherever they were able to do so. Palestinian camps in Jordan, now armed and mobilized by Palestinian paramilitary organizations, began to expand beyond the boundaries of the camps and to seek power in Amman itself.

A war erupted in 1969 in Amman, pitting the Bedouin-based Jordanian army against the Palestinian militias. The army crushed the Palestinian uprising and forced its leaders out of the country. Large numbers of them poured into Lebanon, a liberal, pluralistic and relatively weak state. Palestinians became restless in Lebanon and attempted to realize their goals through other means. They were virtually an army by sheer numbers, and exacted from the weak Lebanese Central Government the right to conduct raids against Israel. The consequence was that every time the Palestinians raided across our borders, the Lebanese reaped massive air retaliation from Israel. Palestinian militants, impervious to retaliation against Lebanon and the Lebanese, continued their raids, and in the process began to alienate a large segment of the local population. Lebanese Muslims tended to side with the armed Palestinians. Christians, fearing Palestinian control over Lebanon, began to arm.

The occupation of academic buildings at the AUB was only one aspect of the rising tension between the two camps. Lebanon, as a liberal democratic country, had always been a forum for Arab ideas and the flashpoint of conflicting theories as they evolved from abstract ideas to stubborn facts on the ground. Phyllis and I were now deeply concerned that this inarguably just cause could destroy the independence, the stability and the liberal culture of our country. In a meeting in our house in Ba'bda that included leading Palestinian and Lebanese intellectuals, we agreed that the occupation of university buildings must quickly end. We naïvely believed that we could deflate the crisis stage by stage. I went to the Minister of the Interior and urged him to enter the campus by force and terminate the occupation. He did so in a dawn operation, and in a few days the university returned to normal.

Encouraged by stage one, we were ready to move to stage two. We saw then the battle at AUB as the harbinger of a bigger battle, an even larger occupation, with more serious consequences. We saw an internal war looming. A prominent Palestinian professor on campus was as disturbed as Phyllis and I were about the course of events. He shared our fear that what was unfolding on campus and the mobilization and militarization of the Palestine refugee camps could threaten the fabric of the Lebanese state. In a discussion by the fireplace in our Ba'bda villa, the following was agreed upon. Our friend was a true patriot and agreed to meet with Yasser Arafat, the uncontested leader of Palestinian militias, to try to convince Arafat not to attempt in Lebanon what he had previously attempted in Jordan. I would meanwhile meet with the leading Lebanese socialist and ally of the Palestinian Movement, Mr Kamal Junblat. My goal was to convince Junblat to disengage from his ruinous alliance with the Palestinians. We strongly believed that this alliance could lead to a disastrous conflict in Lebanon.

Phyllis made a passionate plea to our Palestinian colleague to preserve the purity of the Palestinian cause, not to contaminate it by engaging in wrong battles at the wrong time in the wrong place. Our colleague, who was as strongly Lebanese as he was Palestinian, was in agony about the direction the Palestinian militias were taking in Lebanon. To our deep sorrow, our colleague failed in changing the course of Arafat and I failed in effecting a change in the course of the National Movement.

Like so many other intellectuals in the protective womb of

academic institutions we watched with dismay the rapid spread of the conflagration that transformed our peaceful, cosmopolitan Lebanon into a fierce battleground of brother against brother and neighbour against neighbour. As the war rampaged through the streets of Beirut, it was fought with equal ferocity in the soul of each Lebanese and each Palestinian.

Our children were now attending the Beirut high school called International College, or they were enrolled in the AUB. Phyllis had raised our children to have a strong Lebanese identity. Now they were caught in a conflict in which they became fierce Lebanese loyalists, and fierce defenders of the Palestinian cause. As a family we had to explain the conflict, separate the issues, and attempt to maintain a vestige of rationality in a tragic, highly volatile and irrational situation. Throughout the period of strikes and violence at the university that presaged Lebanon's internal war, I continued as chairman of SAC. The Faculty of Arts and Sciences was a hub of political activity on campus as the drums of war were beating. During this time, the president of the university, Dr Samuel Kirkwood, appointed a search committee to recommend a candidate for the appointment of a dean for the Faculty of Arts and Sciences. For almost a year the committee investigated me, interviewing faculty, students, members of the community and local trustees. Committee members asked to visit me at home in Ba'bda. For hours, members of the committee talked to Phyllis and to me about the many complex issues facing the AUB.

Our visitors were clearly greatly impressed by Phyllis, by the house and by the children, who kept needling their way into the study where the meeting was taking place. The chairman of the committee broke norms and told me the committee would be recommending only one candidate for the deanship – me. The recommendation was sent to the president who could hardly hide his pleasure. Kirkwood told me of his plan to relay the recommendation to the Board of Trustees meeting in New York the following week. The New York meeting must have ended at five p.m. as I received a call from Dr Kirkwood at two a.m. informing me that the board had enthusiastically approved his recommendation. I was to serve as dean of the Faculty of Arts and Sciences as of 1 October 1974.

The appointment of dean at AUB, as in all American universities, is held 'at the pleasure of the Board of Trustees'. Their 'pleasure', however, depends on the 'pleasure' of the president. In the morning, I called my father and announced proudly that his prize horse had been appointed dean. I wanted him to hear it directly from me, before he read about it in the press. Naturally my parents, my wife, my children, and all my extended family were happy for me. At the weekend, as was our custom, we drove to the village. Hordes of people came to congratulate me on my appointment as 'president of the American University of Beirut'. In surprise, I turned to father and asked him the reason for this confusion.

'Oh, this is nothing,' he said, 'I told them so.'

'But, father,' I corrected him, 'I am the dean, not the president.'

'I know, I know,' said the Tiger, 'but you see, when you were chairman of the Political Science Department, I told them you were dean. Do you want to make a liar out of me? Now that you are dean, what can I say? Shall I confirm that you are dean or nudge you upwards? I have told them you are now president.'

Adib's logic was all his own.

Phyllis, with a solid education behind her and with extensive friendships among the faculty, throughout the university and in the greater Beirut community, now took on new responsibilities as the *doyenne* of the largest and most important faculty in the greatest university in the Arab World. Phyllis knew who she was. She knew the role she must play, and the kind of house she would now open to the faculty and to all who cared about the university at its moment of greatest need. I moved into the dean's office on 1 October 1974. I was immediately kicked out physically by students who were, in accordance with Beirut politics, on a new wave of violent strikes. They occupied all the buildings, ousted all of the deans, and confined the president to Marquand House.

As expected, I was now in the midst of a gathering storm that would test the mettle of all of us in the university and in the country.

8

The storm had been gathering since the 1967 war. It was gaining force with the ousting of the Palestinian leaders from Amman and their establishment of their revolutionary headquarters in Beirut. The Cairo Agreement, virtually dictated to Lebanon by Gamal Abdal Nasser and the Palestine Liberation Organization (PLO), made Lebanon a platform for confrontation with Israel. Lebanon was now the rope in a tug-of-war between Israel and the PLO. Lebanon's central government was weak and torn by the fact that the Muslim half of the Lebanese population openly sided with the PLO. Christian groups were therefore building their own militias to prevent what they perceived as a Palestinian-leftist take over of their country. There is in the history of human conflict a deceptive lull between the massing of the clouds and the arrival of the rain. People continue to hope, despite all the signs of war, that war will be avoided. This was the case in Europe in 1914 and in 1939. It was the case in the Middle East in 1936, 1948 and 1967. It was certainly the case in Lebanon in 1973.

While militias were training, the magnificent Lebanese sun continued to shine; the moon continued to grace the mountains with its gentle caressing light. Life in the villages continued at a pace unchanged for centuries – ploughing, planting and reaping. Townspeople engaged in their fervent three-hundred-word dialogue about ploughing, planting and reaping. Parents went on caring for and educating their children and everyone strove for a happy life in the context of their village, their tribe and their extended family. The State was there as an afterthought; a nuisance rather than a constructive force in the life of the people. The proud city of Beirut had seen great civilizations rise and fall from this tiny peninsula that jutted daringly into the sea. Beirut was the successor to Berytus, the Roman city that boasted a university and a law school, the pride of the great Justinian. The city grew slowly and incrementally from a village, to a town, to a major city without losing the spirit of the many villages and the towns that contributed to it. Beirut was like a peaceful pond into which a dozen streams flowed, each retaining its essential character. Villagers from the north, from the south and from the east descended on Beirut to establish their respective communities and, in peaceful and fruitful interaction, created a richly diverse mix. It was quintessentially Mediterranean, but certainly not a melting pot. Armenians, Sunni Muslims, Shia Muslims, Druze, Catholics, Orthodox and a sprinkling of Protestants left behind by the nineteenth-century missionaries from the United States were all Beirutis, but they maintained their connections with their towns and villages and the faith that sustained their communities.

Beirut, the home of poets, philosophers, writers and free journalists; Beirut, the playground of the rich, who fled the arid Arab interior in search of good weather, good restaurants and lively nightclubs; Beirut, the haven of intellectuals and the hope of the oppressed. Beirut was now nurturing in its Palestinian camps and in its basements and sub-basements a new breed of revolutionaries, those who had fled from oppressive regimes in Egypt, Jordan, Iraq and Syria. While Beirut sang, dined and danced, subterranean forces were preparing a powder keg that threatened to explode. While Phyllis and I and most of our friends feared the explosion, we hoped for a reprieve so that we could continue to live as we always had. We loved to study and to teach, to entertain and to intellectualize. We argued and agonized over the fate of Lebanon, the fate of Palestine and the future of our region in the midst of two conflicting ideologies – Zionism and Arabism. It was indeed a challenging time, as Kipling would put it, to keep your head.

In times of great tension people are often driven to extremes, and those in the middle are trampled upon and crushed. To remain pro-Palestinian while Palestinian militants in Lebanon were destroying the country was a challenge indeed. And yet Phyllis and I persisted in our fiercely pro-Palestinian stance. Phyllis was guided by principle to an extent rarely encountered. It was in her Lutheran heritage and nurtured by her father's example. She understood and fully supported the Palestinian cause, as I did. And yet we were also fiercely Lebanese, as we understood and loved our country. Phyllis, the great convert, was if anything even more Lebanese than I was, and more committed to give her adopted country all of her principled strength, intelligence and enormous energy. She sent a steady stream of entreaties to her parents in Melrose Park, inviting them to come and live with us.

'This is a beautiful country,' she would write to them. 'Its loveliness is unequalled, please come. You will live with us. Now that you have retired, you can pursue the hobby of your choice here. You will be our guests – no expenses.' Ernie and Dorothy visited once, twice, three times in the late 1960s, and each time they were confronted with the regional tensions. They concluded that political tension was the character of the region, but joy was the character of the people and beauty the privilege of this little mountain paradise in the plain, pale, arid Middle East.

If the Sells had had any initial doubts about the husband of their daughter, about his country, his values, his culture, those doubts had long since completely evaporated. The Sells adored our children and could not believe that there could be on earth such loving, intelligent, handsome girls and boys as Elie and Phyllis had. Good lineage, good training and a little hurrah to the now old-fashioned Dr Benjamin Spock!

The brave Sells finally sold all of their possessions, packed up their personal belongings and announced to their friends and neighbours that they were on their way. Not discouraged by the lamentable travel experience that Phyllis and Bonnie and the children and I endured in 1962, Ernie and Dorothy came by sea. They brought with them the pride of American industry – a brand-new white Buick. Eat your heart out, O Sami of Haiti, owner of the prized Buick of 1954. By this time, Sami and his Buick were ageing and his marriage to a woman who was centuries ahead of him culturally was rapidly collapsing.

We received the Sells royally. The children hugged and kissed their grandparents and, like everyone, cried for joy. They expressed in tears of joy what children commonly feel when they have their paternal and maternal grandparents by their side. Children need love, the more the better, and no institution could do it better than the extended family. Our children were tremendously fortunate. When young and thirsty for love and attention, they were smothered in affection by my sister and single brothers. Their uncles would come in the evening, tuck them into bed and regale them with endless stories. Philip was and remains a master storyteller. He remembers in great detail every anecdote from the village, and from our parental household. Philip would embellish his tales and theatrically perform them for our children as they struggled to stay awake.

Kamal, the youngest, and an equally theatrical fellow, would play wild games with the children when he babysat. 'Elie and Phyllis have left,' Kamal would sing out, 'let's have a great time. Sleep? Who wants to sleep?!' My brother loved the games as much as the children did. Fawzi lived with us for short periods and was always funny, always making them laugh. Antoun came frequently and with his more restrained humour contributed a certain *gravitas* to our brood. Fuad, known for his love of tradition and his pride in being a Salem, was the most generous of the brothers, always bringing chewing-gum and sweets for the expectant children. Milia and her stout happy-go-lucky husband provided an ideal atmosphere in their quaint village home. As they had no children of their own, they doted on ours with special attention. The extended family was in Ba'bda in full force to welcome the Americans and to suggest a number of sightseeing trips for them. The poor Sells needed to rest and sleep after their lengthy sea voyage. The villagers, however, felt the need to celebrate.

Ernie, the salesman, was a typical go-getter. Whatever we were going to do he would do it. Not Dorothy. She was the stay-at-home type, the bridge player. We moved the Sells delicately into our social life. As they were utterly non-intellectual, we plotted alternative ways to involve them in our community. AUB campus life was rich. There were always American bands on a tour, trips to the country and throughout the region that were arranged by social clubs at the university and in the city. On weekends, we immersed the Sells in our village life.

In the evenings we sat with Phyllis's parents on our balcony, with the spectacular view of the pine garden and Beirut below. We drank bourbon, we chatted and told stories from our past days in Vienna and Arlington. These were great days for the Sells also. They were on their final venture beyond the confines of Pottstown and Melrose Park where they had discussed the dim contours of the Arab–Israeli conflict with their Jewish neighbours. In Beirut they saw it at first hand.

Just as they had loved their Jewish neighbours, they came to love and appreciate the Lebanese and the Arabs. Ernie and Dorothy wrote to their former neighbours presenting their now better-informed point of view. Phyllis and I especially loved one of these former neighbours, a woman named Ham Stern, who expressed interest in coming to visit us.

'Can a Jew come to Beirut?' Ham wrote. 'Is it safe, can I enjoy it?'

'Yes!' we urged. 'And we will make you most welcome.'

And so Ham Stern came to Beirut, and we gave her the grand tour of Lebanon. We took her to the village as a Jewish specimen; she loved the role, and enjoyed her stay. It is a reflection of Ham's optimism as well as her *naïveté* that she so firmly believed that if only Arabs and Jews could get together as she and her friends the Salems did, peace would surely come to this land. After all, wasn't this the land where Hebrews, Christians and Muslims all had their origins?

'Isn't this the Holy Land?' she would ask rhetorically. 'Then why is it that every God-damned thing in the politics of this region is so unholy?'

Ham was utterly fascinated by the historical, political and social facts she was amassing. Her curiosity was boundless. She was a cultured woman, a non-political Jew with a universal agenda. Her naturally expansive tolerance made it impossible for her to understand how such a rich spiritual tradition could degenerate into the parochial, the partisan and the inimical. Ham returned to Melrose Park changed by her experience.

Phyllis wryly observed that the Khalidis at Harvard, after a decade or so, had converted a Jew to the Arab cause. She expected the Salems to do better. But we found the conflict to be so rooted in myth and ideology that it was almost futile to attempt conciliation. We in the Middle East learned long ago to live with conflict and to accept that some problems have no solution. We relied on accommodation, adjustment and temporary truces rather than endlessly searching for ideal solutions.

But the Americans had a different history. As adventurous Europeans faced with a new continent, they had taken on the challenge of this New World and triumphed. Their mostly Protestant orientation was practical, with a faith in God that required hard work on earth that would lead to success, riches and glory. Americans believed that the full application of reason would resolve every conflict. In their view there were no insoluble problems.

In the Arab mind, there is instead a great dependence on Allah, on His will for good or evil, and on the role of fate in the course of human events. The fact that the Arabs are no longer in the ascendant means that history has turned against them. Allah must be punishing them for digressing from the Holy Qur'an. Arabs must return to the Book and obey the will of Allah and history will turn once again in their favour. There is poverty in the Arab World; there is a stultifying desert; there is colonial oppression; there are world powers with great military might, and they are hopeless in the face of such stark realities. Problems of this magnitude are referred to God. They may attempt small remedies to immediate situations, but the pervasive feeling among the Arab people is that they must renew the observance of their religion and all will be well. The successive regimes, from caliphs to sultans, from kings to presidents and colonels, did not effect great change for the people. The leaders may have built roads, hospitals, industries and armies, but the Arab people are left hovering in the twilight zone of suspended destiny, strong in the belief in a transcendent overarching will.

Phyllis fully accepted and respected the tradition she had chosen to live within, and she was eager to add to it rather than abrogate it. Within the Salem family, she goaded, she argued and she added a pragmatic dimension. From her tradition of dedication, hard work and persuasion she worked to make her adopted country a bit more rational, a bit more sane, a bit more principled. But Phyllis was subject to the forces of lateral gravity. One pulled towards the West as she tried to instil some practical American values in us Lebanese. But one also pulled strongly to the East, as she tried to Lebanize her American parents, who were now our charge and our opportunity.

My children named their grandfather 'Bebop', and as Bebop he took Ba'bda by storm. He was the indefatigable doer, a gifted organizer, and had an inexhaustible affection for children. Bebop took full advantage of the opportunity he discovered in Ba'bda to play. Dozens of Maronite Catholic children regularly congregated in our yard. They exchanged sightings of the Virgin Mary and other everyday mysteries. Protestant Bebop had at one time actually entertained the idea of becoming a Catholic. Although he had regained his Lutheranism with vigour after his mother threatened to disown him, Ernie maintained a tolerance of and fascination with the papal creed. He and the Maronite kids were soon fast friends.

Bebop loved American football and baseball – especially baseball. He showed the kids how to divide into teams in Ba'bda, and he organized tournaments. He was a great lover of jazz and encouraged our children to play. Under Bebop's guidance, they formed the finest jazz band Ba'bda has ever seen. Our children dubbed Dorothy 'Momom'. As Bebop flourished, Momom drooped. Our household was an intellectual one, where conversation was often of art and politics. Momon was not a doer and found herself at something of a loss. In Philadelphia, her central entertainment had been her card games and she sorely missed her bridge partners. Apart from our immediate family, Phyllis's mother made no connections whatsoever. Like Phyllis in her first week in Lebanon, Momom read and reread her American magazines and cried often. She could not accommodate such radical change, not in her late fifties, not with her provincial background.

Once, on a skiing trip, we spent an hour dressing her – an effort she barely tolerated. Once she was suitably attired, we led her on to the beginners' slopes.

'Go ahead, Momom,' the family encouraged, demonstrating how to move on the skis. Momom would not move. She would not even attempt the risk, if only for a second. She just stood there with a resigned, stoical smile on her face. Unlike her husband and her daughter, Momom did not like challenges or change.

We were pained and surprised that when we made the excursion to the holy Cedars, the glory of Lebanon, the very trees acclaimed in the Bible, Momon complained all the way. Despite mention of the place in the Bible that she held in such reverence, Momom's fear of heights overcame all else. She was utterly terrified by the journey over winding roads, overlooking steep verdant valleys. If you cannot tolerate heights, if you do not love conversation, if you do not drink arak, if you do not crave the twenty or so *mezza* before lunch, it is very difficult to enjoy Lebanon.

Furthermore, peace in our country was rapidly coming to an end. Conflicts similar to those we witnessed on campus were replicated throughout the country. In Lebanon we have long been accustomed to shooting, and were able to accommodate a certain degree of violence in the routine of life. When a baby boy was born, the father often would draw his pistol – or later his Kalashnikov – to fire shots in the air welcoming the prized male. Friends of the groom would shoot wildly in the air at a wedding to give the groom an aura of power. If a young man were to die, the other young men of the village would accompany the coffin to the grave while shooting rhythmically, now a shot at a time, now angry, rapid shots, reverberating from all sections of the funeral procession. Violence could erupt at any occasion. A glass of arak, a pistol on the side and a highly exaggerated sense of pride were invitations for trouble, and we had lived with such trouble since childhood. Even a church, especially if it was crowded for a special occasion, could be the scene of a violent disturbance. Passions ran close to the surface. An argument might start as a fellow mistakenly stepped on the foot of another. The angry accusation might lead to a denial, an insult, a slap on the face. Soon the right hand found the pistol and screams were heard from all directions. The priest was often among the toughest in the village and was likely to charge into the fray with a pistol of his own, invoking the image of Christ, in a moment of exasperation, lashing at His people in the temple.

Children were commonly beaten if they misbehaved in school. I recall my own schooldays in Aba when a teacher held a knife in his hand to threaten a student who talked back. One of my best friends used his ever-present open knife to be funny. He would hide the blade in an ingenious way and invite a school mate to sit down. The unfortunate dupe would jump up, screaming, with blood flowing from his behind, as my friend choked with laughter. Fights between two villages were common when one of the teams, as is the inevitable rule of the game, lost. These confrontations often involved sticks, daggers and pistols. There were always casualties, but almost never any deaths. And so I and many of my countrymen had a certain tolerance of violence that allowed us to feel somewhat at home dodging bullets, whether they were fired in joy or in anger. Phyllis, of course, grew up with a different experience. Yet her optimism and her love for Lebanon and the Lebanese led her to accept these daily displays of violence. She took them as primitive rituals from an ancient past that did not reflect negatively on the people.

Now in the mid 1970s a new and unfamiliar type of violence was emerging. Public examples of the type we knew were generally of short duration, and of a highly personal or social character. But perhaps because this type of violence was customary, the escalating violence of the mid 1970s permeated our consciousness quite slowly. As we sat on our balcony, overlooking the peaceful garden and the previously peaceful city of Beirut, we began to hear regular bouts of extensive shooting.

Momom became alarmed and agitated one evening as the sky lit up with the comet-like tails of trailer bullets. She screamed and shouted in horrified confusion, 'What the hell is going on?'

'Oh, it must be Palestinians fighting Palestinians.' I tried to fulfil my role as the supposed expert on Middle Eastern affairs by answering as nonchalantly as possible.

The next morning, Momom read the full account in the English paper. An Israeli military unit had arrived by sea and hijacked a taxi. They had driven the stolen vehicle to the target site in Ras Beirut. The Israelis had killed three Palestinian leaders and withdrawn under the cover of night. Momom was terribly worried and edgy.

'This is the beginning of a war,' she declared.

'Not at all, mother,' replied her daughter, the practical Phyllis. 'This is the Middle East, remember, and the battle between Arabs and Israelis goes on all the time. Don't worry, Lebanon is really not involved in it.'

The next evening Momom heard more shooting, and even more disturbing sounds. These were new sounds that she could not associate with pistols, rifles or the machine-gun rattle she had become familiar with.

'Oh, this is nothing to concern us.' Phyllis tried with limited success to reassure her jittery mother. 'The sounds you hear are likely to be explosions, home-made bombs. You know, Molotov cocktails? Or perhaps they are car bombs.'

'Car bombs,' repeated the mother, far from reassured. 'What in the world are car bombs?'

'Well, as I understand it, the bomber gets a car, fills it with explosives, puts a type of trigger in it and positions it in a carefully chosen place. There is some kind of gadget the bomber operates from a distance at a certain moment so that the car explodes, creating havoc as it kills everyone in range.' Phyllis's analytical training made her explanation seem cool and objective.

'My God!' Momom was now more agitated than ever. 'Who does such a horrible thing and why?'

'Take Hani, a friend of Elie's and an active anti-Israeli.' Phyllis seemed to think that if she gave her mother some examples of real people whose lives were affected by targeted violence, Momom would realize that she herself was safe. 'An Israeli gang booby-trapped his car one night. In the morning when Hani turned the key in the ignition to start his car, his world was totally changed. The car exploded, Hani watched his right hand fly out of the car window and his entire body was covered in blood. Fortunately, Hani lived. After a year in the hospital he is now fully recovered and learning to cope without his hand.'

'What!' Momom shrieked, coming to a conclusion opposite to the one Phyllis had intended. 'A friend of Elie's? Then this could happen to Elie.'

'No, Momom, Elie is not involved in this way,' Phyllis soothed. 'Hani was the first to mastermind the hijacking of three aeroplanes. His purpose was to focus world attention on the tragedy of the Palestinians.'

'And did he?'

'We do not know,' Phyllis had to admit. 'In this political climate we no longer know what works and what doesn't.'

Another evening, another vodka martini, and other sounds reached the ears of our Momom in her nerve-shattered state.

'Phyllis, what is this? This is a new sound, not automatic gunfire, not a car bomb and certainly not trailer bullets.'

'This,' answered Phyllis confidently, 'is an anti-aircraft gun.'

'But there are no craft in the air,' Momom asserted weakly. 'Neither friend nor enemy.'

'Well, mother,' explained Phyllis, 'anti-aircraft weapons are now being used in Lebanon against individuals and against small groups. The American Phantom jets that Israel employs are immune to these old-fashioned weapons. But in these battles, weapons are not discarded. They may be demoted, but never discarded. Weapons have become part of the culture, and soon, mother, the tank may replace the machine-gun as the plaything of Lebanese and Palestinians.'

Her look of absolute horror indicated clearly that we were losing Momom. Bebop was losing Momom. Bebop liked action and activity,

208

and he was not especially fazed by the sporadic shootings in Beirut. He wondered if the boys he had trained in American games were now passionate fighters in the Maronite militias that were springing up in defence of the motherland against the incursions of Palestinians and their leftist allies.

Our villa straddled a Maronite-rightist village and a Sunni-leftist Sibnai. Our home became the forum for the few wise heads left in the heat of this bitterly divisive ideological conflict. The Sunnis asked for our intervention in persuading their Maronite neighbours not to fight with them.

'We have been neighbours for a century,' the Sunni leaders pointed out, 'and we should go on being neighbours.'

The Maronite community came to us to express exactly the same feeling, even as both parties took up arms and regarded each other with fear. Something stronger than their individual desire for peace was dragging them into a conflict neither of them wanted. The entire Maronite village walked in a peaceful procession, carrying candles, to Sunni Sibnai to show their good intentions. The Sunnis responded with cheers and extravagant hospitality.

'We are brothers,' the cries rang out, 'we will never fight.'

Momom, however, looked upon these festivities with growing suspicion. She was coming to believe that our very villa, with its spacious garden of trees and flowers, was likely to be the battleground of Christians against Muslims, of rightists against leftists, even of America against the Soviet Union. It did not take long for a visitor to Lebanon to notice that every conflict, no matter how trivial it was, was a mimetic representation of the conflict between the two superpowers.

In the Lebanese troubles that were worsening in the mid 1970s, the Soviets had clearly sided with the Palestinians. The alliance extended to include the socialists, the communists and an array of leftist parties that had coalesced under the banner of the National Movement. America, to Phyllis's sorrow and mine, had always allied itself with Israel. Because of this partnership, the United States favoured the rightist Christian militias now surreptitiously making contact with Israel and gaining its support against the Palestinians. Syria and Iraq were not on good terms at this time. Syria sided with the Muslim left as did Libya, while Iraq sided with the Christian right. Momom's suspicions turned out to be well founded. Without being conscious of it, those who are steeped in a situation of conflict often absorb portentous details. Within a few days, hostilities broke out with a vengeance and Beirut – the peaceful cosmopolitan city of restaurants, clubs and theatres – was transformed into a battle zone.

Now there was no way we could persuade Momom to stay. Even husbands generally reputed to be tough, stubborn and the most opinionated of partners have been known to succumb to the naggings of their wives. Bebop was no exception. While Momom had been in tears for her excruciating 'aloneness' in Lebanon, Bebop was now in tears with the pain of having to leave his Lebanese paradise for the pale, uneventful life he knew he would have in Philadelphia. Ernie had retired, and to return for him meant living in a tiny apartment, with all he could afford on his retirement benefits, and to lead a dreary existence – no real challenges and no excitement to compare with life with his beloved daughter and her family.

He had made a home in Ba'bda, and loved visiting the village of Bterram. He enjoyed his excursions to Beirut, and he wallowed in the warmth of our home. His second daughter Bonnie had become more Lebanese than American and would continue to live by the side of her model sister. Although they were back in Philadelphia, Ernie's son Bill was independent now and so was Peter. Ernie knew that boys in America become their own masters once they graduate from high school. The boys would see their parents, would even visit and occasionally dine with them, but the creed of individualism is American through and through. To make it on your own is a cultural imperative. To fly out of the nest at eighteen is expected. In many nests, to linger past that age of demarcation could mean paying rent and sharing telephone bills and other expenses.

Phyllis and I accepted the inevitable and with deep pain helped as the Sells packed and prepared to return to America. To leave Lebanon in the mid 1970s with the war gaining momentum day by day was itself an operation involving risks. To move even from one village to another was hazardous. Every local group had checkpoints to protect their communities against outsiders. From Ba'bda to Beirut and on to the airport or seaport there were dozens of checkpoints to pass, and it was not always easy to discern the political stamp of each.

For the most part, the Salems had no enemies on either side of the conflict, and we felt in no danger when weaving our way in and out of checkpoints and roadblocks. Our own students or our very neighbours were often sentries stationed there. Irrespective of conflicting loyalties and ideologies, all of the partisans liked us personally. Phyllis's students in the Department of English or Cultural Studies at AUB and BCW idolized her and would gladly take risks themselves in order to ensure her safety.

The American government was urging its citizens in Lebanon to leave. Britain and France sent ships to Beirut and evacuated hundreds of foreign residents, even including some jittery Lebanese. The Sells became part of the evacuation. They left on a British ship, and from Europe were transported by air to Philadelphia. The evacuees sent back colourful letters. In retrospect, they were able to enjoy the excitement of leaving. They exaggerated the dangers they had faced, and the pain of leaving their beloved Beirut. They promised to return as soon as the fighting calmed down. How long can a conflict in Lebanon last, they reflected – a month, perhaps a season, maybe even a year? Impossible that it should be any longer, not in Lebanon, not among the Lebanese. It was unthinkable that it could continue for more than fifteen years. In the midst of the forest one can only discern the trees, the low bushes and the little animals and insects that scurry about. The forest is out of sight.

9

Yes, there was a Palestinian-leftist militia in West Beirut, and a Christian militia in East Beirut. In the west was the charismatic character Kamal Junblat, a wealthy feudal landlord with the most opulent palace in Lebanon. He had turned socialist and allied himself with the *sans culottes* Palestinians. And in the east was the handsome Maronite statesman Camille Chamoun, an ex-president of Lebanon from former prosperous times. By his side was the wiry athletic and energetically passionate Phalangist Pierre Gemayal. Alongside the Lebanese left stood many Palestinian leaders, all carrying the Abu insignia. Arafat was known as Abu Ammar, although he was not married nor had he sired a firstborn son – Ammar. Others of this group included Abu Iyyad, Abu Jihad, Abu al Lutuf, Abu al-Hasan, Abu Mazen and many many others. The Christians branded the group as the Abawat, signifying the plural of Abu.

The Christian militias had no Abu designation, but they had plenty of Ab, or father, to signify a Maronite cleric. In times of conflict the Maronites function as a tribe. Lebanon is their refuge. The Maronites chose the country early on, some fourteen centuries ago, as their safe haven from persecution, first from the Orthodox Byzantines and later from the Muslim caliphs, sultans and amirs. The Maronite Church and the Lebanese state were joined in an inseparable symbiosis. The Maronite Church is hierarchic and militant, and does not shrink from a fight when it feels threatened.

In my youth I saw a movie called *Don Camillo*, whose star was the French comedian Fernandel. Don Camillo was an Ab, a Catholic priest bent on fighting the communists in Italy. He carried the cross as a club with which to batter the heads of infidel Italians, followers of that German Satan, Karl Marx. 'Hold on, Christ,' he would shout as he stormed communist demonstrations in the back-alleys of Rome. In the Maronite tradition the cleric is often a militant father. He counsels, he carries arms, he has visions and he interprets the course of events. Above the Ab is the Abati, the supervisor of Maronite clerics. Any mention of a Maronite militia had to include consideration of their patron, Abati Qassis, followed by Abati Ni'man. One evening in the height of the conflict I saw Abati Qassis in action. I must note that while the war raged on in the streets of Beirut, social life continued as if it were in a time zone of its own. Phyllis and I enjoyed a good drink on most evenings and we hosted many such gatherings ourselves.

On this particular evening, Abati Qassis was standing with the Ambassador of Kuwait, the Ambassador of Egypt and some half a dozen Lebanese, discussing the internal war and weighing gains and losses. The Ambassdaor of Kuwait shook the hand of the Abati and congratulated him on the escape of Camille Chamoun from an assassination attempt that had taken place the day before.

'It was never really a problem,' answered the Abati. 'President Chamoun cannot be assassinated.'

'Indeed, what good news,' was the bemused response from the Ambassador. 'And how does he manage that? Is he not mortal like the rest of us? Since we are all facing these dangers daily, including assassination attempts, I am sure we would all like to know his secret.'

All ears were now attuned as the Abati said in a low and certain voice, 'You see, when President Chamoun gets in the car, the Virgin Mary comes in immediately and sits by his side. She puts her protective arm around his neck. Any bullet fired at Chamoun will be deflected by the Virgin's protective arm.'

The Kuwaiti Ambassador, not schooled in Maronite lore, thought the Abati was joking, and being the good diplomat, laughed encouragingly. He found to his surprise that he was the only one laughing. Everyone else listening knew that the Abati was completely serious, and his demeanour confirmed it. The Abati did not at all appreciate the Kuwaiti reaction. Consequently, it took all the perfumes of Arabia to sweeten the air between the two men.

A few years later, the foreign minister of Khomeini's Iran visited Lebanon, and that same Kuwaiti ambassador, who by now was the dean of Arab ambassadors in Beirut, was assigned to accompany him. The Kuwaiti Ambassador drove the Iranian Minister to the airport on the day after President Jimmy Carter had sent a clandestine military force to free the American hostages in Tehran. The hostages had been taken by Iranian revolutionaries and kept at the command of Khomeini, perhaps as a way of putting pressure on the US to abandon its support of Khomeini's arch enemy – the Shah. The rescue force came in helicopters to attempt a night-time liberation. Somehow the operation was bungled and the force had to withdraw before it even reached Tehran. It was a most humiliating moment for the US. So Mr Uwayjan, the Kuwaiti Ambassador to war-shattered Lebanon, thought it diplomatic to congratulate the Minister on the humiliation of the American force.

'No problem,' the Iranian Minister replied serenely. 'You see, Allah in His Glory fights our wars for us.' He then closed his eyes reverently and recited a surah from the Qur'an attesting to Allah's intervention in saving his people – the Muslims. 'You recall the story of the elephant?' he asked. 'We are told how Allah in His Glory sent a horde of birds. And how the horde pelted the elephant-riders with special stones and totally annihilated them.' The Foreign Minister, Persian-speaking, recited the verse in Arabic of course, as Korani verses are meant to be recited. He did so with confidence, and turned to the Ambassador to acknowledge the latter's approval.

The brilliant Kuwaiti completed the verse with equally strong conviction as a definitive political statement on the American–Iranian conflict. When a few days later, Uwayjan visited us in Ba'bda, he told us of his encounter with the Foreign Minister of Shiite Iran. 'I do not know,' Uwayjan smiled, 'who is crazier, the Maronite Abati or the Shiite minister.'

Which led us easily to a consideration of the broader questions.

'Maronites and Shiites,' Uwayjan pointed out, 'are schisms from mainstream religions. We, the Sunnis, and you, the Orthodox Christians, are mainstream. We fight our own battles with no expectation of transcendental alliances. We are not doing well lately, perhaps we should reconsider.'

For the facts of politics in the Middle East are so permeated by religious considerations that it is virtually impossible to make clear-cut distinctions between them. Often a movement claims a secular format to pronounce its relevance to the modern age, but no sooner is the form revealed then the religious component reasserts its primacy. Such is the bond between religion and politics in our region, that the Book and the street, the fact and the myth, the natural and the supernatural are entirely interdependent and intertwined.

The extreme tensions had caused the president of AUB to become distinctly nervous. Once the internal war erupted, he was not only nervous, but truly fearful for his safety and for the stability of the institution he led. The war in the minds of those who waged it pitted the United States against the Soviets. Whether these superpowers considered themselves pitted against each other or not was not questioned. In war, image can be as important as reality. Because the student body was largely leftist-leaning due to its identification with the Palestinian cause, the president of AUB became the enemy.

Kirkwood telephoned me several times a day. I was the dean closest to him. He trusted me, and I was familiar to all the various factions, right and left. So I was not surprised one evening when he called me at home. 'Elie, will you kindly come down for a meeting?'

Meetings were his most common means of escape from loneliness and helplessness. So I went into Beirut to meet with President Kirkwood. Phyllis anxiously awaited my return. Kirkwood's style was to govern by committee and no one was going to change that. He was originally an obstetrician and though he seemed patient and laid back, in reality he burned with anxiety and frustration. An American Ambassador was killed at a checkpoint. A French Ambassador was missing and found dead. An American businessman was missing, taken hostage. Every day brought with it events and disruptions unheard of in most universities. The American government was urging the American faculty to leave. Government directives encouraged the president to be cautious and not to leave Marquand House where some dozen bodyguards were kept posted. All American wives and children were to be evacuated without further delay.

'This does not apply to me,' said Phyllis. 'I am Lebanese.'

Kirkwood was at the end of his tether and pleaded with me to forgo my Ba'bda villa and move into a spacious apartment on campus. 'We need to run the university, Elie,' he said desperately. 'I need you by my side night and day.'

It really was becoming more difficult to travel back and forth between Ba'bda and Ras Beirut. We decided to move on campus to help keep the battered ship on course through the stormiest waters she had ever sailed. Viewing the move as quite temporary, we took very few possessions. Our cook, called Bashir, had the opposite inclination. Bashir, a Sunni Muslim from the Sudan, was devout. He prayed five times a day, in strict compliance with the rules of Islam. The Maronite neighbourhood children enjoyed Bashir's cookies and loved his company. We asked Bashir to leave the Ba'bda house to Allah's care and come and join us on campus. Bashir agreed but he insisted on bringing his pots and pans and his live chickens.

'How can you do that, Bashir?' Phyllis was sceptical.

'Allah will help,' was the cook's short and confident answer.

Bashir planned to take a taxi to the Green Line, the no man's land separating the combatants of East and West Beirut. It was so called because grass and shrubberies had grown over the paved streets and the exclusive shops of old. We would wait for Bashir on the other side of the line. He would walk the three hundred metres between the lines carrying his possessions. Knowing it could be dangerous for him at a time when people were killed merely on the basis of their identity, we pleaded with him to leave the utensils and the chicken and move with us.

'No.' Bashir was adamant and that was it.

'OK.' I gave in. 'But remember Bashir that God is all-knowing and all-forgiving. If at a Christian checkpoint you are asked about your religion, just say Christian. This is not a sin. It is a mechanism for survival sanctioned by all religions.'

'OK, OK.' Bashir was curt and clearly did not like the way this conversation was going. 'You no worry.'

Worry we did of course. We contacted everyone we knew on both sides of the conflict to please let Bashir cross in peace. At the assigned time and place Phyllis and I waited for Bashir. We strained our necks in the hope of a glimpse of a fat, round, brown man. Bashir insisted he was brown.

'If you think I am black,' he would laugh, 'just wait until you see the cook of Khaireddin – that is black.'

As we waited, we kept the car radio on for any news about check-points, kidnappings, corpses found in deserted places, snipers and other features of the strange times we lived in. No kidnappings or deaths were announced on Bashir's route, but he was late, worryingly late.

'Wait, wait, there is Bashir!' Phyllis cried out joyfully. You could hardly see him. He was loaded with pots and pans of all sizes, all that a trained and accomplished wrestler could carry. Chickens were flapping their wings and screaming for safe passage. Bashir now was certainly not brown. He was yellow. Quickly, we bundled him into the car and raced to our temporary abode on campus.

'Bashir, what in the world happened?' Phyllis waited to hear the details before she could give rein to her feelings of great relief at having Bashir restored to us.

The cook took a deep breath, thanked Allah for His generosity and proceeded to tell us his tale. The first checkpoint in Hazmieh was occupied by very bad people, bad Christians, not really followers of Issa. The cook referred to Christ by his name in the Qur'an. The partisans asked Bashir if he was Muslim. 'Praise be to Allah, I am a Muslim,' our proud Bashir had responded. 'And I am proud of that. Allah is all-powerful, and He will judge the infidels.'

Now it was our turn to take a deep breath as Bashir continued.

'The zealot at the checkpoint cursed me and kicked me and ordered his people to "liquidate" me. I shouted loud then that I work for Dr Elie Salem in Ba'bda and reminded them that they all know Dr Elie Salem.' At this, one of the young boys, who knew Bashir and our family well, had mercifully come to Bashir's rescue. Our friend and three other Ba'bda boys put Bashir in their own partisan car and drove him to the Green Line. 'Allah saved me,' Bashir repeated again and again.

'Yes,' I added, 'with the help of four infidels.'

'No infidels,' protested Bashir. 'Good boys, friends of our children. They loved my desserts, most of all my speciality, umm 'Ali.'

Militias spend half their time fighting and the other half raising money. Money and power are inseparable. Spengler writes that the first election in Rome in the pre-Christian era was bought by cash. Man has experimented with all types of methods to collect funds for government, for party, for institutions and for family. One method, previously unknown to university presidents but then widely in use, was kidnapping. Kidnappings occurred constantly. When they were for political reasons, the kidnappings often ended in assassination. But many were simply for ransom. Sometimes the two objectives got mixed up, as in the case of the AUB librarian. He had no money with him and it was perhaps because he was American that he was unfortunately killed. I learned from a militia leader that a kidnapped person with no money on him was an embarrassment to the kidnappers and was usually badly beaten for wasting their time.

In those awful days I called frequent faculty meetings, depending on the gravity of the current crisis. After two members of our faculty were kidnapped in one day and one of them badly beaten, I called for an urgent meeting. I told the faculty what I had learned from the militia leader, which only confirmed our experience. 'Each of you should carry a minimum of a hundred dollars at all times,' I instructed. 'Then, if you're kidnapped, they will take the money and set you free. If you carry only ten or fifteen dollars, you are likely to be beaten up.'

The faculty members had a tendency common to most teaching staff to make fun of authority. Professor Ted Kennedy, a bearded, scholarly mathematician, took the floor and asked his question in all seriousness. 'Should faculty members carry cash in accordance with their rank. For example, should an associate professor carry more than an assistant professor? How about faculty on tenure like myself? Sir, am I in your opinion valued at a hundred dollars, or at a million dollars, as I value myself?'

As the faculty roared with laughter, I resorted to the trick of timing and I called for an adjournment. Amidst the savagery of war there was always plenty of joking, an abundance of drinking and a rather amazing quantity of good times between killings. Perhaps we tended to celebrate daily to prove that we were still alive.

With her special gift, Phyllis ensured that our apartment on campus was a warm meeting place for faculty and staff. We drank, we told jokes, we recounted the affairs of the day, thus sending out the message that we were here to stay. This is a university worth saving, was our stance – and it is worthy of sacrifice. War is not only a front where direct engagement takes place. War is also a state of mind, affecting each person, and as of April 1975 Lebanon was at war. It is probably more accurate to say that Lebanon was a battleground for warring parties, each with its own agenda.

The most dangerous element in this internal war was the total absence of state authority. As there were dozens of militias, we had dozens of types of order, and therefore no overarching order at all. Perhaps it is impossible to appreciate fully the wisdom and depth of Thomas Hobbes's *Leviathan*, without living through an internal war and the personal experience and terror of anarchy. In that state, Hobbes wrote, man's life is 'nasty, brutish, and short'. When a failing student in the Department of English forced his American professor, with pistol in hand, to change his marks to a passing grade, what could the professor do? What is the appropriate response when a student claiming to be short on cash threatens the registrar, requiring to be listed for graduation or the registrar will be killed? These were daily issues.

My instructions to the faculty were to refer all such cases to me, and I tried to handle them by enforcing some degree of discipline. This often involved the intervention of militia leaders in Ras Beirut – Palestinian, Lebanese and mixed. Often I confiscated pistols and put them in my office until the students cooled off or until the exam was over. Management then was *ad hoc*, entailing much bravado and much fear.

Sitting in my office I heard distant shots, and since they were not particularly impressive ones, paid little attention. They were single pistol shots, which were unfamiliar to ears tuned as ours were to Kalashnikovs, anti-aircraft guns, tank guns and the sort of explosions that brought down buildings and shattered cars. A few minutes later I thought I heard a few more, similarly insignificant, shots. Then the phone rang, and it was Kirkwood. 'Elie, a Palestinian student who was failing an engineering course just shot and killed Dean Ghosn, then proceeded to West Hall where he shot and killed Dean Najemy. The murderer is now outside, in the corridor. He is outside my office and bent on shooting me. He says for all to hear that he will then come to Jesup Hall and kill you, and after you all the other deans.'

When the phone went dead, I assumed the killer had got in and that the president had hung up the phone in fear. I thought Kirkwood must be dead. Raymond Ghosn had been the Dean of the Faculty of Engineering and Architecture and was the leading architect in Lebanon. He was an inordinately gentle soul, young and unmarried, with a brilliant future before him. Robert Najemy was the Dean of Students. He was an American of Lebanese origin, and so proud of his achievements at AUB and his service to Lebanon. Kirkwood, a most dedicated president, an honest, straightforward and puritan man, could also be dead.

My gut reaction in a crisis is to dash towards the scene of the action and take charge. Mad with rage, I raced from my desk in the direction of the president's office. My colleagues in the faculty saw me and read my mind. They knew me well. They also knew what was happening. Some twenty of them got hold of me, literally picked me up and carried me straight to our apartment. Phyllis and Paul were at home, unaware of the murder outside and of the impending danger to me. Some ten of my colleagues stayed with me, physically restraining me, holding me in place. Some ten or more locked the door and guarded it from the outside. Never in the turbulent history of relations between deans and faculty members have faculty members come to the rescue of their dean as my colleagues did on that fateful day. Paul, in his early teens, was most concerned, and lectured me on discretion being the better part of valour.

The series of events that culminated in the assassination of the two deans included the murder of the librarian and a stream of kidnappings of faculty members, staff and students, some for ransom and some never to be seen again. The American government ordered all Americans in Lebanon to leave and many did. Kirkwood was recalled to New York, and the dean of the Faculty of Medicine, Dr Craig Lichtenwalner, was asked to serve as acting president.

We concluded that Lichtenwalner's orders were to close the university, as he went from one faculty member to the next and from house to house on campus, chanting the same refrain. 'Can't you see, the king has no clothes?' he would urge. 'I advise you to leave, to find employment somewhere else. The university cannot continue like this; soon we will be unable to pay the faculty because students are no longer paying fees.'

I led a counter-movement. I decided that it was incumbent upon me as dean of the Faculty of Arts and Sciences, the hub of the university, to do so. I called a series of faculty meetings and invited professors from all other faculties, most of whom attended.

'This university will never close,' I declared. 'The Americans were ordered to leave by their government, but no one can order us to leave. We are staying and will keep the academic programme alive to the best of our ability. If the university cannot pay salaries, we will teach for free until salaries can be paid once more.'

The faculty badly needed unequivocal reassurance and they stood and cheered at these remarks. I offered them a challenge and the entire faculty responded. Phyllis attended these meetings, together with the dozen or so other Americans who refused to abandon ship. Phyllis had an important leadership role in the forefront of our counter-movement. She opened our house for the faculty and created the space for us to meet and encourage one another. A sombre comptroller, who had previously never cracked a smile, came alive at our evening meetings. He drank, he gave his strong opinions, he sang and he danced. To see his two hundred and twenty pounds jumping up and down in drunken happiness was a sign to the faculty that he would pay their salaries on time. Phyllis arranged a series of games and got everyone involved in them.

It was an amazing demonstration of how people rally together in crisis, and how easily they can extend themselves when given an opportunity. Phyllis commissioned a professor to write a play and then she mobilized the ambassadors of Britain, Germany, Italy and Austria to support it and take acting roles in the production. The play was called *The Marchioness of Saden Saden* and was written by Professor Kamal Salibi of the History Department. He even set the piece to music. Phyllis directed the play and staged it to the great acclaim of the Beiruti audience.

Dorothy wrote from her new small apartment in Philadelphia urging us to leave Beirut and join them. 'How close are you to the fighting?' she asked us in one of her infrequent phone calls.

'Don't worry,' we answered. 'We are well out of harm's way. Fighting is at least two blocks from here.'

'Only two blocks away!' We could hear Dorothy scream on the phone. 'Get out! Get out of there right now!'

And Phyllis and I could only laugh. Behind the laughter, we knew, were bitter tears. We felt such deep abiding sorrow to see Lebanon destroyed, to see our liberal democratic order torn to pieces and our civilized image shattered. Lebanon had been known as the land of fun, of peace, the place in the Middle East where a good life was very possible. But this Beirut, this peaceful, pleasant Beirut, had become a symbol of fear and terrorism. At the height of the fighting, almost no restaurants dared to remain open. One of the ones that did was a tiny French restaurant just above Hamra. Phyllis and I would occasionally sneak out around noon to have lunch there and share a bottle of wine. On the way back, driving with Phyllis by my side, I could almost feel happy, full of smiles. On one of these stolen afternoons we drove from the restaurant back to campus with shells showering our path – exploding either a few metres behind us or a few metres ahead.

'Elie,' Phyllis confided, 'are we being irresponsible? After all, we have four children at home.'

'Rely on Allah,' I replied with a grin, 'and let's enjoy what we can.'

And so we did. We were not talking about simple enjoyment or the fun normally associated with it. We were actually talking about responding to the challenge to go on with our lives, to regain our country, once again to control our university, to renew our souls as Lebanese.

As the country divided into various cantons, each under a militia leader, so did the army. If there was a government at all, it was a federal-type structure severely shorn of its powers. Dr Khalil Salem was my cousin and a law-abiding director general of the Ministry of Finance who refused payment to a breakaway unit of the army. The day after his refusal, my cousin disappeared. After days of intensive inquiry, I found him dead in the boot of his own car. A decomposed body after a week in the summer heat is beyond recognition. It took me several hours to confirm that this mutilated corpse was that of my cousin. Although we surmised who the killers were, it was of no use. No government authority existed and therefore no official investigation was possible. No punishment could be imposed and we could only keep quiet and survive. Few indeed in Ras Beirut even dared come to my house to pay their condolences. Still fewer dared to whisper the name of the unit and its leader. While in the midst of receiving the small number of condolences that were offered, I received a phone call. I was now acting president of the university, and I was informed that the same unit had just entered the campus.

They moved in with two tanks, two personnel carriers and a long-range cannon. I ran down the steps to the lower campus, and there was the breakaway colonel with a thick black beard and his troops drawn up behind him. I rushed up to him, I embraced him, deposited juicy kisses on his cheeks, all the while introducing myself and pleading with him to withdraw and keep the campus neutral in this bloody fight. He swore by the Qu'ran he would only fire nine rounds on East Beirut and then he would withdraw. I returned home immediately.

'Phyllis,' I urgently sought her help, 'call the Palestinian professors to meet with me now. Then contact the ambassadors we know well and ask them to interfere.'

When we met, I charged my Palestinian colleagues to go immediately to Arafat headquarters and ask him to remove his ally from campus. Within the hour, Arafat called me and told me he had sent his personal aide to remove the colonel. Meanwhile, the colonel shook the campus and shattered windows, cabinets and other glass with his cannonade. I remained close to the colonel, urging him to hasten his withdrawal and to restrain his wild hashish-intoxicated soldiers from harming the many men, women and children who had gathered on the football field to follow the unfolding drama.

A day or two after we evicted the tanks I spotted a French helicopter hovering over the campus. As the craft landed on our football field, I raced to the site, and in broken French asked the pilot politely to take off at once and never again land on the campus grounds. The pilot was civil, but he had orders to land on campus as the safest place in Ras Beirut for his passengers – a French commission of five officers – to disembark with the minimum of danger. From our campus they planned to walk to the French embassy. As Beirut was a small city, and as fierce fighting was only a block or two from campus, there was no way to ensure the safety of the officers. Bullets were whizzing overhead night and day, and anyone out in the open ran the risk of being hit.

The shelling was so intense as to shatter the nerves of the coolest amongst us. Our eldest child Lisa finally had had enough. 'I must leave now,' she declared after several months of war in 1975. 'I will take the first plane I can get and enrol in an American university.' Phyllis and I opposed her departure, but she insisted to the point of hysteria. We yielded. Our younger daughter, Nina, was in a leftist-liberationist mode, strongly identifying with the Palestinian cause and in no mood to leave. Adib, our older son, was highly political, committed to Lebanon and to its army or what was left of it; he was happy fighting his battles on campus against the Palestinians and their leftist allies. This was quite dangerous for him. Paul, the youngest child, was reflective and concerned about personal consequences – but he worried more about some perceived rashness on his father's part than about his own safety. That is until the afternoon that some local militia boys put a Kalashnikov to his head, and demanded, 'Hey, are you Arab?'

'Yes,' answered Paul. 'I am.'

'Then why are you so fair?' they prodded. 'Are you sure you are not American?'

'I told you I am an Arab.' Paul remained steadfast.

'Are you proud of your Arabism?'

'Yes.'

'In that case, go.'

When Paul recounted his close brush with death, we decided to send him to the United States the very next day. Lisa, in panic from the dizzying drone of the shelling, had left a few weeks earlier to stay with the Sells in Philadelphia. We made the necessary special security arrangements and drove Paul to the airport. Of course, driving in Beirut meant crossing several checkpoints with nervous young men equipped with pistols, hand-grenades and Kalashnikovs. At each checkpoint we had to stop, introduce ourselves, invoke the names of whichever big shots would impress the partisans of the particular stripe we had encountered, and hope for the best. Many of our friends had been killed at checkpoints quite indiscriminately. When law collapses the void is filled according to the mood of the moment. What made these kids even more irresponsible was the hotchpotch of their nationalities. The National Movement, under the rubric of Palestine, socialism and rebelliousness, attracted desperate, often reckless legions. In addition to Lebanese and Palestinians, Syrians poured into the fray, and Iraqis, Jordanians, Sudanese, Libyans and a few Japanese and Latin Americans as well.

The wide network of connections that Phyllis and I had culti-vated served us well throughout the fifteen-year-war. With half of our children in the US and the other half here, weaving into and out of an array of dangerous situations, I urged Phyllis to take Nina and Adib to the US and to enrol them in a normal school. In the mid 1970s the schools in Beirut had become gathering points for demonstrations, for recruitment to any of a number of causes and for back-up support for the various militia groups. Phyllis agreed reluctantly.

She felt she had no choice. She had come as an American bride, but she had become Lebanese. It was against her core principles to leave her country. And yet, she had to ensure the safety of the children. Only by fulfilling her fundamental responsibilities as a mother would she be able to give her best to the situation at hand in the university, in Lebanon, and in the tight community of which she was so integral a part. In deep agony over the need to make such a choice, she departed to the United States with Nina and Adib and established a family home in Doylestown, Pennsylvania. They rented an apartment and she put the children in school.

Phyllis suffered great loneliness away from Beirut. She was totally miserable and bored as well. In our daily phone conversations, she complained bitterly. 'Hell,' she said, 'is not Beirut but the deadly quiet and paleness of Doylestown.'

'You should be happy,' I tried to reassure my wife, 'now you are all safe.'

'No,' she practically screamed, 'I prefer the thud of the anti-aircraft guns to the peace of Doylestown. I am returning to Beirut.'

Each time a brief cease-fire was called, she began packing up the children to return to their lives. Of course the fighting would begin again and she would realize that it was impossible. After a restless three months, Phyllis could no longer stay away. She arranged to leave the children behind in safety with her family and came back to Beirut.

Institutions are usually only as stable as the countries in which they exist. During the war, AUB lost its stability. The Americans who founded it were no longer certain about its continuity. Most of the American faculty had left. After the departure of Kirkwood, the Trustees searched for a new president who was daring enough or crazy enough to take the position. They found one in Dr Harold Hoelcher. Dr Hoelcher, or Hal as he became known to us, was a chubby congenial fellow, prone to tell jokes about high technology, a field he felt comfortable in. The trustees introduced him to the faculty as a daring man, perfect for this difficult phase in the university's life.

The university was governed by the president who was supported by the deans of the various faculties. Once a week, the Board of Deans met under the chairmanship of the president to discuss university issues and make decisions concerning them. In his first meeting with the board, Hal Hoelcher wanted us to admire him as a brave, visionary leader, utterly unaffected by the chaos reigning all about us. He opened the meeting by recounting his bravery in war, although he did not say which war. He was too young for the Second World War and too old for the Korean War. At one point, he solemnly intoned, 'I want you to know that I have killed a man.' Not to miss an opportunity so blatantly offered, I looked at him in equal solemnity and asked, 'Was he a dean, sir?' This led to a great deal of appreciative laughter that had the result of dispelling the awe with which Hal was trying to inspire us.

As the meeting proceeded, he received an urgent telephone call. He listened, his face turned pale and his lower lip began to quiver. I was truly worried. It seemed our new leader was about to have a heart attack. He put the phone down, and with a voice between a choke and a croak, turned to me and said, 'Dean Salem, run home! Meeting dismissed.' Then he did the most extraordinary thing. He put his head between his hands and repeated, 'My God, oh my God.' Our fierce lion of a president turned out to be more like that famous lion in *The Wizard of Oz*.

I was alarmed by Hal's performance and raced home, followed by my colleagues. To my great relief and amusement, I discovered it was only our Nubian cook, Aziz, running in and out of the campus house screaming, 'A bomb, a bomb.' The house looked normal. The only damage, if any, seemed to be in the mind of Aziz. He was a heavy drinker, a hashish smoker and one of the most delightful characters on campus. When Phyllis and I interviewed him, we couldn't distinguish between the fact and the fiction in his world, but we loved him nevertheless. The children treated him like a grandfather. Though in his forties, he looked nearer seventy. Aziz drank all day long, and every afternoon he walked our dog, Blitze, a female Belgian shepherd, in the back-alleys of Ras Beirut. Later we learned that Aziz used these rambles to buy and sell hashish.

One evening, as we approached our house, we saw a dog dangling from our tree. It was a big male dog, and the sight was awful. Phyllis screamed and found the cook. 'Aziz, what is this?'

'I hanged him,' Aziz replied with utter nonchalance, 'because he was pestering Blitze.'

We could believe neither our eyes nor our ears.

'Remove that poor animal before the children see it,' said Phyllis, regaining her composure. 'Go and bury it somewhere, and don't you ever do such a crazy thing again.'

Aziz obeyed and buried the martyred lover, but as for the future, prohibitions meant nothing to Aziz.

On the day of the bomb threat, Aziz was once again totally inebriated. He was his normal self, smiling, humble, eager to please, but with that distant look towards an infinite horizon. After calming him down, I inspected the house, room by room. There was nothing out of the ordinary on the first floor. I went up to the second floor and at first noticed nothing unusual. Then I saw a hunk of plaster from the old ceiling. No doubt when it had fallen it had made enough noise to drive our cook crazy – crazy enough to call the president and in his broken English put an end to what was promising to be an amusing first meeting between president and Board of Deans.

In his strange way, Hal welcomed adventure. He befriended a Palestinian militia leader, who presented him with a sub-machine-gun. Hal was inordinately proud of it, thinking it would add to his power and prestige. There was a convivial side to our new president. He was a *bon viveur* and a generous host. He and his wife Chub felt quite at ease with Phyllis and me, and we socialized a lot. Whether we agreed or disagreed, we maintained good relations. I ran the biggest faculty and he ran the university. We needed each other.

One evening as the Salems and the Hoelchers were drinking at his residence, the stately Marquand House, Hal made a startling declaration after a few drinks. 'Elie, don't be surprised if you find the body of Dean Raja Khoury, riddled with bullets, thrown in a dump in Ras Beirut.'

Raja Khoury was the dean of the Faculty of Medicine and was often at odds with Hal. Evidently the president felt that in the anarchy of Beirut, he could rid himself of a difficult dean. Phyllis and Chub stared at him in startled disbelief. As this to me was not a joking matter, I looked him fiercely in the eye. 'Hal, if a hair is touched on the head of Raja Khoury,' I said evenly, 'I will kill you myself.' Phyllis joined me, and scolded the president for even thinking such thoughts. His ever submissive wife, forlorn and down-trodden, gazed off into empty space.

10

Hal thus reigned unevenly until the Board of Trustees eventually fired him. My good friend Malcolm Kerr was mentioned as a possible successor and I supported him. At that time, Malcolm was serving as a full professor at the University of California in Los Angeles. Kerr always wanted to be president and was eager to accept the offer despite the fact that Beirut was a battleground. He was not daunted by the fact that the university was an endangered American institution in a strongly anti-American war zone.

I suggested that Malcolm should consider living at our house in Ba'bda until he was more acclimatized to Lebanon. He accepted the offer and would venture daily down to the campus with me. In the evening, we would return together to Ba'bda. After several weeks Malcolm was confident enough to move to Marquand House on campus. We all concluded that Kerr had nothing to fear since he was well known to be pro-Palestinian, pro-Arab and anti-Israeli.

On 5 June 1982, the Israeli army invaded Lebanon. On 6 June it had reached Ba'bda. Phyllis's attitudes were so thoroughly anti-Israeli that she could not even conceive of the possibility that the army would occupy the village we had selected as our home. When we drove to Ba'bda that evening, we found our route choked with Israeli tanks, armoured cars, jeeps and ambulances. Israeli troops seemed to be everywhere.

Just before we reached our house, we encountered an Israeli checkpoint. The soldiers were not allowing cars to go beyond their station. Phyllis immediately assumed that the Israelis had taken our house, as the most imposing in that area, and converted it into their headquarters. She screamed at them to let us pass but they would not budge. She threatened, as an American citizen, to call the American Ambassador in Beirut. Still, they would not budge. Instead of negotiating with these young and cocky Israeli youths, I found myself negotiating with my wife, pleading with Phyllis to return with me and not to make a scene. A scene it surely was, however, followed by a Salem retreat to campus. That night Phyllis slept poorly. She phoned her AUB friends to let off steam, raving about the injustice of it all.

I delayed our return to Ba'bda as long as I could. When a few days later we finally made it through the checkpoints and were able to reach our Ba'bda villa, we found the door wide open. The soldiers must have forced their way in, looking for whatever it is that soldiers search for among the civilian populace. We checked carefully from room to room and found nothing missing except two small artistic items of no real value. When we reached the balcony, however, we saw a naked Israeli soldier taking a shower in the garden with our watering hose. Now he received an additional shower, not of water but of insults. He was unfazed and just smiled and continued his watering and soaping as if no one was in sight. Farther down by the tennis court we saw piles of turds and paper tissue all over the place. The scene drove Phyllis utterly mad. Soldiers were walking in and out of our private shady garden, using it as a convenient latrine. Phyllis faced them with insults and shouted threats. 'Where were you raised, to do such a thing?' she demanded.

'I'm from Philadelphia,' answered one of the soldiers.

'An American?' Phyllis was astonished to hear the accent of her own home state. 'What are you doing here?'

The soldier shrugged, 'Ma'am, I am Jewish.'

Despite her entreaties and threats, the soldiers were unaffected and continued their private manoeuvres. In frustration, Phyllis motioned me to make a strategic retreat for now from our overrun house. We left our treasured books, icons and works of art to their uncertain fate and looked for a place to reconsider our options.

It was lunchtime, and we were accustomed to enjoying a nice steak and bottle of wine at our cosy Ba'bda restaurant, Relais de Chasse. But when we arrived at the restaurant we were as shocked as we had been at our house. It seemed that the entire Israeli officer corps was there. The Israeli army occupied all the tables. Dozens of officers waited outside for their turn to savour the fine Lebanese cuisine. The odds were against us. Certain to lose any engagement we might initiate, we withdrew. Phyllis was absolutely furious, but I did my best to remain stoic. Back we went to the AUB campus, which seemed to be the only place that was not occupied by Ariel Sharon's army.

Acutely aware of the potential danger of the war expanding to involve Israel and Syria, the American President sought to avoid any actions that might bring the Americans and the Soviets into direct confrontation in the Middle East. President Ronald Reagan therefore sent his ambassador, Philip Habib, on a mission of peace and reconciliation. Habib's mission was reminiscent of Napoleon's mission to Egypt in 1798. The rulers in Paris wanted to get rid of this ambitious Corsican colonel, so they sent him with fifteen thousand troops and ordered him to build a navy, escape the British fleet in the Mediterranean and destroy the Mamelukes then ruling Egypt. In addition, Napoleon was instructed to cut British communication lines to India, proceed from Egypt to Arabia and Iran, capture India from the British and return to Paris victorious.

Habib was given similarly impossible orders to bring peace to Lebanon, to prevent a Syrian–Israeli war and to ensure Israeli withdrawal from Lebanon. Unlike Napoleon, Habib was given no army! He supposedly had Reagan on his side, but Reagan was always preoccupied. The President liked Habib, and supported him to an extent. But Habib found it virtually impossible to induce Reagan to focus on the problems inherent in the situation or to keep his attention for any length of time.

Phil Habib was a prominent diplomat, born in Brooklyn of Lebanese parents. He loved Lebanon and was mad about Lebanese food. While so many others lost weight in the frustration of the factional fighting on Lebanese terrain, Habib actually gained weight. Phyllis and I met him when Habib first arrived and we liked him very much. He would spend his evenings with us, devouring Lebanese dishes, drinking arak and recalling his childhood. He regaled us with tales of his Lebanese mother and father and the sound of *kibbeh jurns* in Brooklyn. Habib had a frugal wife, who worried about his weight and his inability to stop eating once he started. Habib would walk into our kitchen with delight.

'Oh boy!' he often exclaimed, 'this is how a refrigerator should be – full of food, of cakes, of fruit, not like ours at home. My goddamned wife keeps our fridge nearly empty. Often I open it, and what do I see? – a box of cereal, a piece of cheese, a bottle of milk and, believe you me, a sole apple sitting there on a dish by itself. It makes me sick to look at such a fridge. You know, this may be one reason why I am always on a mission abroad.'

Phyllis was direct with Habib, as one blunt American to another. 'Phil, what are you doing about the cease-fire, about Israeli withdrawal?'

'I am doing my best,' was Habib's customary reply. 'I take one step forward and the Zionist lobby in Washington pulls me back two steps. I have a direct line to Reagan. The question, however, is how to keep Reagan focused. His attention-span is so damned short that I virtually lose him a minute after I start talking.'

Habib described a typical phone conversation with Reagan.

'Mr President,' he told us he would shout down the phone, 'you have got to call Prime Minister Begin in Israel. You must insist that he honour the cease-fire as he promised.'

'Oh, there is cease-fire,' Reagan answered calmly.

'No, there is not one yet,' Habib's voice rose in frustration.

'Yes, there is cease-fire,' Reagan would insist, 'or so I am told by my chief of staff.'

Habib put the phone receiver outside the window and told Reagan, 'Mr President listen to the cease-fire.' He held the phone so that Reagan could clearly hear the planes circling, the shells exploding and automatic weapons stuttering. Returning the phone to his ear, Habib heard Reagan saying, 'The bastards are lying to me.'

11

In the spring of 1982, fortune intervened and changed the course of my career. I was invited by a Washington think-tank to lecture on Lebanon and the Arab–Israeli conflict. It was a time of great tension in Lebanon and in the Arab East. Lebanon was in the midst of a vicious internal war, and the Middle East was boiling. The PLO was mounting raids against Israel from Lebanese territory. Syria and Israel were exchanging fire, and rumours of an imminent Israeli invasion of Lebanon were rapidly taking serious form.

An emissary from Bashir Gemayel visited me at home and most politely informed me that if I were to go to Washington to talk on Lebanon Bashir would not be at all happy.

'No?' I enquired gently. 'And what would he do?'

'He would kill you,' came the polite but firm answer.

This was too heavy a price to pay for a lecture, I told myself. And there was not even an honorarium. In our war, killing was a normal, everyday occurrence. Because there were no courts, no real state and certainly no effective national police, justice was administered by whichever militia controlled the immediate locale. Bashir's militia was called the Lebanese Forces and it was a strong, efficient machine, capable of doing whatever its leader commanded. I asked the emissary to arrange for me to see Bashir. I had never met him although his image was entirely familiar. His picture, with a machine-gun on his lap, decorated all the walls of Christian East Beirut. The meeting was quickly arranged.

Bashir's father, Sheikh Pierre Gemayel, founded the Kataib Party in the 1930s. It started as a boy-scout organization and grew into a disciplined, largely Maronite political party. In the 1970s the Kataib Party formed a militia to counterbalance militias formed by the Palestinian refugees in Lebanon and their leftist allies. Sheikh Pierre became the spokesman for the Christians in Lebanon. He was rightist by inclination and pretty close to France and the other Western powers. He had two sons, Amine and Bashir. Amine was the more intellectual and refined, Bashir the more militant and the more action-oriented. He was confident and charismatic and allowed no one and no institution to stand in his path. In this way he was quintessentially Ottoman, sidestepping even the authority of his own family by establishing a power base of his own.

Our meeting had been arranged at the house of a mutual friend. I arrived a few minutes before he did. Bashir strode in with quick steps and shook my hand firmly, a signal I thought of who carried the sword, who the pen.

'Let's get straight to business,' Bashir said.

'Fine with me,' I agreed.

'I heard you are going next month to give a lecture on Lebanon.'

'Yes, I have been invited by a Washington think-tank and I was planning to go.'

'Are you aware that I will allow no voice on Lebanon in Washington at present except my own or that of my representative?' Bashir demanded firmly.

'No, I was unaware of that,' I replied. 'And why is it so?'

'Because I want to be president of Lebanon in a few months,' he announced, 'and I want Washington's support. Therefore, I can risk no independent voice in that critical capital.'

'Do you expect to be president now?' I asked, taken aback. 'You are hardly thirty years old, the country is so heatedly divided and you are right smack in the middle of the reasons for the division.'

'Now or never,' he answered with assurance. And again Bashir stared me deep in the eye, defying opposition.

Bashir was largely ignorant of Islam and the Muslim perspective, had little experience of the Arabs and Arabism, and consequently he feared Islam and the Arabs. It is common for ignorance to result in fear. Bashir vehemently opposed any Palestinian influence in Lebanon. He was against the alignment of Muslim parties with the Palestinian cause. In the same spirit, he opposed the Syrians who supported Muslims, Palestinians and leftists of all colours. The young militia leader knew power by exercising it, and the more uncompromising it appeared, the stronger and more effective was its impact on the masses. Napoleon first attained fame by shooting at the Parisian mob. He did not waver, did not compromise and certainly did not negotiate. Bashir admired Napoleon, and if he read at all, his reading was probably limited to biographies of great military leaders – men whose rise to power involved the ruthless deployment of the bayonet.

Within the Christian coalition, Bashir tolerated no one else's leadership. He, Bashir, was the leader, regardless of age, education or wisdom. He held the gun, spoke with the decisive voice and attracted a large following of young men and women yearning for robust leadership. His followers looked to Bashir for certainty and relied on his willingness to take risks on behalf of the Lebanon they dreamt of.

The traditional Christian leaders were the elders, the wise men who organized political parties. Bashir's father, Sheikh Pierre, was one of these, as was Camille Chamoun, the former president of Lebanon and head of the Ahrar militia. For a time Suleiman Frangieh had influence as a former president with a militia in North Lebanon. The philosopher statesman Charles Malik led with a pen rather than a sword. Before long, however, these leaders and others became ciphers as Bashir Gemayel, young and charismatic, seized control of the Christian region of Lebanon.

When the Chamouni Ahrar militia contested Bashir's power, he liquidated them with one decisive *putsch*. When his father cautioned compromise, Bashir threatened to lock him up. Clearly, he was in the game for the highest stakes. Bashir was at war, and took no prisoners.

While Bashir stared at me, his gaze spoke volumes with confidence, passion and determination. While his tone was somehow harsh he did not intimidate me. Unconsciously, I assumed a fatherly role. I love this guy, I thought. I like his style. He did not have much intellectual discipline, but passion he had in abundance. Here was good material, I thought. Perhaps it can be moulded. I was the inveterate teacher, the hidden Messianic, the counsellor.

In looking at Bashir I saw the young revolutionaries on AUB's campus, the militant Palestinians, the ideological socialists and the dreamy Arab nationalists. They too were fighting for causes that seemed to them fair and just. But of all the revolutionaries I had encountered on and off campus, Bashir stood out. I liked the fellow at first encounter although we virtually had nothing in common; except perhaps passion and commitment to Lebanon. And even then, we disagreed about the Lebanon we envisaged.

Bashir spoke with vigour. At times he seemed to be lecturing. His hands sliced the air, enlarging his thoughts. He brought his fist down hard on the table for emphasis. Then he allowed the silence to linger. He had delivered the message and now was all ears.

To soften the atmosphere and in the hope of preventing it from deteriorating into one of unpleasant mutual animosity, our host had invited our wives for the luncheon meeting. Phyllis and Bashir's wife Solange were doing their best to make a social occasion of the event. When either of them attempted to change the conversation to something less urgent, less direct, Bashir ignored the attempt and returned to the focal point. When the women failed to engage us, they searched desperately for ways to engage with each other, for they lacked a common language in which to express themselves as Phyllis was Anglophone and Solange clearly Francophone. Phyllis was truly concerned. She knew that many a wife had lost a husband for a lesser cause than was at stake on that night.

'I admire your passion for Lebanon,' I told Bashir, 'and I congratulate you on your success in becoming the uncontested leader of Lebanon's Christian community. You are young. Your love for Lebanon is exemplary. Like you, I love my country. I respect your father and his view of Lebanon as an "icon" that must be cherished, loved and prayed for. I have been writing and teaching about Lebanon for twenty-five years. In addition, during all that time I have written and published pieces on Lebanon's neighbours – Syria, Iraq, Palestine, Jordan, the Arab Peninsula and Arab North Africa. In Washington I am regarded as a leading expert on the Middle East. Many of my students from my Johns Hopkins days are now prominent officials in the State Department, in the Department of Defense and in the White House. They may also be, and most likely they are, in the FBI and in the CIA. America's Ambassador to Lebanon seeks me out to solicit my counsel.'

The more I revealed, intentionally emphasizing my role and avoiding false modesty, the more he pricked up his ears and the more attentive he became. When I realized that he was impressed and knew that he had nothing to fear from me, I suggested another option.

'My dear Bashir,' I counselled, 'you should be influenced by me rather than I by you. Were I to speak in Washington I would say what is right for Lebanon.'

Phyllis heard that and signalled caution. Great was her relief and mine when Bashir jumped to his feet, and hugged me closely in a warm embrace.

'I respect your courage,' the young man said. 'No one speaks like that to me. I am young, and perhaps I have some things to learn, but one thing I need from you. When you speak well of Lebanon, as you will, please speak well of me.'

And so it was that the dean and the young rebel became friends. Weekly I would slip out of West Beirut and into East Beirut to meet with Bashir and review policy options. We discussed the tactical moves that would propel him to the presidency in the elections that were to take place in a few eventful months. Sneaking away is easier said than done. The two wings of Beirut were separated by dozens of checkpoints – some with clear colours, some with grey colours and some with no colours at all. At each checkpoint, a different story was required, and it was best to hide your identity. Whether on foot or by car, crossing the Green Line entailed dodging bullets. Not only did snipers hide clandestinely in ruined buildings, but there was constant rocket-propelled-grenade and cannon fire exchanged between the two armed camps. Often the fighting became so intense in the no man's land separating two sectors that I had to abandon the car and take refuge in one of the deserted shuttered buildings in the middle. In eight years of continuing battles these buildings had become monuments to the devastation and destructiveness of war. They had shed their colour and faith years ago, their balconies hung by just a few persistent iron bars and dangled precariously over the road. A building with a gaping hole appeared as an architectural cyclops. Another was so pitted with holes that it recalled a face stored in my distant memory of a man with a severe case of smallpox.

Eventually I would make it to Bashir's military headquarters. Once there, we often argued, sometimes we even screamed at one another. We disagreed on virtually every point, but I was not discouraged. The fellow was pragmatic, not ideological. He could change positions without batting an eyelid if it helped his climb to power. Philosophically, Bashir and I came from opposite poles. Often I could not believe what my ears had actually heard him say. Was it for effect? Was he testing ideas he had picked up here and there? Was he sincere? Bashir tended to lecture, to orate and to impress. With the public, his style was effective. With me, it was less so.

The Lebanese people were looking for a forceful person to lead them, one who was committed to strong management and reform and who could secure the independence and stability of Lebanon. Bashir's thoughts seemed to explode when he was with me. His ideas would surge forth, unformed, unstructured and unruly. He struggled to give them expression and in doing so he often worked up a temper. The face of the young leader would turn red, his neck muscles would tighten and his veins bulge. At some point, he would suddenly fall quiet, amazingly quiet, and he would listen.

My meetings with Bashir were the best seminars I ever held. In university classes we deal with theories and hypotheses, we examine historical events and we attempt to draw lessons from them. My discussions with Bashir dealt with live issues, ones that entailed brothers fighting against brothers, the immediate manipulation of militias by external forces and foreign armies invading our once peaceful country from all directions. We tried to arrive at a rational position from which he could formulate policy once he became president.

The Palestinians, now mobilized under their leader Arafat as a powerful militia, saw Lebanon as their stepping stone to the liberation of Palestine. This logic was not sound, but there it was. Iranians supported the Shiite Muslims of Lebanon that they might attain a higher degree of political power. The Syrians had an army in Lebanon, and with it they had a number of leftist allies who took orders from Damascus. And the Israelis, even before their invasion of Lebanon in 1982, had maintained a military presence in south Lebanon since 1978 and a political presence through their sympathizers, including the Lebanese Forces. These were a few of the many issues at stake which we discussed exhaustively.

Into this highly complicated situation, the massive Israeli invasion of June 1982 introduced another lethal layer of complexity. Ariel Sharon led the invasion and was in collusion with Bashir. Both leaders regarded the PLO as their mortal enemy. Coming from the other camp, it was impossible for me to accept the Sharon alliance and I told Bashir so most emphatically. He held my arm and led me to the spacious piazza by the sea. He continued to grip my arm as he whispered in my ear, 'Who was Machiavelli? He was not so important. It's true I haven't read him, but they tell me a lot about him and his methods. I am much shrewder than he was. I am tough. I am a realist. I play games that neither Machiavelli nor the medieval popes could fathom. Machiavelli dealt only with Italians. I am dealing with Americans, French, Israelis, Syrians, Iraqis and Palestinians. More difficult than all of these, I am dealing with the Lebanese.'

'Some come from mountain tops, some from caves. Some look to the Vatican, some to Mecca. Machiavelli had a stew you could hold in a spoon. I have a salad without a dressing. It is impossible to hold it together. With a fork you could pick a piece here, a piece there. I will mesh the salad and hold it firmly in my grip. Sharon is a key ingredient. I will wring him dry and throw him away. He is crucial for me to reach the presidency. Once I am there I will turn against him. I have one love, one icon – "Lebanon 10,453 km^2". This is a slogan I coined, and I am proud of it. The Palestinians are bent on taking Lebanon. As they cannot regain Palestine they have opted to take over Lebanon instead. I will not let them. I will use the Israelis to get the Palestinians out. I will use the Americans to get the Israelis out, and I have my own plans how to get the Syrians out.'

He went on and on. I learned an enormous amount from Bashir. I came to know much about who he was, what he was doing and the vital activities going on behind the scenes. The boy warrior learned something from me as well. I spoke to him with a different language and from a different perspective than any he had ever encountered. We were close and yet far from each other. Close in passion and commitment to Lebanon, far on regional perceptions, on tactics and on methodologies.

I told him how completely I agreed with him on the independence and sovereignty of Lebanon, but I also explained to him that all the others had their own causes and their own perspectives. It was important to try to our utmost ability to understand them objectively and to support them as we extricated them from their entanglements in Lebanon.

Bashir urged that we get together daily.

'Daily!' I objected. 'Just try to cross the danger zone as I have to to be with you! No, I will risk it only once a month.'

'OK then,' Bashir reconsidered, 'twice a week.'

And this is how it was. After each of my visits to Bashir, Phyllis waited anxiously with a drink, as my return was usually in the early evening. I recounted to her the details of my arguments with Bashir, the facts and plans that he shared with me in confidence. Phyllis was awed. She was brave and ready to take great risks. The country she had grown to love so passionately, the land she had made her own, was crumbling before her eyes. Like me she was eager to do something, to take a step that might break the vicious cycle of violence and renew our hope. We believed then that Bashir was a potential leader.

Phyllis too was learning more about the Palestinians and their frustration. She contemplated the complex Lebanese mosaic and the external connections of each piece in it. She felt that she and Bashir had much in common. Though he had been born in Lebanon, his horizon was limited, since he was insulated and schooled with no external Arab connections. His peers gave little or no consideration to the needs and aspirations of Palestinians, Syrians or Arabs in general. Phyllis was dedicated to learn formally and informally, and as she learned, her perspective changed and her horizons broadened. She cared passionately about Lebanon, but her innate adherence to principle and her willingness to solve problems objectively embodied the broader perspective I was trying to convey to Bashir.

Lebanese of all faiths and colours listened to Bashir's highly pitched and passionate speeches. Some were his followers and listened openly and proudly, but many others listened clandestinely and in suppressed admiration. Phyllis probed, questioned and formulated new ideas and approaches for my future meetings with him. She knew as well as anyone how extremely dangerous it was to cross the war zones and yet she never succumbed to fear or doubt. She was always by my side in moving from Beirut to our home on the other side in Ba'bda and to the village in the al-Kurah region.

We did not fear because we were not partisan. Even in talking to Bashir, I felt more like an intermediary, an interlocutor or an ambassador from the leftist–Islamic–Palestinian camp. Shooting continued night and day. The stammering of machine-guns constantly filled the air. Attacks were met with counter-attacks. Village after village collapsed and was emptied of its population. Desperate refugees sought temporary shelter. Displaced people often become angry, and they too begin to carry arms and seek revenge against those who have evicted them. Some are kidnapped for ransom or prisoner exchange and some are liquidated. Torture comes easily to the angered horde, to the zealot of both religious and ideological conviction.

We tell ourselves that the cruelty of man to man has been tempered by the so-called march of civilization. But what we did to each other in the 1970s and 1980s in Lebanon was no less barbaric than what our ancestors in our dark and distant past did to each other. Images of civil and internal war paraded through my mind as I daily witnessed the cruelty. In an internal war, all rules are suspended. The more savage the act, the greater the effort to justify it using warped perceptions of a politicized religion. And the one God who dwells in highest heaven is pulled apart by his zealous adherents on this tiny strip of the spectacular planet.

I thought of the ingenious De Guillotine who actually prided himself on inventing a decapitating machine that severed the heads of royalists, aristocrats and eventually the very revolutionaries who manipulated it. I thought of the American Civil War, the bloodiest in that nation's history. The myth tells of a Christian population escaping old fractious Europe to build a paradise of peace, stability and tolerance in a newly found land across the dark and forbidding ocean. After less than a hundred years, this promised land was suffused with blood shed by bayonet and fuselade just as effectively as by the awful guillotine or the sharp swords of the French Revolution. When humanity needs a reminder closer to the present, it may consider how the more recently conceived paradise of Marx and Engle fared under Stalin.

The more I reflected on revolutions and their utopian aspirations, the more I yearned for a more old-fashioned society. I renewed my admiration of the deep, cynical and sarcastic observations of Thomas Carlyle, conveyed in literary form, on the triumphant revolution carving its path in tears and blood on a continent from which he felt blissfully separated by a God-given sea. To the passionate youth of a nation in the making, the fight itself is enthralling. Testing every possibility to the absolute limit in the hope of realizing a dream must give him a buzz like an aphrodisiac or an intoxicant. I have seen the faces behind the barricade – young men and young women. They had a cause, or so they thought, until the cloud was dispersed by stronger winds and they found themselves to be mere players in a game bigger than they bargained for, and in causes far different from the ones they were ready to die for.

There is something fascinating in internal war. People seem to be happy and content, living together in peace, in affection and in a high degree of mutual respect. Society may in fact be a paradigm of mother nature. All seems quiet and at rest, until suddenly an earthquake erupts, destroying peaceful villages, scattering helpless towns, opening gaping holes, subsuming both the good and the bad and engulfing the fleeing mortals among rocks and boulders.

Such was the fate of Lebanon, previously the envy of the region, the playground of the rich and the 'Switzerland of the Middle East'. The young men and women who partied together the night before were pitted against each other the next day, ready to kill and mutilate one another. The war devastated the nation, ruined the economy, dispersed the population and killed and maimed the young, so passionately committed to their causes. In a flash love turns into hatred, friendship into enmity, trust into fear. Nothing is what it seems. Fact is distorted into rumour, the small takes on a gargantuan garb and the slightest incident is exaggerated beyond recognition.

It was up to the old and not-so-committed to determine the climax and cool its fury. During our internal war, we Lebanese seemed to be proxies for Syrians, for Iraqis, for Palestinians, for Israelis, for Iranians, for Libyans, and more grandiosely for the Americans and Soviets. How to end such a war? We hoped that young charismatic Bashir could unify the Lebanese. And so the youth from behind their barricades as well as those of us seeking a way to end the fighting all looked to Bashir for salvation.

The fortunes of war bring major surprises. I was not at all certain that Bashir, the passionate partisan, would be willing to build the coalitions necessary to attain the presidency in a country as divided and as diverse as Lebanon. Yet Bashir campaigned hard. The incumbent president, Elias Sarkis supported him. The American envoy Philip Habib adopted him, and subsequently no other Maronite dared to announce his candidacy. By persuasion, by threat, by charisma and by cash Bashir was elected president. Phyllis and I were jubilant. We began to spend more time with the president-elect. The partisan was now called upon to be the unifier, to become the president of all the people in a nation half-Christian and half-Muslim. Not only would he have to deal with the Syrians and Palestinians whom he loathed, but the new president must also evict the Israelis who until recently had been his allies.

Bashir asked Phyllis to help him learn how to talk to Philip Habib and to the Americans. The Francophone was eager to learn from the Anglophone how to ally himself with the superpower. Television networks vied with each other to get an interview with the energetic young leader. The president-elect worked hard and learned fast. He began to reach out to former enemies and successfully to broaden his base of support.

Bashir asked me to stay close to him, to help him formulate his position with respect to regional powers and to the two superpowers. ABC, a major television station, asked for an interview with the young president. He agreed provided I was present and that ABC would correct any statement identified as needing revision by the president and me. As the interview proceeded I noted eighteen points that I felt should be revised. When the interview ended, the president asked if we needed to make any changes.

'Yes,' I answered, 'there are eighteen misstatements.'

'Fine,' President Bashir replied, 'let's hear them.'

'First,' I said, 'you were negative about Muslims and on Islam. You are now president of a country that is half Muslim. They are your citizens and you are their leader. You should be speaking well of them and of their great religion.'

'Of course, you are right,' the president responded.

'You spoke of the Syrians,' I continued, 'and you attack them in exactly the same tone and same language as you did when you were the head of the Lebanese Forces. This is dangerous. You will be negotiating with them soon. Send them a more positive message.'

'You are absolutely right,' he replied. 'I thought I had changed my tone, but obviously I had not.'

And thus we proceeded. He accepted every correction I made, until we reached point number eighteen. He looked at me, faking anger, and said this must stay. 'I will not correct this one even if a regional war erupts as a result.' We both laughed and ended the correction session. I no longer recall what the eighteenth point was, but I was pleased by his flexibility and his readiness to change tack when an error was pointed out to him. I thought this was a sign of strength, and hoped he would exercise it in office.

I had tried to be a counsellor to President Suleiman Frangiyeh, but he was not at ease with me. President Elias Sarkis who succeeded Frangiyeh in 1976 explored the possibility with me but nothing ever came of it. From time to time I wrote a speech or prepared a brief for him. Occasionally I had undertaken a confidential mission, but no more.

When I left America in 1962 I told Phyllis that one of the reasons I had to leave was that I could not live in a country in which I could not be president. Phyllis thought this was reasonable but years later would use the decision in an anecdote to friends.

'Elie lied to me twice,' Phyllis declared. 'He said he could not live in a country where he was not able to be president, and for this reason we returned to Lebanon. But he never told me about the National Pact.' The Pact of 1943 reserved the presidency of Lebanon to a Maronite. The highest office obtainable by a Greek Orthodox, like me, was that of Deputy Prime Minister or Minister in the cabinet.

'The second lie was when I asked him what his father did for a living,' Phyllis continued. 'Elie told me his father was in oil. He never told me it was olive oil.'

Oil and the presidency aside, I was not at all political. Running for office or serving in the bureaucracy had never held any attraction to me. Nevertheless, Phyllis prompted me, urging that I would be a good counsellor to the new president. She found him to be intelligent, pragmatic, eager to learn and surprisingly open to alternative ideas. Never did we discuss the possibility of resigning my deanship at AUB to take a governmental position.

A few short days before he was to take office, Bashir Gemayel was assassinated. The tragedy was compounded when Bashir's death provided General Sharon with an opportunity to avenge himself. Vengeance comes naturally to a man like Sharon with a mono-maniacal perspective. Though it was not yet known who had planted the bomb that killed the newly anointed leader, Sharon and his friends in the Lebanese Forces assumed that it was the Palestinians. Sharon's tanks rolled into West Beirut followed by the Lebanese Forces. And in the heat of the anger generated by the assassination, Sharon signalled his friends to enter Palestinian camps and murder men, women and children in cold blood.

The world quickly learned with horror of the Sabra–Shatila massacre. The more it learned, the more the world wondered. How

243

deep, how endemic, how ferocious was this conflict between Arabs and Jews? Was it Arabs v. Jews? Was it Arab v. Zionist? Was it Palestinian v. Israeli? Was it the historic conflict over gods, caves and rivers? Has mankind made no progress at all?

Is it the fate of man to excel in technology and fail in theology, to indulge his appetite for the visible and the material and to discard universals that had once focused his mind and captured his imagination? The century once hailed by dreamers as the century of hope had turned into a period of unprecedented violence and crimes of immense proportions. The excesses of Atilla, of Hulagu and of Genghis Khan seemed to pale before the horrific feats of Fascists, Nazis and Communists.

To placate the civilized world that recoiled in condemnation and revulsion at what took place in the camps, Israel investigated the massacre. The judgment was a mere slap on the hand for Sharon. Lebanon was too weak and rudderless to act. The country spoke with too many voices, and the one voice that could have spoken with the power of legitimacy had been silenced. Bashir won the election by extracting it from the contradictions on the ground. The light of hope had been so intensely focused on Bashir that even in death it continued to shine on those closest to him in blood, and particularly on his brother Amine.

Bashir and Amine had gone separate ways during the war. Bashir became entirely militaristic. Amine, perhaps by logical reaction, became the aesthetic and intellectual. Bashir I knew only for a few months and then he was killed. I had never met Amine. The wheel of fortune that catapulted Bashir into centre stage, now made one more turn and elevated Amine into the presidency of Lebanon. Amine did not have many friends, but he also had few enemies. He emerged as a consensus figure, hailed in Muslim West Beirut a bit more than in the Christian part of the capital. The Christians clung to the saintly image of their fallen hero Bashir, their martyr.

When Bashir died, I concentrated on my position at the university as Dean of the Faculty of Arts and Sciences, a position I may have compromised by my frequent visits to the president-elect in East Beirut. One works most when one is hurt most, and there was a lot for me to do at the university. Phyllis, too, concentrated with redoubled efforts on her position as director of AMIDEAST Lebanon. AMIDEAST is the American Mideast Educational Office. It is a private American foundation with headquarters in Washington DC and branches in several Arab countries. As director of AMIDEAST Phyllis made her dream of helping Lebanon a reality. Her love for her adopted country was expressed as she gave counsel to young men and women, many of them anxious to leave after years of war and despair. Most expressed a great attraction to America, seeking what Lebanon lacked – peace, stability, opportunity and advanced education. Many students wanted to leave our country and never return. The devastation of the war had so shaken their confidence that it seemed to have robbed them of their very identity.

I became accustomed to hearing the voice of Phyllis counselling coming from her office when I stopped to pick her up and head for home. 'You're right. You need a good education,' Phyllis encouraged her current applicant. 'I will tell you about the universities to which you should apply, and help you get into one of them. Keep in mind, however, that you are going to America to study, to get a good degree that will stand you in good stead here in Lebanon. Always remember that you are Lebanese. Lebanon is a glorious country. It is beautiful, the people are wonderful and its needs are immense.

'You are needed here,' Phyllis reminded her young listeners. 'No one needs you in America. You are mad at everything in Lebanon because of the war, I understand that. I, too, am mad at the way things have turned out. But we are all Lebanese and we are going to change things. We have a dream for Lebanon, and only you – your generation – can realize that dream. I am an American converted to Lebanon. I counsel my four children like I counsel you – go to America, study. But come back. Do not be fooled by the comforts of America. They are not for you. You have comforts enough here in Lebanon and you have more challenges, more than you can now imagine. I recommend that you take your BA here first, and then go for higher education in America. The older you are when you land in New York the better off you are. My husband had many problems as a young student in America. I will try to prepare you in such a way as to minimize your problems.'

Quite often their parents accompanied the students who came to seek Phyllis's counsel. Lebanese mothers are possessive and only rarely are able to cut the umbilical cord entirely. These mothers, as desperate and as wounded as their children, were mesmerized by

Phyllis. Here was an American, speaking American English, and yet the content of her speech was pure Lebanese. They had rarely encountered a foreigner holding forth with such confidence, such hope and such passion about the country that had fallen around them in ruins. As Lebanese from every nook and cranny in the country were searching for escape routes for their sons and daughters, a great many of them ended up in the AMIDEAST office seeking help. Phyllis's name had become familiar to every household. People recognized her in the streets, in supermarkets, in any public place and rushed over to her. Many would touch her, hugging and kissing her in their eagerness to appropriate part of her faith in a country torn apart by irresistible centrifugal forces.

In the evening Phyllis came home emotionally drained. She recounted one story after another of families trying to escape, of children totally confused, of a people who had lost their faith in their own country. 'How can we restore faith?' she sighed. 'How can we restore the people to their country, and the country to them? Elie, the issues are too complicated, too difficult to explain to these people who are at my door from morning to evening. I am amazed at how passionate they are. Their commitment to education is awesome. If I tell them the cost of education in a university on the East Coast, the parents vow to pay the fees no matter how. "We will sell land," they say. "We will mortgage the house." One way or another, education they are determined to get. They so believe that education is the true passport. All other solutions are transitory, illusory. I admire the Lebanese so much. I admire their tenacity, their scope of vision. They look at the wider world as their salvation. Many of the people I see have lost not only their home but their whole village. They have been refugees running from one shelter to another. The son or the daughter is their entire hope. They are willing to invest absolutely everything in the education of that child, that child who will in effect be their true country, their safety net, their insurance policy.'

It is said that converts tend to be uncompromising in their faith. Phyllis was a convert, and about Lebanon and what it stood for she was absolutely uncompromising. God help the Lebanese, the French, the German or the American who belittled Lebanon in the presence of Phyllis. She allowed no one to criticize the Lebanese in their social or even political habits. Like Carl Schurz, a nineteenth-century

American soldier and politician, Phyllis proclaimed, 'My country, right or wrong!' Phyllis defended the Lebanese to any non-Lebanese, even where the Lebanese were truly most vulnerable. Lebanese are known as wild drivers, as truly anarchic, as insanely individualistic behind the steering wheel. Yet, I heard Phyllis shout down the Austrian neighbour who so often cursed Lebanese drivers. 'You are just wrong! They are good drivers, they are polite. They are not nearly as rude, selfish and impersonal as Austrian drivers.' I listened, knowing that she was not addressing the facts as they were but rather as she hoped they would be in her idealized Lebanon of the future. It was this vision that motivated her and coloured all the harsh realities around her. To Phyllis, 'This is Lebanon, love it or leave it!' was much more than a slogan, it was a genuine conviction. When she spoke on Lebanon, she was a charismatic and persuasive lecturer. Lebanon to her was a total love affair.

Speaking of her extended Salem family, she would say, 'The Salems are a great clan. They are fine people. They are educated. They cling together. They accept diversity. They are honest, just, fair. There are not many clans that have these characteristics.'

As friends compared various ethnic cuisines, I could count on Phyllis to declare, 'Lebanese food is the best. Poor are the people who have never had raw meat with a glass of arak for breakfast; deprived indeed are those who have not eaten *mjdrah* and *burghul* with raw onion. And how, how can one live and claim to be civilized if one has not tasted raw *kibbeh*?' Not only did she love traditional Lebanese dishes but she perfected her technique of cooking them until native Lebanese were after her for her special recipes.

On the geography, she was equally eloquent. 'The mountains are truly unequalled. They are not embarrassingly low like those in Pennsylvania, and not as obscenely high as the Hindu Kush. They are spectacular, sitting majestically by the sea. Within an hour you can bathe in the Mediterranean and ski on the mountain tops. And the mountains are museums of quaint villages, of diverse religious habits, ancient traditions and rules of hospitality, a refuge from cosmopolitan Beirut.'

Nature has seen to it that Lebanon is truly unparalleled. There are four distinctly different seasons: the summer is warm and yields a generous harvest of every kind of fruit; the autumn is a cool breezy delight; the winter is rainy and windy, with thunderstorms and heavy snow on the mountains; and the spring with its gentle weather brings a spectacular profusion of wild flowers. Phyllis loved the river valleys and the mountain peaks for the different types of beauty they offered, but the seashore was to her the home of civilization. Here, on the easternmost shores of the Mediterranean, stood Tyre, Sidon, Berytus, Byblos and Tripoli, legendary towns of biblical and mythical fame.

Phyllis the teacher and the counsellor was also Phyllis the proud guide, who showed off her mountains, her villages and her people to all newcomers. Her knowledge and understanding were so extensive that often she illuminated their own country to native Lebanese. For there are those that have eyes yet do not see and ears yet do not hear.

12

As Dean of the Faculty of Arts and Sciences I entertained daily. Conditions in Beirut were extremely dangerous and so we stayed on campus to celebrate every evening the simple fact that we were still alive. While there was life there was hope. Contrary to my natural habits, we went to bed late most nights. Guests enjoyed themselves. The revellers were all living on campus so did not have to run the gauntlet of the militias to venture home.

Each intersection had its militia and its checkpoint and it was not easy to discern who was who. In early October 1982 new Israeli checkpoints were added to those of the trigger-happy Palestinians, Maronites, Shiites, Sunnis and Syrians and of a dozen agents of various foreign countries and competing ideologies. Amine Gemayel had just been sworn in as the new president. Unlike the election of Bashir, Amine's was by consensus. He was respected by most competing factions. He was not as partisan as his younger brother. The assassination of Bashir must have created sympathy for Amine and his family. The new president, we read in the press, had asked Chafic Wazzan to serve as Prime Minister. Wazzan was a neutral Sunni Muslim from Beirut. As Prime Minister designate he was expected to consult widely with the members of parliament and recommend a cabinet to the president. In fact, it is the President and the Prime Minister designate who together select a cabinet, usually with extensive consultation.

At about ten p.m. on 8 October, our phone rang and Phyllis answered. It was the operator at the presidential palace asking me to come to the phone and talk to the aide-de-camp. I did. I was requested to get into the car alone, tell no one, and drive to the palace.

'Tonight?' I asked. 'At this hour?' The shelling was as intense as ever; I was not sure I would ever reach the palace. 'Can't the matter wait till tomorrow?'

The stern voice at the other end let me know that when the president calls, one must respond. The President's command required me not to ask questions or to hesitate.

Nevertheless, I procrastinated. I had been out at night but no farther than a few blocks from the university and always before nine p.m. To drive alone – and I was a miserable driver – especially at night, was unthinkable. It was difficult under normal circumstances to travel to the presidential palace in Ba'bda some thirty minutes away across town. Now, it was utterly impossible.

'The president is expecting you.'

'O.K,' I surrendered. 'I'm coming.'

'What's going on?' asked Phyllis.

'The president wants to see me now.'

'I'll go with you.'

'No, no.' I could not permit it.

Some of our guests suggested that a few of them accompany me and wait for me in a safe place near the palace.

'No, that would not do,' I remembered my instructions. 'I will go alone.'

Phyllis led me to the study, closed the door and together we speculated. 'What does the president want? He doesn't know you,' my wife pondered. 'You have never met. Maybe Bashir told him about you, maybe Philip Habib, maybe he has read some of your papers. To call you at this hour, it must be important. He may want you to be his advisor; he may want you to serve as his ambassador in Washington, now that he needs the US to help him evict the Israelis from Lebanon. On no account accept an appointment outside Lebanon. We left Washington to live in Lebanon, to raise a family here, and if we are to leave some footsteps, it is here.'

'Yes, yes, I understand,' I assured her. 'I agree, let's not rush into appointments that no one has offered.'

The drive to Ba'bda was predictable. At each checkpoint I gave the appropriate answer, the appropriate identity. This was relatively easy with the Palestinians, and with the Lebanese of all colours. It was not so easy at the three Israeli checkpoints. There I claimed to be a Maronite close to the Lebanese Forces, and proudly mentioned my friendship with the martyred president. I arrived at the palace just before midnight.

The place seemed quite deserted. A light flickered here and there. At night it seemed serene, lonely, and pretty much irrelevant. A young man paced back and forth in the spacious entrance. He carried his keys at the end of a chain which served as his worry beads. This is a good sign, I thought, he does not carry a *masbahah*. The key chain seemed a symbol of humility and perhaps of rebellious modernity.

'I am Amine Gemayel,' the young man said as he extended his hand. After the introduction we paced for an hour together. He spoke about the burden of the presidency, the dangers facing Lebanon and the prevalence of militias and occupying armies. 'We have little left,' he said, as if speaking to himself, 'except legitimacy. The state, shattered as it is, is the only legitimate force that can speak in the name of the country.'

This clearly was not an interview. He had hardly asked me a single question about me or my interests or even my opinion. Amine was full of ideas and full of worries. He was reflectively probing for a handle by which he could grab a country that had slipped from the hand of its government and was quickly being snatched at by every other hand around. After what I thought was an eloquent soliloquy, he told me the reason for the summons.

'Tomorrow at ten the Prime Minister designate, Chafic Wazzan, will come to the palace,' the new president told me. 'He and I will attempt to form a government to deal with the "mission impossible" that we are faced with. I want you to be present. You will serve as Deputy Prime Minister and Minister of Foreign Affairs in the new government. There are to be no questions, you have no choice.'

Nevertheless, I asked one question. 'Are you committed to signing a peace treaty with Israel?'

'No,' Amine answered.

'Fine, then. I am with you.'

I navigated my way back to the campus, employing all the tricks of dissimulation that we had learned in surviving a war fought among buildings, on the streets and in back-alleys.

Far from thinning out, the crowd at home had grown, attracting all the bored, scared, lonely and semi-employed denizens of the campus. The questions rained down immediately. 'What did the President want? Did he offer you a job?'

'Yes,' I nodded. 'Meet the new Foreign Minister of Lebanon.'

A round of applause thundered through the crowded hall, a gratifying gesture for me to enjoy before the full burden of office fell upon my shoulders. Phyllis was jubilant. She called for champagne but there was none. Cautioning everyone that this might all come to nothing, I told them that the government would be formed the next day, with or without me. 'But it seems,' I continued, 'I will be there with the President and the Prime Minister designate forming the new government.'

I have written a political memoir *Violence and Diplomacy in Lebanon*, (1995) and I shall not attempt to duplicate that account, nor do I intend to dwell on the political and diplomatic issues that I believe I have covered to the best of my ability in that book. Conscious of the difficulty of separating the personal from the public, I shall nevertheless attempt the task.

In the new government I was clearly the strongest after the President and the Prime Minister. In a few days the old ministers handed their posts to the new ones. Meanwhile, I was settling my affairs at AUB to ensure the continuity of the dean's office, especially since my secretary, Ms Itamar Diab, was coming with me as my assistant in the Ministry of Foreign Affairs. For the next few days my office was virtually an Arab coffee house. I welcomed colleagues from the university, friends and politicians. On such occasions, the dangers that lurked outside the protective womb of the campus were forgotten or boldly disregarded. In this festive mood I was congratulated. Had the mood been more reflective, I should have been condoled. Either way I did not feel I had a choice. Here was a national job, the most difficult since the founding of our country, and someone had to do it. I would do it. Once the announcement was made, Phyllis was as committed as I. She began immediately to plan our new life.

On my first day in office, the Secretary General of the Ministry of Foreign Affairs entered and asked to speak with me. He was a polite and very refined gentleman who was about to retire. He was a product of the ministry. French-educated, French-dressed, French-speaking, he was an extremely elegant fellow. He came gently to my desk and sat down. In a soft voice and with a most humble manner, he proceeded to the task in hand.

'In the name of my colleagues I welcome you,' said the Secretary General. 'We are lucky to have a person of your high qualifications. You are a man of substance and of learning.'

Hearing this introduction, I wondered about what was to follow, sensing that this was the positive preamble that warned of the negative to come.

'You see,' he continued, 'we at the Ministry follow the French tradition. While you do not speak French, your English is strong, and perhaps we need a bit of English now that we have to negotiate with the United States to help us end the Israeli occupation of Lebanon.'

'Thank you for the compliment,' I thought, as I listened to his obviously well-rehearsed speech.

'Clearly we are proud of you and will work hard for you,' he assured me. 'However, there are a few unimportant points I would like to raise, if you do not mind.'

'Not at all,' I answered affably, feeling somewhat amused.

'You see you come to us from the American University of Beirut,' he signalled his understanding of my background. 'You come from an academic ethos, and you have a style of your own. This is good. In substance you are unequalled. In form we may suggest a few things regarding dress.' Seeing that I was still attentive, he continued. 'You see, sir, your necktie is too wide. Look at ours, they are less wide and of good French quality. Yours looks cheap, too cheap for the Minister of Foreign Affairs.'

'Fine, ' I replied without hesitation, 'I will change it.'

'Also, sir,' he was emboldened to add, 'your shirt has a button-down collar. We do not wear American working-men's shirts in the Ministry. Please look at mine, sir.'

'Good, I will change it,' came my response now more amused than before.

'Also, sir, your shoes are too heavy, too wide,' he continued earnestly. 'We wear the softer, thinner French variety.'

'I will change them. Just tell me all the things I need to buy and where to buy them,' I lied, 'and I will be pleased to comply.'

The Secretary was plainly happy with his triumph. As he looked at me to thank me for my understanding, and without any conscious intent of deflating the ossified self-importance of the Ministry, I raised an item on my own immediate agenda.

'Mr Secretary,' I told him loudly and clearly, 'I need to piss. What shall I do?'

He was taken aback but immediately his training took over and, 'There is a way, sir, don't move,' he said.

'By God,' I exclaimed, 'what are you planning to do?'

He calmly rang the bell that sat on my desk, and a doorkeeper, who was called the *planton*, entered immediately. The Secretary spoke in a whisper to the *planton*. 'His excellency wishes to wash his hands,' he said.

Thereupon the *planton* produced a huge key of medieval appearance and asked me to follow him down a number of corridors, shaking hands along the way with the many people waiting to meet the new and different minister. We finally arrived at a pre-medieval lavatory. I learned later that the poor Secretary General had been asked to have a discreet word with me by the President himself, who was concerned by my lack of attention to protocol. I also learned then after the Secretary left my office, the President called him to enquire how he did.

'Sir, he is a hopeless case,' was the Secretary's rueful reply.

In matters of protocol it seemed as if I was destined to fail my President, as I did once at the Elysée Palace at dinner with President François Mitterand. Not only did I arrive for dinner unshaven and with rumpled clothes from flying straight from Washington DC, but I committed the ultimate sin at a French table. When dinner was over and the time for the toasts arrived, the waiters poured champagne. As soon as my glass was filled, I emptied it with not a care in the world, to the horror of President Gemayel and our own protocol man. No one had thought to tell me that the champagne was to be drunk only for the toast. After hundreds of mistakes the president left me alone when it came to protocol.

As we began this new phase of our lives, Phyllis and I made plans to leave campus and live in our house in Ba'bda, only a mile from the presidential palace. The Ba'bda house was commodious, old and elegant, and had a large and lovely garden. It was a good place for entertaining, should it be possible to entertain under the existing drastic conditions. An officer from Army Intelligence visited us and asked to talk to us in private. He talked. Phyllis and I listened.

'As of now your life has changed,' the officer informed us. 'You require protection, lots of it. Two units will be assigned to you. One from the Sûreté Generale of sixteen members, eight at a time, on a twenty-four-hour basis. They are to protect your person and to accompany you at all times. One from the army. This is a larger force of some thirty-five personnel. They will live in tents in your garden. They will have one troop carrier and three armoured cars.

They are to protect the family, the house and the area from any major attempt on your lives.'

'But we have no enemies,' Phyllis interrupted. 'Why all this security?'

'Perhaps no personal enemies,' answered the officer, 'but there are at least twenty intelligence units operating in Beirut committed to disrupting the government. These units represent foreign and regional powers, and they thrive in the chaos that currently prevails. Your husband is third in importance after the president and the prime minister and these two have even larger military units protecting them.'

This all seemed a bit surrealistic until we moved to our house in Ba'bda. As we opened the door, an army truck behind us disgorged eight heavily armed Sûreté men. The men were all quite large and looked bigger and heavier with their gear – pistols, M16 rifles, machine-guns, hand-grenades – and they just walked with us into the house. We had no idea where to put them, how to feed them and how to keep them out of the way. We had at that time one skinny Filipino maid who was terrified by the invasion. Without asking, the occupying force took the first room on the left, and they seem to overflow its bounds into the living-room and into the other rooms as well. Eight young men, average weight eighty-five kilos, mostly from poorer families, with little or no training in the niceties of modern living; to the contrary these young men were trained to be rough and tough, to sleep in trenches and to eat live snakes if the chips were down. Phyllis and I tried to ensure that we had at least one room – the bedroom – all to ourselves. Occasionally we even managed to occupy the living-room, but rarely. These men needed to move, and they had orders to keep an eye on me, and the living-room was spacious enough for them to escape the claustrophobia of one bedroom.

The eight assured us that they would be with us for the night. Another set of eight was scheduled to arrive in the morning. They would have two cars, one to drive in front of me and one behind, whenever we left the house. Each car would carry three men. A driver from the Sûreté would drive my car. An officer from the Sûreté would sit by the driver. I would have the back seat to myself.

An hour or so later three army trucks disgorged the promised thirty-five soldiers, together with their tents and their weapons. A tank took up position outside our gate as a troop carrier drove into the garden with two armoured trucks.

Their officer consulted with me as to where the tents could be pitched to minimize disturbance to ourselves and to the neighbours. He then chose a number of positions around the outside of the house that would be manned night and day. Our house had become in effect an army camp. The officer and his soldiers looked down on my Sûreté detail. Their disdain was reciprocated. A vague tension hung over the two guardian contingents but fortunately never broke into open warfare.

Living in Ba'bda was complicated by the ubiquitous deployment of the Israeli army. The Israelis were all over Ba'bda, controlling all of the routes to the presidential palace. Their Mirkave tanks were so huge they scraped the walls of the ancient alleys of Ba'bda. One such tank with its full detail chose to park a few metres from our gate. As I came and went from my home, the Israeli in the tank's cannon seat hailed me.

'Hello, Mr Foreign Minister,' the Israeli tank driver called out, 'how are you, sir? When are you going to visit Israel?'

I usually just pretended not to hear him and continued on my way. One day the tank commander decided to test my patience. He parked the tank so that it blocked my route. I saw it only after my car had driven a few metres. My security man asked the Israeli to open the way. 'Gladly,' answered the Israeli, 'but the tank has developed a problem, it cannot move. We have called for specialists to fix it but it will be hours.'

I pretended to hear nothing. Priding myself on my patience, I left the car and walked past the tank, followed on foot by my security people who were visibly affronted and angered. Another car picked us up for the rest of the trip. When I returned in the evening, the tank had moved.

Phyllis did not share the patience I exhibited with the occupying force. Somehow, she conducted her own war with the Israelis and fearlessly picked fights with them at every possible opportunity. As a woman and as an American she was in a relatively good position.

'What are you doing in Lebanon?' she would challenge them. 'Why do you irritate the population? Is this how you spend the money we Americans give you? You should get out of Lebanon fast, this country has suffered a lot all because of you.'

The Israelis often tried to answer, but Phyllis would not listen. She meant to lecture, not to engage in dialogue.

Ba'bda was a peaceful Maronite village near Beirut. Its people occupied petty jobs in local administrations. As the seat of government of one of Lebanon's five *muhafzats*, it serviced employees and the citizens seeking their help. As a result, small shops catering to diverse needs arose in the town's charming narrow alleys. Israeli soldiers took advantage of these tiny shops, especially the ones that sold watches, glasses and souvenirs. They would crowd the shop and fill all the space. As one negotiated for an item, the others picked what they could and silently walked away. We heard that this was a common game that occupying armies play. When the people complained to the commanding officer they were advised to file a petition. Hundreds of such petitions were submitted, and naturally ignored.

On our President's first official trip to the United States to consult with President Ronald Reagan, I asked Phyllis to accompany me. I had reserved a Lebanese 747 plane to carry the President and his team, and it was important to me for Phyllis, a small-town girl from Pennsylvania, to return to her native country as the wife of the Foreign Minister. She was in effect a high-powered consultant on how best to negotiate with the Americans. America, under President Reagan, adopted an initiative to evict all foreign forces from Lebanon and to help the country end its internal war and recover its lost democratic legacy. American troops were in Lebanon as part of a multi-national force to help Lebanon regain its sovereignty. Reagan was pivotal in our diplomatic effort, and I was to see him again and again throughout my political days.

The Lebanese President's team of fifteen people was swallowed by the huge 747. Our team included the President, myself, my wife and my assistant. We were accompanied by two consultants, a medical doctor and several reporters. The President and I spent most of the trip in the upper deck writing speeches, preparing statements and sharpening the tiniest details of our one-week visit.

Security in the US for visiting dignitaries is proverbial. Our plane was directed to a military airport where an elegant woman entered the plane and took over. She was Salwa 'Lucky' Roosevelt, the chief of protocol at the White House. Salwa is of Lebanese origin, Druze from the Shuqyar family – 'Shawkar' in the States. She was married to a descendant of the famous warrior President Teddy Roosevelt, who famously advised, 'Speak softly and carry a big stick.' It so happened that Salwa was the sister of a girlfriend of mine from SAIS days, Kay Shawkar.

Two special presidential helicopters were waiting for us. One transported the president and me. The other took the rest of our party. The helicopters were luxurious and spacious and even fitted with tables. Jars of multi-coloured jelly beans, favoured by President Reagan, decorated every little space inside. The helicopters landed on the grounds of the Washington Monument. Tourists visiting the Monument were cordoned off. They stared at us as if we were travellers from outer space. In my younger days I had climbed the infinite number of steps that wind up to the top of the Monument, challenging to the limit my latent claustrophobia. The Monument, built to honour George Washington, the Father of the Nation, is the most visible and spectacular monument in DC. The grand monuments built for Presidents Abraham Lincoln and Thomas Jefferson lack its lofty magnificence.

As we landed, Secretary of State George Shultz and other officials and hordes of secret-service officers were on the ground to meet us. Salwa made us feel at home, and she bonded straight away with Phyllis who became her Virgilian guide as to the needs and expectations of the delegation. After brief words of welcome, President Gemayel was directed to his limousine, Phyllis and I to ours. The limousine that we rode in was especially built for visiting dignitaries. It was a stretch model and entirely bullet-proof, a sleek black machine with a seating area more like a luxury lounge in a five-star hotel, well stocked with spirits and the finest liqueurs, glasses and an icebox in case the traveller felt the need to relax in Washington traffic. Two secret-service men occupied the front seat. One was the driver and the other was in charge of the detail assigned to protect me. I never knew exactly how many secret-service men and women were assigned to me. A car travelled directly in front of us and another directly behind, each carrying five officers. There were invariably at least two or three more waiting at our point of destination.

The head of the detail was in continuous contact with the two cars and with the officers at our destination. The officers included both men and women who wore civilian clothes and carried hidden pistols. From time to time I spotted an officer shift an innocent-looking bag that concealed a sub-machine-gun. The travel routine began as the officers opened the door of the limousine and we entered the car. They closed the door, and the limousine immediately began to move. As we accelerated, secret-service officers on each side of the vehicle placed one hand on the car body and one hand on their side arms. They ran with the car until it gained sufficient speed. Then they jumped into their own car behind us. There was no difference at all between the functions performed by the male and female members of the detail. The women, with heels high enough to be feminine but low and sturdy enough to permit running, kept up with the men.

Other than an occasional enquiry from the head of the detail, protocol discouraged communication of any form between the visitor and his guards. The guards had undergone the finest professional training and were entirely focused on security, leaving no room for the distraction that could result from a lapse into the informal and the friendly. We realized that this entire unit was totally committed to our security and that our safety was exclusively their responsibility. We were not allowed to make a single move unless it was coordinated with the head of the unit. They required us to remain in the limousine until they had checked out the area where we were to disembark. They were the ones who opened the door and decided when to lead us into our suite at the hotel. Three of them remained at the door. The final decisions were always with them. They opened the door for us, if we had to leave, and for any visitors who were permitted in.

As we were whisked to our suite in the Madison Hotel, I told the officer in charge that we had family and friends here in the United States and that our children, my wife's relatives, many of our friends and some diplomats could all be coming to see us. The security people were cooperative and gracious, asking only that we provide the name, the visitor's relation to us and a basic description of the physical features of each of our expected guests, as well as the time they were expected. As friendly as they were about the arrangements, they had iron-clad rules and there would be no lackadaisical Lebanese way around them. I quickly adjusted to the system, providing them with all the information they required, and Phyllis and I were delighted to be able to see our children and relatives and friends for the few minutes of private time available during an official visit to Washington.

Security rules were so tight that I wondered whether I could have any extra private time with my family. The only person I could ask such a question was Reagan's envoy, Philip Habib. 'Are you dreaming?' my friend replied when I asked him. 'Are you aware how many people would want to assassinate President Gemayel? And do you know, if they cannot get him, how many would settle for the Foreign Minister? There are dozens of groups who want the Lebanese war to continue and who therefore would like to disrupt the process. Forget you were a professor. You are now in the front trenches and your safety is as much in the hands of your security detail as in those of Allah. That is if you believe in Him.'

Nevertheless, on one of my later trips to the United States, I informed the head of the security unit that I intended to pay a personal visit to my daughter's family in Houston, Texas. They expressed no objection to my plans, and no one asked any further questions. They bought the airline tickets and reserved as well the seats in front of me and behind me. When I volunteered to tell them about my daughter, her married name, her address and so forth, they smiled gently. 'No need for that, sir,' I was told. When our limousine arrived at Nina's house in Houston, two security cars were already there and more than ten officers were positioned all around the house. This was a complete surprise to Nina and her brood. The neighbours were agog and peered curiously from behind their curtained windows trying to guess what the hell was going on. They must have sighed a huge sigh of relief when we departed the next day.

Security in a peaceful and stable society like America was quite different from security in Lebanon. In the midst of our internal war and throughout the 1980s every evening's news featured stories of kidnappings, assassinations, hijacking and other forms of lawlessness. I was instructed by my local security detail to change my route daily as I travelled between my home and office. I was told to stay inside my bullet-proof car until my guards had surrounded me. I was told not to indulge in my habit of pacing around on our tennis court at the end of the garden. I rarely complied with these instructions.

We Lebanese had become so fatalistic since 1975 that we were sometimes tempted to push our luck to the limit. I paced regularly on our tennis court. In congested traffic, as we neared the Ministry of Foreign Affairs, I often jumped out of the car and raced to my office, followed by guards with guns ready to shoot. I was sometimes more afraid of my guards than my enemies, if enemies I really had. In their anxiety to remain close enough not to allow another car to get in between, the back-up car would repeatedly bump into my car, irritating me to high heaven. The least unusual act was thought by my guardians to be an attempt on my life. They often jumped from both cars, shooting right and left, mostly for the fierce impression they hoped they made, until I could calm them down and persuade them to get back into their cars.

The head of our army intelligence tried to impress upon me the real danger facing me. He often came to our house to make me listen to tape recordings of militia leaders instructing their forces to adjust the angle of their cannons to better aim at us. Our house was a target for several of the many armies and militias ravaging Lebanon. Phyllis collected shrapnel from our yard and from the balconies until she wearied of the task. You collect only items that are rare. Shrapnel was entirely too common. For a while we exhibited hundreds of shrapnel pieces, ranging in size from an inch to twenty inches. Phyllis also collected bullets. Once bullets began arriving by the kilogram, however, she abandoned the effort. Whenever our house was under fire, which was often, Phyllis just dived under the bed, knowing full well that the bed was no protection, but feeling a greater sense of safety nevertheless. Often at home we just drank arak and sat it out, listening to the bullets crisscrossing our house from all directions. We learned that security is concerned as much with mind as with matter.

Anyone thoroughly determined to kill me would be likely to succeed, I reasoned, and lived therefore under the tension of that possibility. Like many Easterners I surrendered to fate, to kismet. What will be, will be. There is also a kind of satisfaction, a certain assertion of the rightness of your position, if you test the odds. Often I would escape from my security detail in Beirut and walk the familiar streets just to regain a sense of normality. If you venture out when and where you are least expected it is not only safe but therapeutic.

One day I was reading through the dozens of intelligence reports from government agencies, as I so often did, when I came across one relating to me. I quickly skimmed through it and deposited it in the out file. Upon reflection, I retrieved the report and read it again. 'The higher council of the Amal militia met last night,' it read, 'and made a decision to assassinate the Minister of Foreign Affairs, Dr Elie A. Salem, in order to derail the peace process he is pursuing.'

Well, it is true nothing focuses the mind like the threat of imminent death. I was electrified, and without the slightest hesitation I asked one of my guards to drive me straight to the Amal headquarters. Within just a few minutes I was there, facing the leader of Amal, Mr Nabih Birri.

'Here I am,' I stated baldly, 'kill me.'

'What are you talking about?' he said. 'I respect you, I would never harm you.'

I showed him the report I had just read. Birri was indignant and said that the document had clearly been sent by one of dozens of intelligence services in Lebanon, not only to scare me but also to cast doubt on his own noble organization. We exchanged a few hugs and kisses, drank coffee together and said our goodbyes. But this was not the last of such written alerts. Indeed they became routine. I learned to ignore them for the most part. But it was much more difficult to dismiss the actions of militia members who blatantly set up their equipment within a hundred yards of our house. We watched as they positioned two rockets and shot them straight at the building. Fortunately, one of the rockets missed entirely, but the other devastated our wooden red-tile roof. In some ways the worst thing of all was the constant barrage of leaflets all around the house accusing me of treason. Every act of mine was an act of treason to one or more of these armed gangs of militia.

If it was dangerous to live in our house in Ba'bda, it was more dangerous to work at the presidential palace and to stay overnight. Ariel Sharon once threatened the President directly that if Lebanon failed to sign a peace treaty with the Israelis, Sharon would not allow Gemayel to govern beyond his office desk. There were many others like Sharon, with their own military forces, each one fighting his own war within our country. None of them had any interest or stake in the survival of the president or in the return of legitimate government. To protect ourselves in the palace, we fortified the roof and positioned armaments around the building. Security forces deployed several types of cannon, anti-aircraft guns, tanks, troop carriers and an entire army regiment immediately around the home of the president. Shelling of the palace was constant but we were able to ignore it, so inured had we become to danger by this time. I was often required to stay there overnight and was accustomed to the music of shelling. In fact, we only became nervous when it stopped.

One incident of those that occurred daily illustrates our situation. Libya's leader Muammar Gaddafi regularly called for a revolution to topple our regime. His foreign minister spoke harshly and threatened to direct Libyan paid militia to storm the palace. In a lull in the war of words between us, Gaddafi sent his foreign minister to negotiate a Libyan proposal with us to bring peace to Lebanon. I welcomed the foreign minister in my office at the palace, and then invited him to have a working lunch with President Gemayel. As we were enjoying food and wine (yes, he drank) a shell hit the wall of the dining-room. As the wall caved in, the brave Libyan just threw himself on the ground and hid under the table. In vain we tried to settle his nerves and to bring him back to the table, at least to finish his wine. But he was thoroughly shaken and had turned as white as a sheet. I called for a tank to carry him back to his embassy. After his departure the President and I returned to the table to sip our coffee and wonder out loud about the armchair revolutionaries who talk big about bravery and sacrifice, and yet fail the first test in an actual situation. But perhaps it was not courage so much as the routine of the war that allowed us to remain in a room that had just lost a wall and was likely to be hit again. Perhaps we were the target. Perhaps the Libyan guest. We never knew. We never bothered to ask.

When I returned home that evening I described to Phyllis the behaviour of the theoretical revolutionary. She burst out laughing and didn't ask one question about the shell, or the crumbling wall of Jericho. Lethal danger was such an accepted part of our lives, we were all anaesthetized more than we knew at the time.

I do not mean to give the impression that my political years were entirely concerned with danger and insecurity. In fact, the opposite was often the case, since security was generally the last of my concerns. The years between1982 and 1988 were tremendously challenging for Phyllis and me personally. We were at the very centre of decision-making for the future of our country. Our book-lined study, designed to be a cosy place for research and reflection, became the reception room for special envoys from the United States, including Habib, McFarlane, Rumsfeld and Draper. We also welcomed envoys from France, Italy, the Vatican, Egypt and Saudi Arabia, to meet with us at home in Ba'bda. At first, we hesitated to hold meetings at home because the Israelis had chosen the building just behind our house as their temporary listening post. Philip Habib in his distinctive Brooklyn accent expressed a sentiment shared by many. 'Hell, Elie, how can we talk here,' he demanded explosively, 'while David Kimche and the rest of the Israeli intelligence are just a few yards away with their ears to the wall.' Habib used the influence of the United States and soon succeeded in removing Kimche's station from its position nearby. He was also able to eliminate the Israeli checkpoints on the way to the presidential palace.

Of the many heads of state with whom I negotiated, the most memorable would have to include Ronald Reagan, the quintessential choreographer. At breakfast in the White House he would regale his companions with stories, funny ones, with the intent of making you feel at home. He left the work to his assistants. They would hand the president an index card on which a question had been written for him to ask. He would put the provided question, and then sit back and enjoy the proceedings, always with a broad smile on his face.

At one time a former Lebanese Prime Minister and I met with Reagan. As my companion explained the difficult process facing our country and praised the President for his commitment, Reagan's eyes were on me and he was not hearing a word. His stare was so focused and intense that my companion found it useless to continue and simply stopped speaking. Reagan broke the silence to address me.

'Mr Foreign Minister,' he said with that same broad smile, 'you know who you remind me of?'

'Yes, Mr President,' I said, 'I believe I do.'

'Who do you think?' he asked triumphantly as if I would never guess.

'Danny Thomas,' I answered.

'Damn right,' he hollered, full of life and humour. He continued by relating anecdotes about his friend Danny in Hollywood and how he pretended to be Jewish to please the Jewish studio heads. Of course, they were not fooled, but they all loved Danny never-theless.

Once at a luncheon, Reagan took me aside and confided to me that there was one act he would really like to perform, except that he was terrified of the consequences. The Reagans owned a ranch in California and sometimes allowed photographers to come in. As he rode his horse he often saw them perched high on the rocks above, using binoculars and long-distance lenses to watch his movements. 'I would love,' he said, 'to act as if I had been hit by a bullet. I would throw my head back, scream and slowly slide off the horse. Wow, wouldn't that be an item on the evening news?' He laughed uproariously before telling himself regretfully, 'No, no, it would be too dangerous.'

He recalled to me an incident that occurred as he was preparing to give a talk from the Oval Office. He was asked by the technician if he would say a few words to test the sound system. 'So I said something about preparing to bomb the Soviet Union,' he told me. 'And the next day it was reported in the press by an irresponsible reporter.' Subsequently the remark was interpreted as a joke by some and as an act of senility by others.

Another leader I met with often was President Hafez al-Assad of Syria. Assad was known for his single-mindedness; on all issues his mind was made up. He could very rarely be affected by what his visitors had to say. Nevertheless, he would meet with them and at least listen to them. Assad would keep his visitors for long periods, indeed as long as they wished. He would regale them with stories of ancient Arab times and amuse them with anecdotes to make sure that little time was left to attend to the purpose of the visit. I quickly learned to play the game with him, and we became seemingly very much at ease with each other. Once, however, when I showed him a draft of an agreement we were going to sign with Israel in order to get the Israeli army out of Lebanon, Assad became visibly angry.

'Do you know,' he said, 'that when President Anwar Sadat came to tell me that he was going to Israel the next day to address the Knesset, I made a big mistake.'

'What was that?' I innocently enquired.

'I should have shot down his plane,' he answered vehemently.

'Oh, well,' I interjected and I hoped I was joking, 'you do not need big guns in my case. I came in a Gazelle helicopter, the most vulnerable of all machines that fly.'

'Don't worry,' he laughed. 'You're a friend, a good friend.'

As I flew back to Beirut and looked down at the Syrian army deployed everywhere, I saw the mouths of cannon aimed upwards and wondered will they or won't they. I reflected on the comforts of being a dean in a university and the hazards of government in times of war.

Phyllis spent half her time with AMIDEAST promoting her educational agenda and the other half with me sharing in the discussions with the parade of special envoys. And as we were truly in a multi-dimensional situation we got advice from all directions. From one perspective, we were urged to conduct direct negotiations with Israel. Another one counselled distance from America and closer cooperation with the Soviets. Yet another insisted on exclusive support of the Arabs, in contradiction of one who cautioned against too much involvement with the mercurial Arab regimes. One advised full compliance with the Syrian position while another felt Syria was the problem.

Throughout these conflicting pulls and shoves our administration had to maintain a steady Lebanese policy course despite the weak centrifugal forces in our young country. Amazing how frail was the national loyalty, how shallow and diluted was our local identity and how fragmented were the partisans. Not only was it necessary to extricate the country from the web into which it had fallen, the very identity of the state had yet to be firmly established. We needed to decide who we were as a nation before we could focus national attention, reconstruct the country and work on substantive reforms.

As a student I was convinced by the Socratic method, by the technique of dialogue in Plato's *Republic* and the arguments. The Platonic method of discourse held a special appeal for me. My political years confirmed my belief that politics should be the domain of the educated, those whom Plato identified under the broad designation philosopher kings. I was truly shocked by the provincialism of politicians, by their corruption, and by their tendency to accommodate and dissimulate. I was awed by the weakness and backwardness of our political and administrative institutions. I wondered about an educational system that sent so many lawyers and seemingly educated people to the public domain with little interest in truly altruistic service. The Lebanese passion to excel seemed to me to be concentrated in the private sector. There were very, very few who could truly analyse a situation, write a serious report or provide you with useful information. The officials seemed to me to be more concerned with form than with substance.

There were only a few leading politicians in Lebanon who earned my affection and admiration. Sa'ib Salam occupied a special position as a statesman of the highest calibre. History will remember him well and recognize his heroic role at a time bereft of heroes. I admired the young president with whom I worked for six years – Amine Gemayel – who deserved greater respect and a more serious evaluation of his presidency than he has ever received. Camille Chamoun earned my regard. Among religious leaders, I revered Patriarch Ignatius IV, Metropolitan Elias (Audi), Patriarch Sfeir and Al-Imam Muhamed Mahdi Shams al-Din. And I loved Chafic Wazzan.

Wazzan was a Lebanese patriot, earthy, the son of a baker. On every occasion he could quote a wise dictum that he had heard from his late father. Wazzan was a traditional Sunni Muslim. He spoke French, but not English. For his American visits he depended on me to translate for him. Once in discussions with United States Secretary of State George Shultz, Wazzan asked me to convey to Schultz his urgent desire for the Israeli army to leave Beirut.

'Don't worry,' the Secretary assured us, 'we will get them out.'

Encouraged, Wazzan asked, 'And how do you plan to do it?'

'Tell the Prime Minister,' Schultz directed me, 'that there are many ways to skin a cat.'

When I translated this difficult idiom, Wazzan muttered, as if to himself: 'I hope it is not going to be hair by hair until the end of time.'

Wazzan always wondered how I managed to stay cheerful through all the rough days we encountered as a government in the raging internal war of the 1980s. He would look at me and shake his head.

'Mr Minister, I envy you. You are always smiling in spite of the huge problems that face us. You do so perhaps because you came into politics by parachute from a university. I got into politics by working at it. I came from below, from the street. When our turn is over you will go back to the university. Where shall I go?'

His toughest days, however, were when he came to Washington and discovered that his security detail contained as many women as men. We joked with him about it – a manly Muslim figure protected by women. 'Your excellency, you know me,' I teased. 'I will never tell Mrs Wazzan that the guard who kept the key to your suite was a woman, but I cannot guarantee that the ambassadors accompanying us will be so discreet.' That was not a subject for levity to Wazzan. He reprimanded me most gently but most firmly. 'This is no joking matter. The ambassadors must not utter one word that might reach my wife.'

Before I bring down the curtain on my political career I must note that I played a central role in 1987 working out a reform document that had a lasting impact. President Hafez al-Assad approved it but insisted as a condition of its implementation that we deliver the assassins of Prime Minister Rashid Karami. The Prime Minister was killed by a bomb placed behind his seat in the military helicopter that took him back and forth between Beirut and his hometown of Tripoli. As we actually did not know who the killers were we could not deliver them and President Assad was not satisfied by our response. A year later I handed the document to the Arab League conciliator, al-Akhdar al-Ibrahimi, and in a slightly modified form it was submitted to a peace conference held in Taif, Saudi Arabia, under the auspices of the Arab States, and was adopted.

The Taif Document ended Lebanon's internal war in 1989 and ushered Lebanon into a new era of peace and reconstruction In a highly politicized country like Lebanon – and I am inclined to believe in all small countries – politics is the game that is most admired. Most Lebanese conceive of politics as meaning running for a seat in parliament, establishing a political party, seeking a provincial office or serving as a member of the government. Politics in this sense consists of obtaining a visible post to exercise observable power in the community. To reflect on the substance of the nation, however, and to be concerned about national identity, our place in the region and our role in world affairs did not come under the common definition of politics. To be obsessed with reform, to write about it, to organize institutions with the view of translating ideas into reality, these activities were not considered politics by most Lebanese. For me, however, and for Phyllis this was the only political activity of lasting interest.

13

We left government in 1988. With the help of my good friend Issam M. Fares, I established a think-tank in Lebanon, the first of its kind. Phyllis was the lead organizer and motivator and we had the support of our daughter Lisa and our two sons Adib and Paul in establishing the Lebanese Center for Policy Studies. Our daughter Nina, an active medical doctor, encouraged us as well with her thoughtful enquiries about our progress. The Center filled an urgent need in the reconstruction of Lebanon after a fifteen-year war. We held seminars and symposia to encourage constructive thinking. The Center sponsored lectures and promoted extensive research into all aspects of national development. We published books and pamphlets, research papers and a political journal.

The Center began doing budget analysis, recruiting financial experts to prepare extensive scrutiny of the budget proposed by parliament and often recommending changes based on Lebanon's needs and its priorities. The Center's analysis was put in a written report or booklet that was distributed to all concerned. The same process was followed on issues such as decentralization, electoral law, administrative reform, technological innovations, etc. In time, the Center became the major reference point for embassies, professors, journalists and government officials.

Many ambassadors told me that they consulted the studies issued by the Center before they prepared their own reports to their respective governments. Many told me that it was the most serious, the most comprehensive and the most objective research centre in the Arab World. This was so because the Center was highly professional, scientific and strictly non-partisan. In addition to the dozen researchers employed on a full-time basis, the Center called on a host of experts in all fields and from all the universities operating in Lebanon. As well as producing publications on specific subjects, the Center held international conferences on issues such as Middle East peace and reconstruction efforts in the Arab World. The Center's projects were generously supported by United Nations agencies, the European Union, the World Bank and a number of foundations and Arab philanthropists. Undoubtedly the Center filled a national need and in so doing reflected my own interest in contributing to the political process through careful research that pointed the way to reform and democratization.

Our government, finding the Center independent and productive, chose to ignore it completely. Our efforts to secure a licence from the government were rigorously blocked. It was amusing to observe that while ambassadors, foundations, researchers and journalists were extremely interested in our publications, our own government feared us as if we were the hand hired to destroy the temple.

One common feature of national underdevelopment is a complete separation between government and university, governance and knowledge. We who live off the olive tree and who live in the olive press at harvest time know first-hand the function of the transmission belt. Oh what pleasure we derived as children when the belt was diverted gently from the idle wheel to the active wheel that crushed the olives and directed the flow of the oil. There are belts and wheels a-plenty in Lebanon, but the mechanism, indeed the will to hitch the belt to the active wheel, is not there. It was our hope that the Center would serve as a mechanism to connect the centres of knowledge in Lebanon to the centres of action. I believe we made some headway, but there was still a long way to go before the belt was firmly in place.

After our political years, Phyllis and I were looking for a project in our village, Bterram. Father had bequeathed to my two sons an old vault house in the village, of a type that Phyllis dearly loved. It had undergone the transition from the earth-on-beams roof, to the red-tile-on-wood roof, to the cement roof. The earthen type roof had completely disappeared by the 1950s. It must have been thousands of years old. It was way back in time that Bterram began to build its houses in the vault style, with the stones of the vault held together by the arch principle.

Generally each family in our village had one vault house, a spacious area with a high ceiling. The interior was not divided into living-room, kitchen, bathroom and bedrooms. Mattresses were piled on top of each other against the wall. At bedtime, the whole floor would be covered with mattresses and the beds would fill up on a first-come, first-served basis. There was no privacy at all. Father, mother, a grandparent or two and some five children or more would sleep like this. I remember it well as we lived that way till 1938 when I was eight years old. It was simple, warm and rather pleasant. At night we boys jumped out of the window to relieve ourselves in the garden. The sisters, and I believe fathers and mothers, resorted to the chamber pot. When cement made its début in the village, my father had two rooms built on top of our vault, and in time we evolved from the vault to the red-brick culture, and eventually to the cement.

As the village 'progressed', the quaint and intriguing vaults were torn down and replaced by cement monstrosities. Phyllis and I were dismayed at the rate of destruction, and we planned to pre-serve as many of these vaults as possible. We would start with our own. Our idea was to preserve the vault and to add bedrooms, bathrooms and a kitchen to the main structure in a graceful, unob-trusive fashion. It was to be a restoration without desecration. We felt that if we succeeded in this project, and were able to create a thing of beauty as well as functionality, then other villagers would follow suit. Phyllis scanned the village and was impressed by the number of houses that had escaped the wrecking balls of 'progress'. She planned to buy as many of these structures as we could afford, convert them for modern living, and then sell them to friends and acquaintances who appreciated this old form of architecture and who loved village life.

For some four years, and with the help of two empathetic archi-tects, we worked on our project. The result was a piece of art. Villagers, too shy to have a look when we were on site, took advan-tage of our absence and came in hordes to see and admire the house. Like so many people, the villagers were often eager to discard the old and show off with the new. Once they saw what we had done, however, they began to appreciate their vaults and to envision the potential of these houses. Many came to regret their error of judgement in destroying what they had inherited from their parents and grandparents. Phyllis, the reformer, the restorer, the authenticator had won them over.

Our Bterram house had its own gravitational pull on our family. Our children loved it, and eagerly awaited the weekend when we gathered there to spend time and bask in the simplicity of rural life. It was truly fortuitous that as we were about to complete the restoration of the vault, I was asked to serve as the president of a new university just six miles from Bterram. The University of Balamand was founded in 1988, during the Lebanese internal war, by Ignatius IV, the Greek Orthodox Patriarch of Antioch and all the East. The patriarch was unusual in many ways. Of all the scores of Orthodox Patriarchs who had occupied the ecclesiastic throne of Antioch since the Apostles Peter and Paul, only one patriarch, Ignatius IV, had ever built a university. I knew who he was, I admired his standing in the history of Christianity, and I approved of his political position on virtually all major issues facing the Arab World.

I admired in particular the depth of the Patriarch's mind, the purity of his faith, and the monastic mystic simplicity of his way of life. We knew each other distantly through chance encounters. I knew him as a daring reformer. He knew me as an academic administrator, as an author on the Middle East, as Foreign Minister, and as Advisor to the President of the Republic on foreign affairs. We had met one evening at the presidential palace, perhaps in 1986 when the patriarch came to ask the President, Amine Gemayel, to be fair to the Orthodox in making appointments in the administration. In Lebanon, each religious denomination had its quota in the bureaucracy and in the political system. The President told the Patriarch that the Orthodox were well represented.

'You need not worry about the Orthodox share in the government,' Gemayel assured Ignatius IV. 'My two closest advisors, Ghassan Tueni and Elie Salem, are both Orthodox.'

The Patriarch, wistfully sceptical of politics and politicians, answered the President with a dubious smile. 'You have not given me the assurance I was seeking,' the Patriarch gently asserted. 'Ghassan Tueni is your personal friend. He comes for dinner, for a drink and for conversation. He is neither in the cabinet nor in state administration. As for Elie, how Orthodox is he? Ask him does he have any idea where the bishopric is located?'

Although we all laughed together, I understood the Patriarch well. He respected me for who I was, a professor of politics. He knew that I was Orthodox, but also that I was not active in the Church. When, years later, the Patriarch asked me to serve as president of the university, Ghassan Tueni had already completed

273

his third year in that position. Ghassan had given the university visibility, and now the patriarch was ready for an academician to take charge. The idea of capping my career as president of a university, the first one in a rural region in Lebanon, and just a few miles from the very house that Phyllis and I had restored, was a temptation impossible to resist.

In October 1993, the Board of Trustees elected me to the post that I now fill with a great deal of passion and commitment. My son Paul took over the management of the Lebanese Center for Policy Studies. From time to time my son Adib came in for short stints at the Center. Phyllis continued as director of AMIDEAST and provided counsel to the Center.

Our visits to the village became more frequent, now that village and office were only a few minutes apart. To write about the complex task of building a university, to tell the story of the University of Balamand, would be an attractive project but one that must wait for another time.

14

Phyllis was confidante and mentor to hundreds of people through-out all these years. Her job at AMIDEAST, of course, was to counsel students, which she did with honesty, warmth and intelligence. For those in all the many other realms of her life – for the members of the extended family in the village, for the faculty and staff while we were at AUB, for the neighbours in Ba'bda and, of course, for me and our children – she created a sense of belonging and deep connection. She listened and she advised others with compassion and care. She seemed to derive her own spiritual sustenance from these diverse communities that she created and served.

It was very hard on her spirits as these communities changed or even broke up. As the war wore on, the AUB group dispersed, I was away more often with political life, the children spent years at a time in the United States for school and work, friends died or left the country and she was growing older while the future of the country that she loved so much was still uncertain.

Phyllis found herself fighting at the end of the 1990s on two fronts – her office and her health. AMIDEAST was undergoing rapid change and was becoming thickly bureaucratic. The Washington office was suddenly trying to micromanage the regional one from a distance. The freedom that Phyllis had enjoyed in running the Beirut office in her inimitable efficient and empathetic style was being challenged on a daily basis. She would arrive home in the evening exhausted and bitter. She began to talk seriously of resign-ing. 'All I want to do is restore old houses in the village,' she declared. 'I am ready for a new venture.' Of course, I encouraged her.

It seemed to happen quite suddenly that I noticed Phyllis looking tired, her face drawn. My always-young-looking wife was rapidly looking older. Phyllis had been a heavy smoker from the age of sixteen. Of course, she knew the dangers of smoking. Deep down, however, she was hoping to be spared any ill effects. After all, disease seemed to be a matter of luck. Some got sick, some didn't. She was an avid reader of the *Herald Tribune* and regularly searched for any scientific articles that seemed to challenge the prevailing intelligent opinion on any topic, but especially this one.

'Elie, I'm sure,' she would claim with amusement, 'that soon they'll discover smoking's good for you.'

'Never!' I would scoff. 'You should stop and stop now. You're a strong person, you can do it.'

'Yes, I suppose I can,' she sighed, 'but I really don't want to. I so enjoy smoking. After all, I keep reading that the habit is likely to take five or ten years from your life, but that's not a bad trade-off. I love smoking, and really can't live without it.'

I had learned long before not to pressure Phyllis. The best I could do was gently prod, counsel and mobilize children and friends to do the same. Some of her closest friends smoked, and just as heavily as she did, which only strengthened her resolve.

Phyllis resigned from AMIDEAST and we celebrated the event as though it were a great victory. Plans to help in the university and to restore more old vaults were put on the primary track. I was struck once by the thesis that you can never examine history from a beginning. You always get into it at mid-course. Similarly, you cannot choose or plan a point of exit from your life. My favourite Arab poet is al-Mutanabbi and he once wrote, 'We saddle our horses and prepare for battle, but death strikes us down before we engage.'

As lovers Phyllis and I had rehearsed over our vodka martinis all types of scenarios – the beautiful, the sensual and the morbid. 'If I die first,' we asked each other, 'how do you plan to complete your journey?' Phyllis had an easy answer. She was a matter-of-fact woman. 'If you die first,' she told me, 'I will spend my time between Ba'bda and Bterram. I will take care of grandchildren, I will restore old houses in Bterram and attract my American friends to buy them. I will create a Lebanese–American community in the Kurah and try to put some sense into you Bterramis. You need change, you need new ideas. Reform is on the way.'

In one's life there is always a telephone call you wish not to receive, yet the call must come. It is in the scheme of things. My medical daughter told me in a choking voice, 'Mother has cancer.'

A few years earlier she had called me in similar circumstances to tell me that she had diagnosed my prostate tissue as cancerous. Now again the news was bad and Nina broke down. Why would a father allow his children to study medicine? Worse, why would he allow a daughter to pursue the medical profession only to have her carry the cross of her parents' health as they grew older? Phyllis and I had always said that we would not allow Nina to be in charge of us or to oversee our medical check-ups. When the time came, however, theory was abandoned in the face of reality and both times we had called our daughter.

Now we were comforted to know that at the very least she would be our primary advisor. Who should examine Phyllis? Who should operate? Where will the treatment take place? Phyllis insisted that she wanted to be treated in Beirut, and that under no circumstances would she seek medical aid anywhere else. Under her daughter's supervision, she was confident of getting the best medical treatment possible. Enfolded by her husband and children, in the warmth of her home and in the company of her many friends and admirers, she had all the solace she wanted.

She well knew what was happening and that the odds were against her, and yet she remained most cheerful, most serene. Her unfailing humour was her weapon against the pain of the thing that was killing her. I do not wish to write about her last three months with us. There is too much pain for me, too much of the private to put down on paper. In time she succumbed, as we all shall. Our children, who had been far flung in natural pursuit of their own lives, gathered around her once again. For the days and weeks they had together, she was joyful. She was able to put aside all distractions and simply love her children and be loved by them. They were all there to give their mother an adieu exceeding in pomp and glory the reception their father had given his young bride half a century before.

When Phyllis came to Lebanon as a hopeful bride-to-be, the entire village of Bterram was there to welcome her. For her departure, all of Lebanon came to say goodbye to the woman they knew, that they dearly loved and that they honoured with all their hearts. The highest officers of state came to pay their deepest respects. The President of the Republic added one more medal to the many medals Phyllis had received in her lifetime. Former President Gemayel walked behind the coffin from village to village, the tears flowing down his face. When Gemayel had returned to Lebanon after a long exile two years earlier, Phyllis had been there with thousands of the Lebanese people to welcome him home with tears of happiness in her eyes. Now he came to say goodbye.

The family received mourners for seven days. Thousands of people came from all over the world to pay tribute. The funeral procession was the wedding procession in reverse. There were the family, the friends, the villagers, this time silent, despondent in unbelief. As my mother had wept with joy, there were now copious tears of sorrow. The mother and father who welcomed her with hugs and kisses had already departed. I am glad they were spared the agony of separation from the one they loved as life itself.

Some three kilometres before we reached our village for the burial rites, villagers on the way stopped the procession, removed the casket from the hearse and carried it by hand, raised high above the gathered mourners. Thus, borne on the shoulders of youths from the neighbouring villages, the casket entered Bterram. In compliance with tradition, we carried the casket to the home that Phyllis loved and made a farewell tour of the house amid the weeping and lamentation of the many, many people who grieved for her and walked behind her. In the same church where she was married, wearing the famous wedding dress that she had carried across the ocean, we performed the funeral rites.

My mind wandered during the service to that time, half a century before, when in this same place Norman Burns had so nervously recited his truncated version of the Lord's Prayer. I smiled in spite of my grief as I thought of Norman fooling with the recording in a desperate attempt to save his Christian image by filling in the part of the prayer that he forgot.

At her wedding, Phyllis had no family. As she departed, she was with her four wonderful children and a horde of grandchildren, all carrying her genes and imprinted with her love, reason and principled determination. There is a saying in my village: 'Man Khallaf ma mat' – 'Those who have begotten children do not die.' Phyllis loved village sayings and repeated them often in her inimitable Arabic, this one in particular. It is true that we live on in our progeny. A little more than a year after Phyllis died, my son Paul and his wife Maggie presented our family with a set of remarkable twins – a boy and girl. The parents named them Elie and Aya. The baby girl is the image of Phyllis at the same age. With their blond curls and bright blue eyes, these Lebanese children receive an outpouring of love from the extended Salem family that their grandmother held so dear throughout her life.

This is the way it is with us mortals. We love and are loved in return. We do good works, and we reap goodwill. Yes, I am an optimist. Like so many men of my generation I carried a heavy load of scepticism about life and its meaning. In despair I became an existentialist. We are born, we thrive, we endeavour to leave a mark and then we vanish. All living things vanish. The lovelier the flower, the more heartrending its demise.

Of the existentialists I loved two – Dostoyevsky and Nietzsche. The first was hopeful, yearning for a paradise beyond this vale of tears and aspiring to attain it. The latter relished and brilliantly expressed the hopelessness of it all. As a young man I read and reread the Bible. Genesis captivated me and kept me awake at night. The prophets inspired my imagination. The Psalms elevated my soul to great heights. These beautiful songs were also prayers and supplications that carried within them the accumulated wisdom and the spiritual insights of the civilizations that rose and fell in the ancient Middle East. I read Ecclesiastes many times and wondered who wrote it and when. What was the author's purpose in placing those verses that tell us 'there is a time to every purpose under heaven' at the very heart of the Holy Book? There I read the inescapable truth that there is a time to laugh and a time to weep; a time to plant and a time to reap; a time to be born and a time to die . . . I turned to the New Testament to take comfort in a Lord like no other Lord, the Son of God, the incarnation of God here on earth. He taught, He stirred things up. He was crucified. He died. He was buried, and on the third day He rose from the dead. O death, where is thy sting? Christ has conquered you. Christ has risen. No one has better expounded the historic victory of Christ over death than that eloquent, passionate Bishop of Antioch, St John Chrysostom. His Easter sermon on the Resurrection of Christ is a masterpiece. I memorized it as a child and have reflected long on it as an adult.

From the Orthodox perspective Christ died and in His death He rendered matter holy. All things in existence were glorified and sanctified by His Resurrection. And as Christ's followers tried better to understand and better to preach the story of the Son of Man, they reached a formulation of Christian faith at a meeting in Nicea.

I knew the Nicene Creed from my early youth, when I served in our village church. Indeed, I memorized the entire Orthodox service and hold a paraphrase of the Creed in my own heart to this day: 'I *believe* in one God, Creator of all things. I *believe* in one Lord, the Son of God, who is one in substance with God. I *believe* in the Holy Spirit that guides the prophets and the believers. I *believe* in one Church, Holy, United, Apostolic. And I *hope* for the resurrection of the living and the dead on Judgment Day.'

There is a world of difference between the conviction of 'I *believe*' and the yearning of 'I *hope*'. An Arabic poem speaks to me with the line, 'Oh how meaningless life is without that spark of hope.' With the death of Phyllis I was hurled by destiny into the realm of 'I hope' within my Orthodox Christian faith. With faith, that kernel of hope may become a rock on which a church is built and from the church a beacon may pierce the darkness of space and time to guide a solitary voyager.

Death, I came to realize, is the problem of the living. To die is to sleep, to rest or, as we Orthodox believe, to lie gently dormant in Christ's bosom until the time comes to rise from the dead with Him. In our faith, people do not die, they only deeply sleep. Words, of course, are what we use to attempt to explain our being. We invent our own constructs, and we have to live with them and by them. We have no other vocabulary. Even the most mysterious of revelations must be conveyed in our words, according to our own astigmatic perception of what goes on inside us and all about us.

With words we live and with words we die. With words we construct meaning, we weave visions, and we build castles in the air. No wonder St John, the most beloved of our Gospels, starts: 'In the beginning was the Word, and the Word was with God.'

I do not possess the right words to define where I am after the departure of Phyllis. Death deepens. Death imposes on the survivor a loneliness with no discernible boundaries. A reflective mood, a sad one at that, traverses again and again the infinite space of the lonely soul. Something in this mysterious space pulls at your sleeve and whispers of a beginning. You suddenly awake as if from deep sleep and scream, 'When? Where? How?'